Sharon Lockhart | Noa Eshkol

SHARON LOCKHART
NOA ESHKOL

Organized by

Talia Amar, Stephanie Barron, and Britt Salvesen

Edited by

Stephanie Barron and Britt Salvesen

With contributions by

Talia Amar
Stephanie Barron and Britt Salvesen
Eva Díaz
Sabine Eckmann and Sharon Lockhart
Michal Shoshani

Los Angeles County Museum of Art
The Israel Museum, Jerusalem
DelMonico Books • Prestel Munich London New York

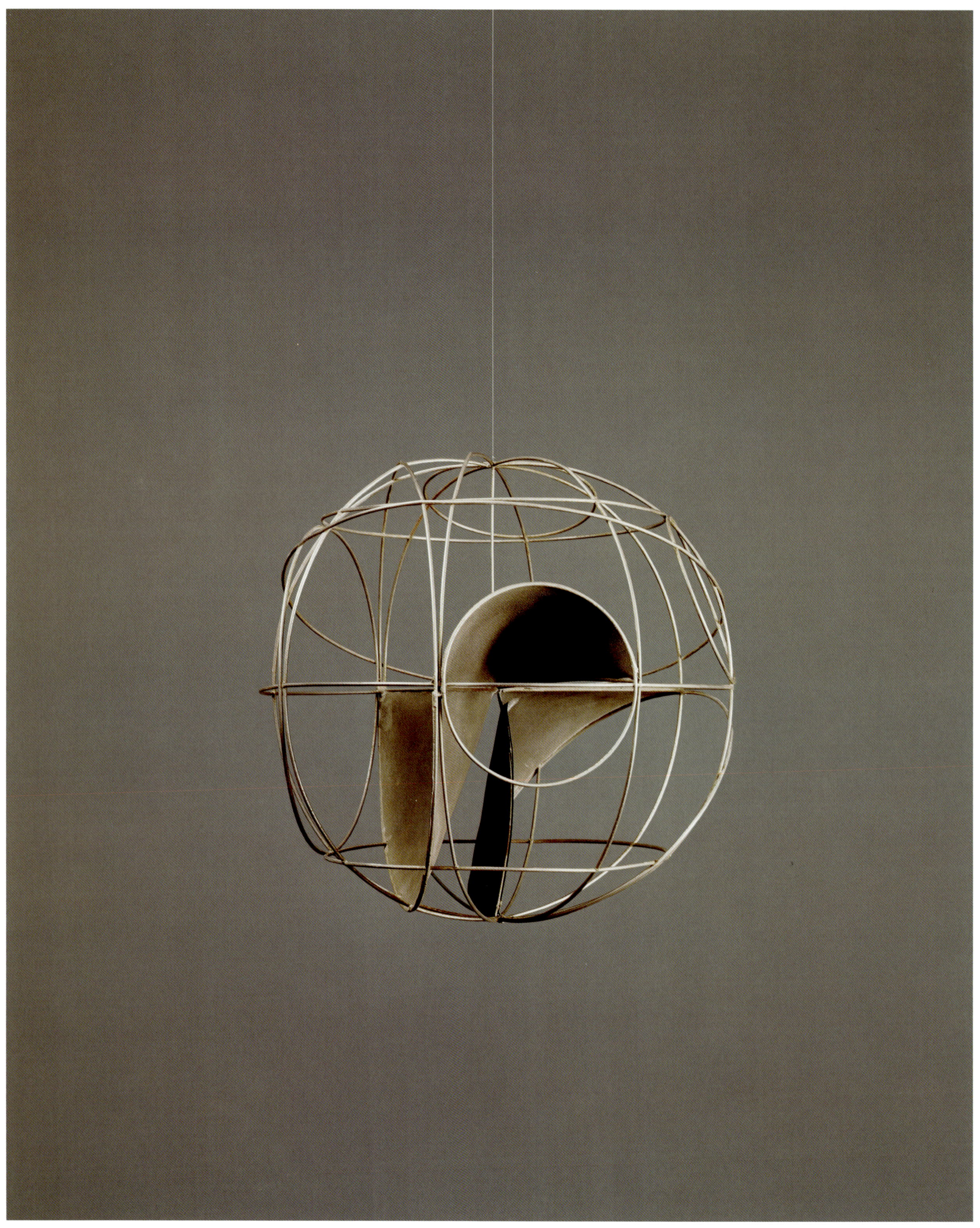

Sharon Lockhart, *Models of Orbits in the System of Reference, Eshkol-Wachman Movement Notation System*, 2011, *Sphere Three at Five Points in Its Rotation* (detail)

Contents

Directors' Foreword

In 2008, Los Angeles–based artist Sharon Lockhart visited Israel on a research trip sponsored by The Jewish Federation of Greater Los Angeles's Tel Aviv – Los Angeles Partnership, guided by an interest in exploring textiles, ethnography, dance, and conservation techniques. Logic brought her to the storerooms of the Israel Museum's Ethnography Department. Serendipity took her thereafter to the Noa Eshkol Foundation for Movement Notation in Holon, which is dedicated to preserving the legacy of the Israeli movement and dance theorist, dance composer, teacher, and textile artist Noa Eshkol. Lockhart was entranced by her encounter with Eshkol's world, touching as it did on so many of her own interests, and the *Sharon Lockhart | Noa Eshkol* project was born.

Eshkol was a remarkable personality in her own time in the Israeli cultural world, best known for developing in the 1950s, together with architect Avraham Wachman, a groundbreaking movement-notation system capable of describing virtually every perceptible movement of the body. Less well known were her talents as a textile artist, informed by the early twentieth-century European modernism that was a part of her heritage, together with other artistic sources.

For Lockhart, who works in film and photography, Eshkol offered a perfect new subject. Lockhart's research on Eshkol's practice—as well as her extensive work with members of the foundation, including several dancers from Eshkol's Chamber Dance Group—enabled the artist to celebrate her own deep affinity for movement and dance, anthropological exploration, and communal collaboration. From this collaboration she developed the project that is the subject of the present exhibition, which she conceived as a two-person show.

Lockhart's film installation *Five Dances and Nine Wall Carpets by Noa Eshkol* (2011), the centerpiece of the exhibition, features several dancers, including longtime members of Eshkol's Chamber Dance Group, performing five of her dances within a "set" organized around a selection of her "wall carpets," the term she used to describe the textiles she created. Reflecting Lockhart's special insight, the film installation brings together for the first time two aspects of Eshkol's creative output—her dances and her carpets—and draws resonant connections between them. It also highlights connections with contemporaneous traditions elsewhere in the world, notably Merce Cunningham's and Yvonne Rainer's engagements with visual art as a central component of the modern-dance experience. Displayed in the exhibition as well are a group of Eshkol's carpets and a collection of scores, drawings, photographs, and other items from her archive, together with a series of photographs Lockhart made of several wire-and-mesh spheres she discovered in the archive.

Our project has benefited immeasurably from the partnership between the Israel Museum and the Los Angeles County Museum of Art—in some ways twin institutions, both founded on May 11, 1965, and both campus museums with an encyclopedic purview. And there could not have been more natural partners for this enterprise, with Lockhart's deep roots in Los Angeles's cultural community and with Los Angeles's long-standing ties to Tel Aviv as its sister city in Israel. Following its second presentation, in Los Angeles, a version of the exhibition will travel to The Jewish Museum in New York, where it will be presented in the fall of 2012, and we gratefully acknowledge Claudia Gould, Helen Goldsmith Menschel Director, and Ruth Beesch, Deputy Director for Program, for their efforts.

Our thanks go first and foremost to Sharon Lockhart, whose vision has synthesized Noa Eshkol's achievement in an intrinsic way, while also bringing it to the attention of a broader international audience in the course of creating a new chapter in Lockhart's own work. We are also deeply grateful to the members of Eshkol's Chamber Dance Group and the Noa Eshkol Foundation for Movement Notation for enabling us to enter their world and for their cooperation in so many ways, not least in lending the carpets and archival materials that are central to the installation. And we owe an important debt of gratitude to Sergio Edelsztein, Director of the Center for Contemporary Art in Tel Aviv, for the CCA's seminal role in our project and for its concurrent presentation, while our exhibition was being premiered in Jerusalem, of a companion exhibition featuring Lockhart's film *Four*

Exercises in Eshkol-Wachman Movement Notation (2011), accompanied by an extensive series of performances, workshops, lectures, and other public programs. In addition, we thank Diana Shoef, Production Manager at the CCA, who first introduced Lockhart to the remarkable world of Eshkol's work.

This complex enterprise could not have succeeded without the generous sponsorship of many individuals and institutions. Nancy Berman has supported the project from its inception, initially within the framework of the Tel Aviv – Los Angeles Partnership—a collaborative project of the Jewish Federation of Greater Los Angeles, the Municipality of Tel Aviv-Yafo, and the Jewish Agency for Israel—and has also made this publication possible. In Israel, an important group of donors rose to the occasion to underwrite that presentation in full: Dorit Gary and Modi Segal, Los Angeles and Tel Aviv; Judith Yovel Recanati, Herzliya, in memory of her beloved husband Israel (Rolly) Yovel; Rivka Saker and Uzi Zucker, New York and Tel Aviv; Rachel and Moshe Yanai, Tel Aviv; anonymous donors from Caesarea and Tel Aviv; and the donors to the Israel Museum's 2011 Exhibition Fund: Claudia Davidoff, Cambridge, Massachusetts, in memory of Ruth and Leon Davidoff; Hanno D. Mott, New York; and The Nash Family Foundation, New York. At the Center for Contemporary Art, Tel Aviv, Lockhart's film was produced with the support of Outset Contemporary Art Fund; The Philip and Muriel Berman Foundation; Ostrovsky Family Fund; and Art Partners; the programs were made possible thanks to the generosity of the Weil Family. In Los Angeles the exhibition has been made possible by the generous sponsorship of Wells Fargo. The significant contributions of Daniel Greenberg, Susan Steinhauser, and The Greenberg Foundation; Audrey M. Irmas; Alice and Nahum Lainer; Drs. Rebecka and Arie Belldegrun; The Philip and Muriel Berman Foundation; and The Photographic Arts Council, LACMA, have helped to realize the project. Additional support was provided by Helgard Field-Lion and Irwin Field; Laura and Jim Maslon; and the Consulate General of Israel, Los Angeles. To all we express our most profound gratitude.

It has been a great pleasure for our two museums, with their shared history of collegial engagement, to work together to realize *Sharon Lockhart | Noa Eshkol* so completely. In Israel, our warmest thanks go to Suzanne Landau, Chief Curator of Fine Arts, and Tania Coen-Uzzielli, Head of Curatorial Services, for their leading assistance at all stages of this project, and especially to Talia Amar, Associate Curator of Contemporary Art at the Israel Museum, for her talent, dedication, passion, and enthusiasm, which helped bring this complex endeavor to its successful conclusion there. At LACMA, Stephanie Barron, Senior Curator of Modern Art, first brought this project to our attention and together with Britt Salvesen, Curator of Photography, spearheaded the production of this publication in a timely fashion so that it could coincide with the exhibition's presentation in Los Angeles, reflecting installation photography from Israel. Their enthusiasm, expertise, and managerial skills made for a seamless collaboration. Finally, we thank Lockhart's galleries—Blum & Poe of Los Angeles, Gladstone Gallery of New York and Brussels, and neugerriemschneider of Berlin—for lending their full support to our vision for Sharon Lockhart's project and its successful presentation.

Michael Govan
CEO and Wallis Annenberg Director
Los Angeles County Museum of Art

James S. Snyder
Anne and Jerome Fisher Director
The Israel Museum, Jerusalem

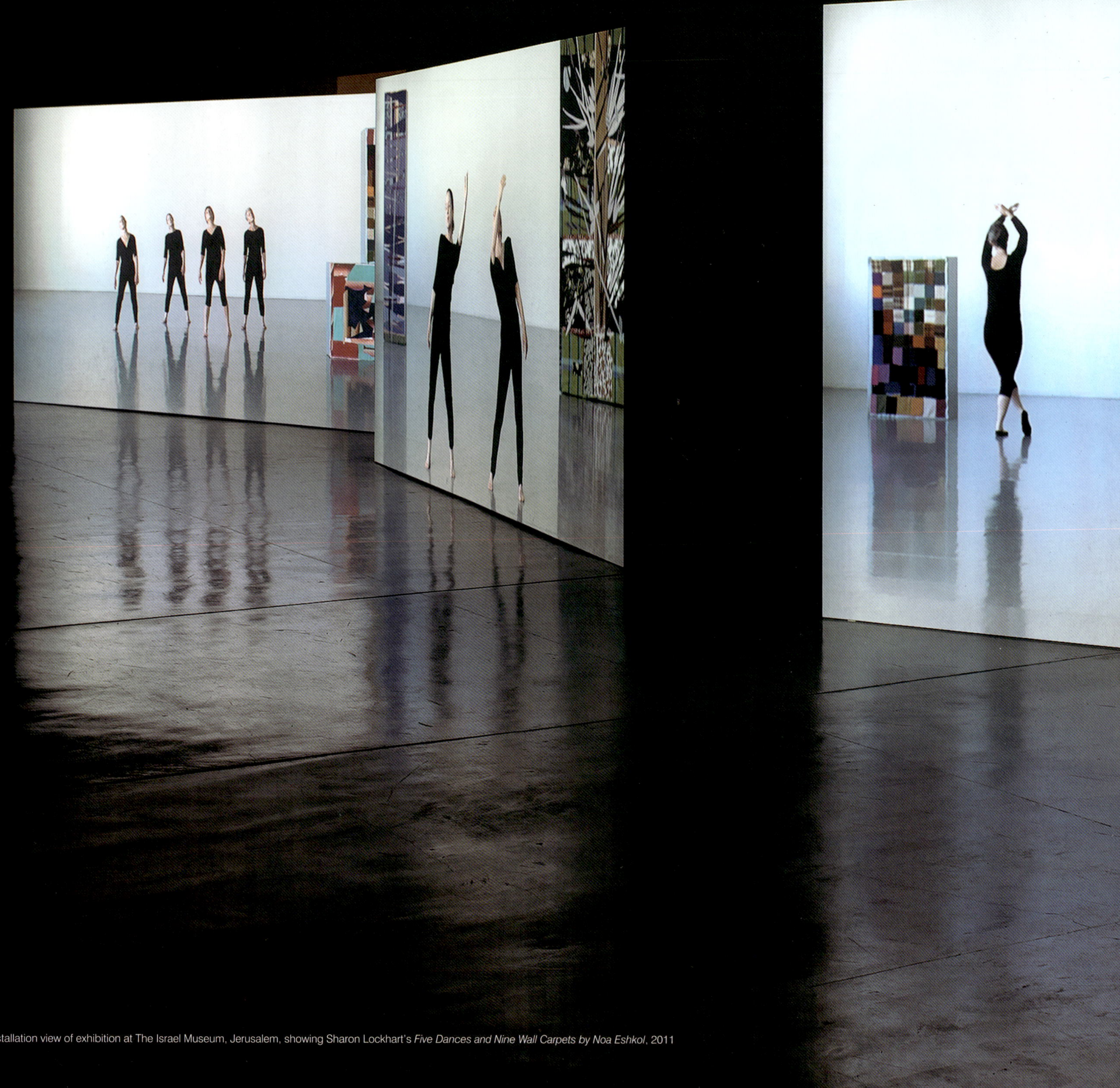

stallation view of exhibition at The Israel Museum, Jerusalem, showing Sharon Lockhart's *Five Dances and Nine Wall Carpets by Noa Eshkol*, 2011

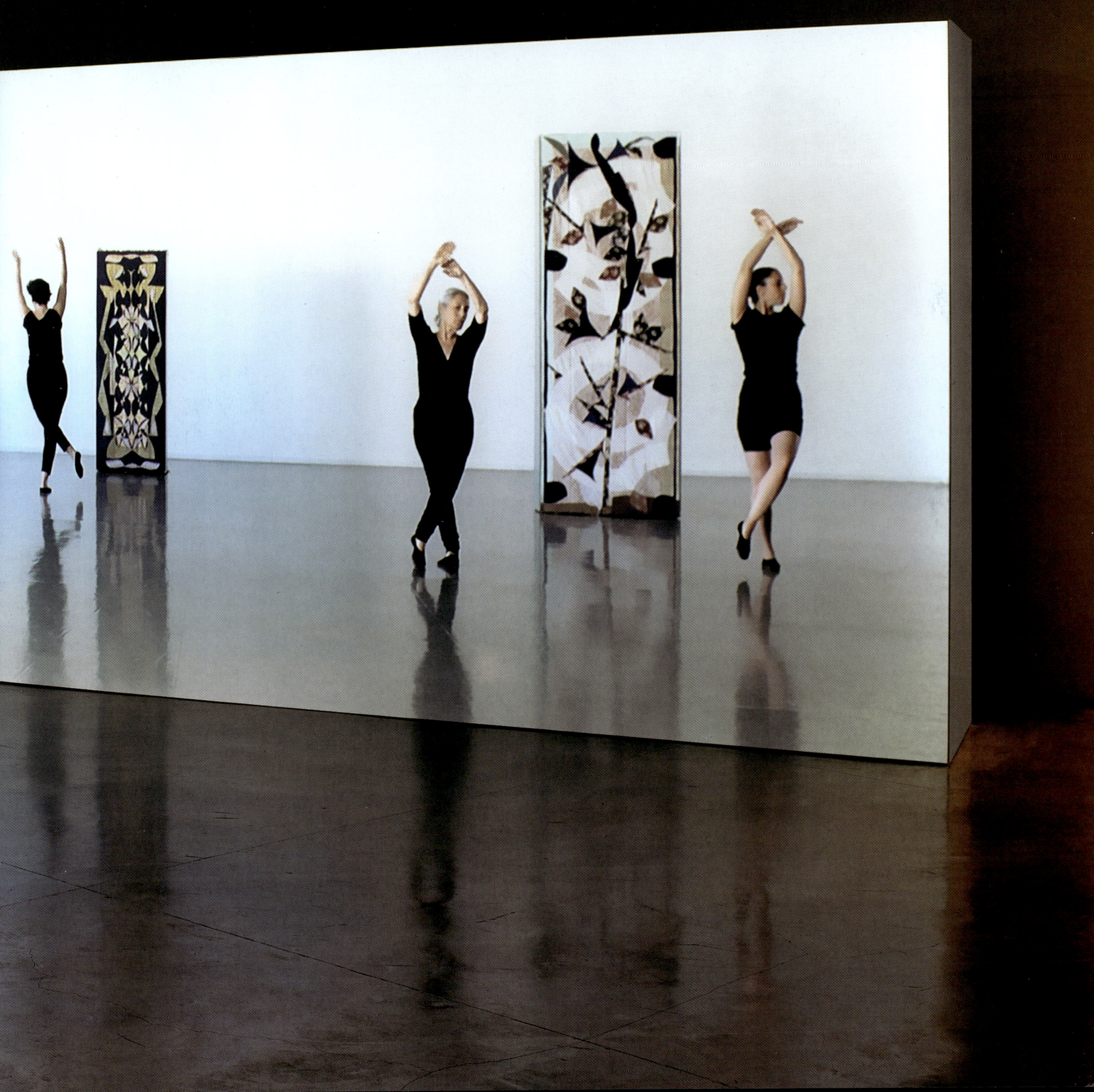

Sharon Lockhart's Historical Choreography; or, the War of Remembrance That Is History

Eva Díaz

Sharon Lockhart's staging of Noa Eshkol's *War Dance (Heraldic)* is *fierce*. One portion of this dance is particularly striking (fig. 1). Three dancers are shown in a triangular arrangement—two in the foreground, one several feet behind—in a spacious, battleship-gray rehearsal room. Dressed simply and uniformly in black tops and black ankle-length pants, the dancers assume an identical pose: with weight balanced on their right legs they tilt back, extending left legs heel first toward the viewer while brandishing right arms above their heads in defiant fists. Though their bodies confront the viewer, their eyes look leftward, trained on an object out of frame in the near horizon. One can easily imagine spears grasped in those raised arms, or arrows deftly moving from quivers at their scapulas to bows held in their outstretched left arms. Here are three hunters stalking in the night, three fighters challenging a common enemy.

It is a forceful image. This is a dance of silent and powerful union: a warrior dance.

(If I told you two of the three dancers are women, would the dance be any less martial, any less fearsome?)

(If I told you that all three dancers are in their seventies, would that make them any less imposing, any less dancerly?)

It is an arresting image. Arresting, too, in another sense of the word: this is a frame from a film Lockhart produced for her five-channel film installation *Five Dances and Nine Wall Carpets by Noa Eshkol* (2011), the centerpiece of the exhibition *Sharon Lockhart | Noa Eshkol*.[1] Though it is an excerpt—a frame from a film—it appears final and complete. It has the look of what has been called a "cinematic photograph": when time is halted in a static image, it allows for a precise composition that proves deeply satisfying, while still offering a promise of narrative fulfillment.[2]

For this film installation Lockhart restaged five dances, including *War Dance (Heraldic)*, from the dance suite *Theme and Variations* by Israeli dance and movement theorist, dance composer, and teacher Noa Eshkol (1924–2007).[3] The three dancers were once members of Eshkol's Chamber Dance Group and worked with Eshkol in her studio in Holon, Israel. In the concord of the three bodies I can sense an ethic of martial discipline characteristic of Eshkol's choreographic style. The metaphor of the body in war—dance corps as military corps—is central to Eshkol's dance technique and, indeed, could be said to define dance training more generally; precise instruction and rigorous rehearsal separate professionals from those of us who traverse the world with rather less physical preparation. The metaphor of battle also offers a point of entry into Lockhart's reconsideration of Eshkol: the exhibition, which she has conceived as a two-person exhibition consisting of works by

1. Lockhart designed the exhibition in collaboration with the Los Angeles–based architecture firm EscherGuneWardena Architecture. The description of the exhibition in this essay is based on the version presented at The Israel Museum, Jerusalem, which I viewed in December 2011. Both the film and the selection of Eshkol's wall carpets and archival material vary with each venue.

2. See Corey Creekmur, "The Cinematic Photograph and the Possibility of Mourning," *Wide Angle* 9, no. 1 (1986): 41–49. George Baker adopts this phrase in "Photography's Expanded Field," *October*, no. 114 (Autumn 2005): 120–40.

3. Eshkol did not like to be described as a "choreographer"; following the terminology used in this book, I refer to her as a "dance composer." The dances from *Theme and Variations*, which Eshkol premiered in 1965, are: *Ländler* (arranged by Racheli Nul-Kahana; dancers: Mor Bashan, Noga Goral, Or Gal-Or, Ruti Sela); *Fugue* (dancers: Nul-Kahana, Sela); *Strolling (Promenade)* (dancers: Nul-Kahana, Hamutal Peled, Sela, Sara Sheffi); *War Dance (Heraldic)* (dancers: Nul-Kahana, Sela, Shmulik Zaidel); and *Duet* (Nul-Kahana, Sela). The introduction to the book *Theme & Variations: Dance Suite, Book 1* (Holon, Israel: Movement Notation Society for the Noa Eshkol Foundation for Movement Notation, 2010) states that in "the suite '*Theme and Variations*' . . . (or in its first name, '*Preludes and Fugues*'), Eshkol emphatically relates [the form of the dances] to serial orders, . . . fugue, etc. These musical forms served her in building a polyphonic composition, both among the single dancer's body parts, as well as among the dancers as a group" (6). Lockhart conceives her five films of these five dances as separate parts of one film; Nul-Kahana, who worked with Eshkol from the 1960s and possesses a deep knowledge of her dance compositions, staged the dances for the film.

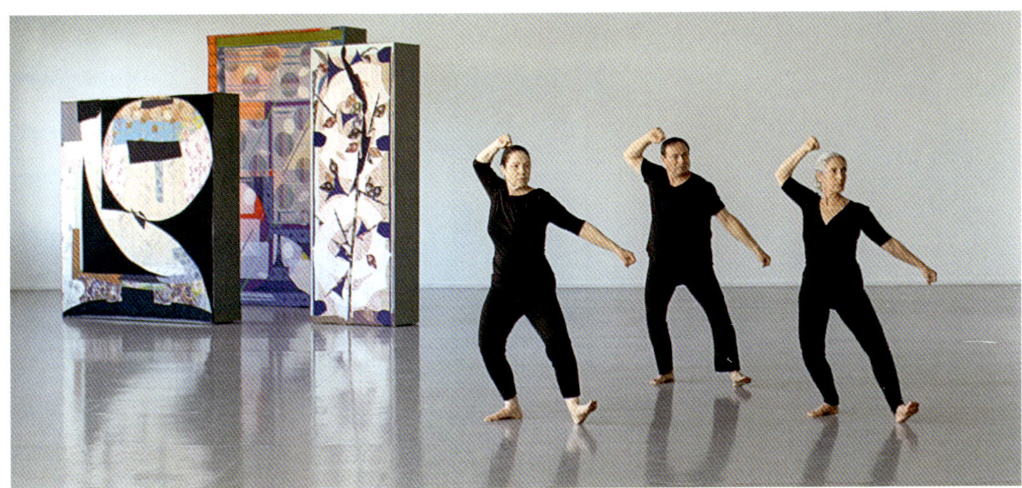

Fig. 1. Sharon Lockhart, frame from *Five Dances and Nine Wall Carpets by Noa Eshkol*, 2011

both artists that mutually inform each other, can be interpreted as an exercise in "historical choreography," in which Lockhart fights to remember, and to have us remember, past histories through the recovery and reinterpretation of objects, experiences, and people that "progress" has left behind.

•

Stand in front of Lockhart's film of *War Dance (Heraldic)*, projected onto a large gray rectangular volume in the installation, as are the other four parts of the film, and you'll see something even more incongruous than three mature dancers garbed in black performing a warlike line dance.[4] In the left half of the projected image are three large "wall carpets," the term Eshkol used to describe the textile works she began creating in 1973, mounted to vertical slate-gray volumes set at a 45-degree angle to the viewer (and the projection); these volumes evoke the form of the structure on which the image itself is projected. The carpets are bright and bold, all abstract designs, though they range from geometric figures to vegetal patterns.[5] The arrangement of these three volumes within *War Dance (Heraldic)* parallels the diagonal orientation of the three dancers at stage left; together they appear like three additional (silent and immobile) participants in the dance.

These carpets—examples of which are found in each of the five projections as well as being physically installed on plinths in an adjacent room of the exhibition—are part of Eshkol's decades-long practice of collecting fabric oddments and laying out the unaltered scraps in compositions stitched together by her dancers and friends. In contrast to the strict adherence to choreography that Eshkol demanded of her dancers, her acceptance of accidents of discovery in her carpets is a kind of contingency-through-control that attracted Lockhart to the works. Until now these carpets, hundreds of which exist, had never been publicly combined with Eshkol's more well-known work as a dance composer.

When the projected textile and dance components are seen together within a single projected field, a bundle of contradictions emerges. Immediately obvious is how traditional gender and age roles in dance are troubled. Yet other sets of concerns are at stake here, too: the relationship between craft (as tradition) and art (as innovation); between dance (as choreography) and visual art (as composition); between film (as movement) and photography (as stasis); between originality and repetition, control and freedom, chance and design, collectivity and singularity. (In discussing these contradictions, these paired relationships, let us not understand them as antinomies, binaries, or oppositions. Each term can and should be seen through the lens of its couple, as a dynamic, mutually informing

4. Lockhart uses the term "volume" to describe the structures featured in the film and the structures on which the film is projected.

5. *Dolphin with Ball*, the squarish carpet to the left, is dominated by a giant circle. *Tree*, the narrow carpet to the right, depicts a more all-over twig-like floral pattern. *Nine Moons*, the large carpet in the center, is composed of a tessellated group of blue, white, green, and orange fabric blocks.

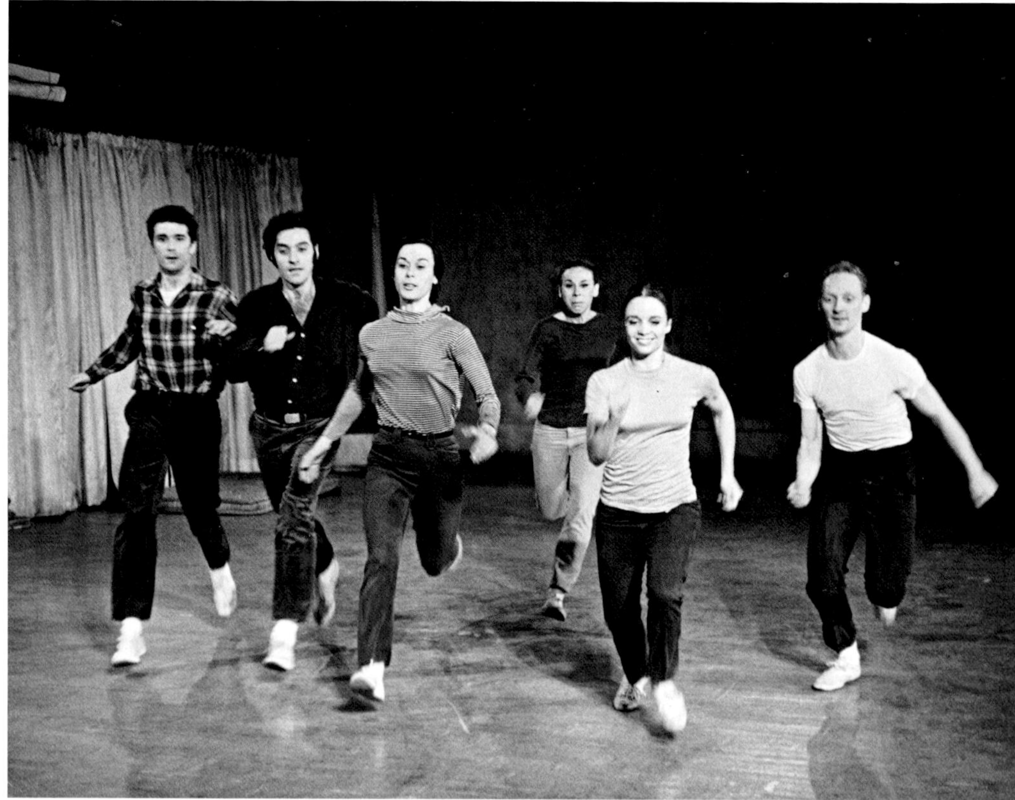

Fig. 2. Yvonne Rainer, *The Mind Is a Muscle*, as performed at Judson Memorial Church, May 24, 1966, photo by Peter Moore, © The Estate of Peter Moore/Licensed by VAGA, New York, NY. Courtesy of The Getty Research Institute, Los Angeles (2006.M.24)

relationship, as part of a dialectic whose terms collaborate to produce a synthesis.) These dynamics are all at play in the exhibition, swirling through the designs of the textiles and in the gestures of the dances, in Lockhart's return to practices now forty-plus years old and largely unknown outside of Eshkol's circle. To understand why Lockhart brought these people and objects related to Eshkol together, the most important relationship to consider is the one between "then and now," between modernism and contemporaneity, the dialectic between actions past and present that expresses a paradoxical "fact of contingency" (to use Louis Althusser's phrase): that is, the ability to revisit and rethink histories in light of our own dynamic relationship to actions and events in the present.[6]

Reconsidering the work of Eshkol, Lockhart intertwines tropes and techniques of modernist art: social documentary practices (site visits, interviews, work with original company members) with nonnarrative explorations of durational and aleatory events.[7] She asks what the stakes of these strategies of representation are today, connecting them to the broader set of interrelationships I mentioned above. Her selection of elements and artifacts from her subjects' physical world, and her combination of them with her own representations of their actions and gestures are strategies she has adopted in previous projects. It might be called a kind of "social choreography."[8] Like Lockhart's work on Eshkol, in recent years other artists and filmmakers have turned to social choreography, specifically in dance, as a kind of hybridity beyond hyperspecialization, and as a model for collaborative practice and interdisciplinarity. Social choreography in Lockhart's work can be understood as a blurring of "the lines between ritual and recreation," a practice in which commonplace or familiar actions are reframed and revealed as loaded with social meaning.[9] In this reconsideration she mines the rich and only recently historicized concerns of the Fluxus "event" score as a kind of paradoxical scripting of ordinary actions. She also revisits the related concerns of Judson Dance Theater, such as Yvonne Rainer's framing in *The Mind Is a Muscle* (1966, fig. 2) of

6. In a series of late essays from the 1980s, Louis Althusser addressed criticisms that his view of determination overemphasized the reproduction of existing structures of domination, thereby diminishing the role of human agency in effecting structural change. In his reassessment of this necessitarian logic, Althusser introduced the idea of a "fact of contingency." Expanding on the concept, he maintained that in each event there are singular uncertain and unforeseeable elements that result in a "void essential to any aleatory encounter." Althusser, *Philosophy of the Encounter: Later Writings, 1978–87*, ed. François Matheron and Oliver Corpet and trans. G. M. Goshgarian (London: Verso Press, 2006), 170, 202, 264.

7. Lockhart's commingling of order and chance, as George Baker has noted, "[c]ombines that ethnographic tradition with a completely opposed set of codes, often from Cagean avant-garde aesthetics. Various types of avant-garde strategies are layered in her project that were formerly . . . incompatible. The work's challenge turns on whether and how these opposed legacies can be brought together. *Teatro Amazonas* (1999) is an ethnographic film that's also a Cagean event; *Goshogaoka* is an Yvonne Rainer dance performance as much as an ethnographic film." Baker in Baker et al., "Round Table: The Projected Image in Contemporary Art," *October*, no. 104 (Spring 2003): 82. See also Linda Norden, "So Here's My Holiday," in *Pine Flat* (Milan: Charta, 2006), 128–32.

8. Examples include *Goshogaoka* (1997), *Pine Flat* (2006), and *Lunch Break* (2008). In *Goshogaoka*, Lockhart worked with both a Japanese teenage-girl basketball team and a professional choreographer, Stephen Galloway, who choreographed basketball routines that have affinities with the dances of Yvonne Rainer.

9. Bernard Joisten, "Interview with Sharon Lockhart," *Purple* (Winter 1998–99), reprinted in Jenelle Porter, ed., *Dance with Camera* (Philadelphia: Institute of Contemporary Art, University of Pennsylvania, 2009), 140–42.

everyday actions to dehabituate not only habits of spectatorship, but tics of performance, such as the virtuoso flourish or the photogenic "ta-da" moment of self-presentation.[10] One is reminded, too, of Bruce Nauman's filling the void of an empty studio with a dance exercise, as in his *Dance or Exercise on the Perimeter of a Square* (1967–68).[11]

In the present exhibition, however, social choreography might be more accurately termed "historical choreography": art-historical research combined with reenactment. To understand how this thinking-historically-in-the-present works, it is essential to conceive of the dynamic interrelationships I invoked—stasis and movement, design and chance, collectivity and singularity—as themselves collaborations. For various reasons, this way of thinking of collaboration either as social choreography, or as the temporally specific contextualization of bodies of historical choreography, was fraught if not impossible in Eshkol's career as a dance composer and textile artist. It is important to note that such a hybridization of craft, dance, photography, and film as the shared practices of modernist experimentation is pressured by contemporary artists such as Lockhart, whose work asks that the contemporary museum rethink medium-specific separations in the interest of presenting more complex histories of how things *really* went down.

•

Eshkol—arguably Israel's most innovative modern dance composer and the creator of Eshkol-Wachman Movement Notation in collaboration with architect Avraham Wachman—has been relatively overlooked outside of her home country. She undertook her work from a studio based in her home in Holon, where she lived from the 1940s until her death.[12] A tight-knit group of dancers formed around her. Many of them joined her Chamber Dance Group, which she established in 1954. Her exacting rehearsal schedule and outspoken, galvanic personality made her a polarizing figure in her day, a reputation that continues into the present. The Noa Eshkol Foundation for Movement Notation now maintains her archive, preserves and re-creates her dances, and cares for the carpets.

Lockhart made multiple visits to Israel over a three-year period, where she worked in the archive and with members of the foundation. Five main elements from this research and discussion emerged as central to the concept, design, and appearance of the exhibition. First and most important was the collaboration with several dancers, many of them longtime members of the Chamber Dance Group, to reconstruct Eshkol's dances for the five-channel film installation mentioned above and the "exercises" for the single-channel film installation *Four Exercises in Eshkol-Wachman Movement Notation* (2011).[13]

Second, Lockhart combined a selection of Eshkol's carpets with the dances, using the specially designed volumes as physical objects placed in the dancers' mise-en-scène. Third, she selected and brought three of the carpets into the exhibition space, installing them on large plinths. Fourth, she included in the exhibition her photographic series *Models of Orbits in the System of Reference, Eshkol-Wachman Movement Notation System* (2011), which she produced by photographing seven wire-and-mesh spherical models Eshkol designed to represent the possible movements of any limb.[14] And fifth, she brought selected notes, programs, posters, original publications, and photographs from Eshkol's archive for display in specially designed vitrines.

The largest part of the exhibition is taken up with a snakelike sequence of five rectangular volumes upon which the five parts of Lockhart's film of the dances are projected. Two of the dances are duets, two feature groups of four women, and one is the trio, *War Dance (Heraldic)*, described above. All the dances are performed to the synchronized sound of a metronome set at 120 beats per minute, as Eshkol intended. Because of the zigzagging flow of the five projections—three to the right when entering

10. See Carrie Lambert, "Moving Still: Mediating Yvonne Rainer's 'Trio A,'" *October*, no. 89 (Summer 1999): 87–112.

11. Lockhart's former student Elad Lassry's restaging of Balanchine choreography from multiple perspectives also comes to mind. In addition, think of Catherine Sullivan's simplification of theatrical gesture into a series of choreographed movements enacted by both amateur and professional performers, Joachim Koester's exploration of choreographing spontaneous dance in his recent film installation *Tarantulism* (2007), and filmmaker Pierre Coulibeuf's work with various modern dance companies throughout Europe. If one appended contemporary artists who use coordinated gestures on the part of performers, combined with the popularity of the biennial Performa, the list surely swells. We are truly in a dance-theater-art-film nexus. For further examples, see Catherine Wood's article "The Art of Writing with People," in *Tate Etc.*, no. 20 (Autumn 2010), available at http://www.tate.org.uk/tateetc/issue20/artanddance.htm.

12. Eshkol's father, Levi Eshkol, was the finance minister of Israel for twelve years and served as prime minister from 1963 until his death in 1969. For more information on Levi Eshkol, see Terence Prittie, *Eshkol: The Man and the Nation* (New York: Pittman Publishing Corp., 1969).

13. Eshkol used the term "exercise" for stage events performed by single dancers, in contrast to "dance" for pieces with more than one performer. Ruti Sela is the dancer featured in *Four Exercises in Eshkol-Wachman Movement Notation*.

14. For an in-depth discussion of the photographic series, see Stephanie Barron and Britt Salvesen, "Drawing in Space," in this book.

near the introductory wall signage, and two to the left on the far side of the room—the viewer is in a consistently dynamic relationship with respect to the movements depicted on the screens. Negotiating the space of the exhibition involves a series of physical recalibrations on the part of spectators as they orient themselves to each screen. The size of the projections figures each dancer at an approximately "real" human scale, which puts viewers into a relationship of physical equality, in a partnership of sorts, with the dancers before them.

In some of the dances of *Theme and Variations*, dancers mirror one another's gestures, creating patterns in the gray spaces as they harmonize or deviate from their fellow performers' actions. This sense of a community of movement is extensive: in the dances with four performers one is invited to imagine how those patterns of movements depicted could extend into the space before the projection—the diegetic space of the film leaks into the space of reception. In particular, the warrior dance is a dance of coalition and equality; each performer's actions conform precisely to the shared choreography in a way that nearly impels viewers to join the march. The ticktock of the metronome imbues the performance with the urgency of a heartbeat pounding, anticipating the climax of the hunt, or the adrenaline rush of battle, that, in this film, infects the viewer with a sense of intensity, of bodily identification.

Yet the metronome's monotony, combined with the deliberation and lack of haste in the dancers' movements, refuses dramatic arcs or narrative catharsis. Even in their most literal moments, like the one signifying attack in the warrior dance, the metronomic linearity of time in the dances implies that events can unfold endlessly, punctuated only by the repetition of certain cyclical gestures—arms swinging overhead, weight toggling between extended legs, or hips slowly rotating. Eshkol's characteristic pattern of choreographed movement is the form of the revolving circle, a circle encompassing the body's own rotational joints (neck, waist, shoulders, elbows, wrists, hips, and ankles), circles rolling into smooth progressions without flourish. Lockhart's decision to loop each of the five parts of the film, each of a different length, emphasizes this weave of time and space. The sound design, in which the metronome can be heard throughout the gallery, yet in actuality is concentrated in speakers inside the volumes that act as screens, lends viewers' movements through the space a sense of increasing rhythmic intensity upon approaching each volume, heightening the phenomenological siting of spectatorship in the body.[15] This mode of spectatorship is further accentuated by the viewers' relationships to the volumes themselves as objects, which evoke Minimalist sculptures, particularly Robert Morris's gray-painted plywood sculptures of the mid-1960s.[16]

•

In bringing Eshkol's textile and dance works together, Lockhart situates Eshkol's production within a complex interdisciplinary performance tradition it refused in its time. This tradition extends from Oskar Schlemmer's and Vsevolod Meyerhold's works of the 1920s to Merce Cunningham's work of the 1950s—particularly his collaborations with Robert Rauschenberg. Think, for example, of Rauschenberg's *Minutiae* (1954, fig. 3), an early Combine created as a set piece for a Cunningham dance featuring a musical score by John Cage. As the dancers remarked to Lockhart, the project of joining the different components of Eshkol's career would have been vehemently opposed by Eshkol, though the resulting contextualization within other modernist explorations of movement delighted the dancers themselves.

It is through these strategies of making the objects a part of the dancers' (and viewers') subjective experiences that Lockhart opens up the proscriptions of Eshkol's separation of the

15. Lockhart created the minimalist musical composition for the film with composer Becky Allen and sound engineer Dane Davis. It consists of two tracks audible from three speakers embedded in each of the five volumes onto which the five parts of the film are respectively projected: the beat of a metronome set at 120 beats per minute (the same for each part of the film), and a mix of the sound of the dancers' movements as they perform each individual dance (different for each dance) and the reverberations recorded in the performance space during each individual dance and then amplified (also different). Just as Eshkol's dance scores map the dancers' movements in space graphically, the tones of the musical composition map their movements sonically. The musical composition further relates to Eshkol's dance scores and notation system to the extent that it consists of different elements all coexisting and brought together into a unified composition.

16. One is reminded of Michael Fried's (disparaging) characterization of the spectatorial relationship produced by Morris's sculptures in particular and Minimalist sculptures in general in "Art and Objecthood": "Whereas in previous art 'what is to be had from the work is located strictly within [it],' the experience of literalist [Minimalist] art is of an object *in a situation*—one that, virtually by definition, *includes the beholder*." Michael Fried, "Art and Objecthood," in Gregory Battcock, ed., *Minimal Art: A Critical Anthology* (Berkeley: University of California Press, 1995), 125. Although beyond the scope of this essay, the relationship of Lockhart's work to Minimalism, including the work of artists such as Morris, Rainer, and Steve Reich, is a rich subject for further exploration.

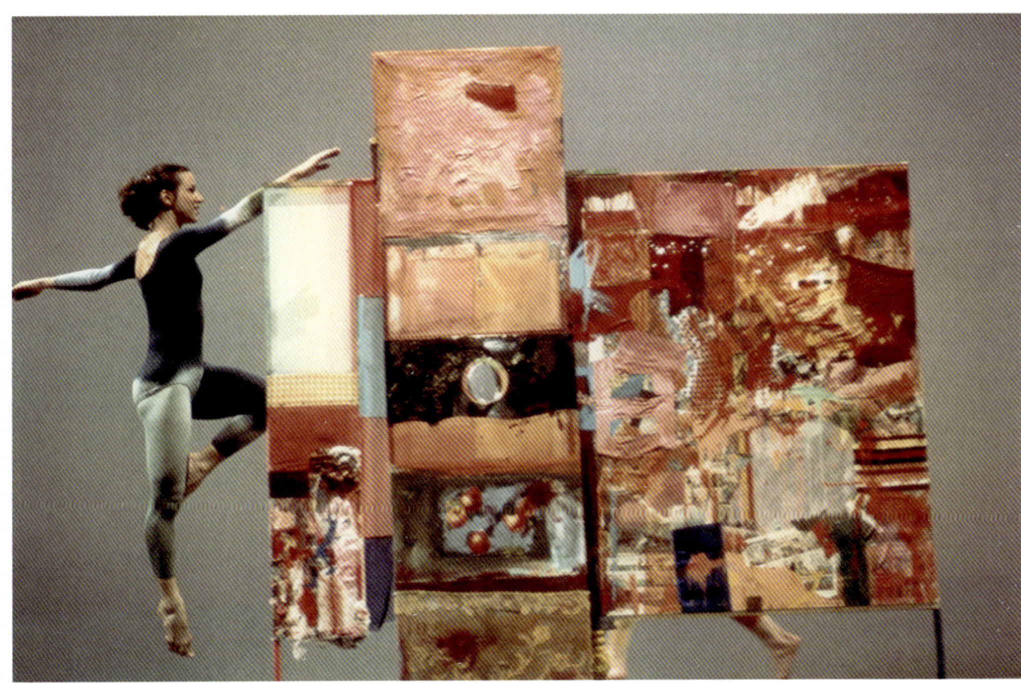

Fig. 3. Performance of Merce Cunningham's *Minutiae* (1954) for the PBS television series *Dance in America: Event for Television* (1977), showing dancer Ellen Cornfield with Robert Rauschenberg's Combine *Minutiae* (1954)

dances from the carpets. Other prescriptions (the prescribed gesture through notation, the prescribed movements of the dancers) are opened up by Lockhart's camera through framing, by bringing the carpets into a relationship with the dancers. This new relationship with the subject folds back to the chain of dialectics I mentioned before: perhaps a key dialectic is not merely *time* (then and now), but also that of the *subject*. You or me, them or us; the subject/object relationship constructed as a polarity is perhaps what Lockhart disrupts the most. The "objects" in the images (for example, the carpets) are as much subject as the dancers.[17] Contrariwise, "you," as subject, are physiologically implicated as an object of the performance in the way the phenomenological effects of the sound and the human scale of the projections act on you.

•

For Lockhart the representation of these objects and experiences is a kind of advocacy. She has taken disparate threads of Eshkol's work and put them into the museum as contemporary art. Thus, Eshkol's diverse practices, in their interdisciplinarity, may now be found where they never had a home before. Is it now the role of contemporary art to fight for the kind of interdisciplinarity and hybridity that modernist figures in dance like Schlemmer, Meyerhold, Cunningham, and others practiced, which Eshkol herself practiced, in a half-expressed manner, in her work as a dance composer and textile designer?

Is *this* the battle being contested in Lockhart's staging of *War Dance (Heraldic)* and Eshkol's other dances? Is this why Lockhart has chosen to return us to these acts and objects? Let us consider these questions in relation to another work of art on view at the Israel Museum, the site where *Sharon Lockhart | Noa Eshkol* was first presented: the small Paul Klee work titled *Angelus Novus* (1920, fig. 4) in the museum's permanent collection. Walter Benjamin once owned this work, and his now-famous interpretation of it in his "Theses on the Philosophy of History" (written in 1940, the year of his death) has made it "an icon of the left."[18] Here is Benjamin:

17. Likewise, Lockhart's photographs of the Eshkol-Wachman spheres initially seem to present these objects neutrally against a gray background. Yet the gleaming metallic suspended forms are shot with an eerie frontality, as though they were portraits. Each form is photographed turning on its longitudinal axis, highlighting its dimensional complexity, rather than the cursory visual inventory the object catalogue or database provides.

18. Otto Karl Werckmeister, *Icons of the Left: Benjamin and Eisenstein, Picasso and Kafka after the Fall of Communism* (Chicago: University of Chicago Press, 1999).

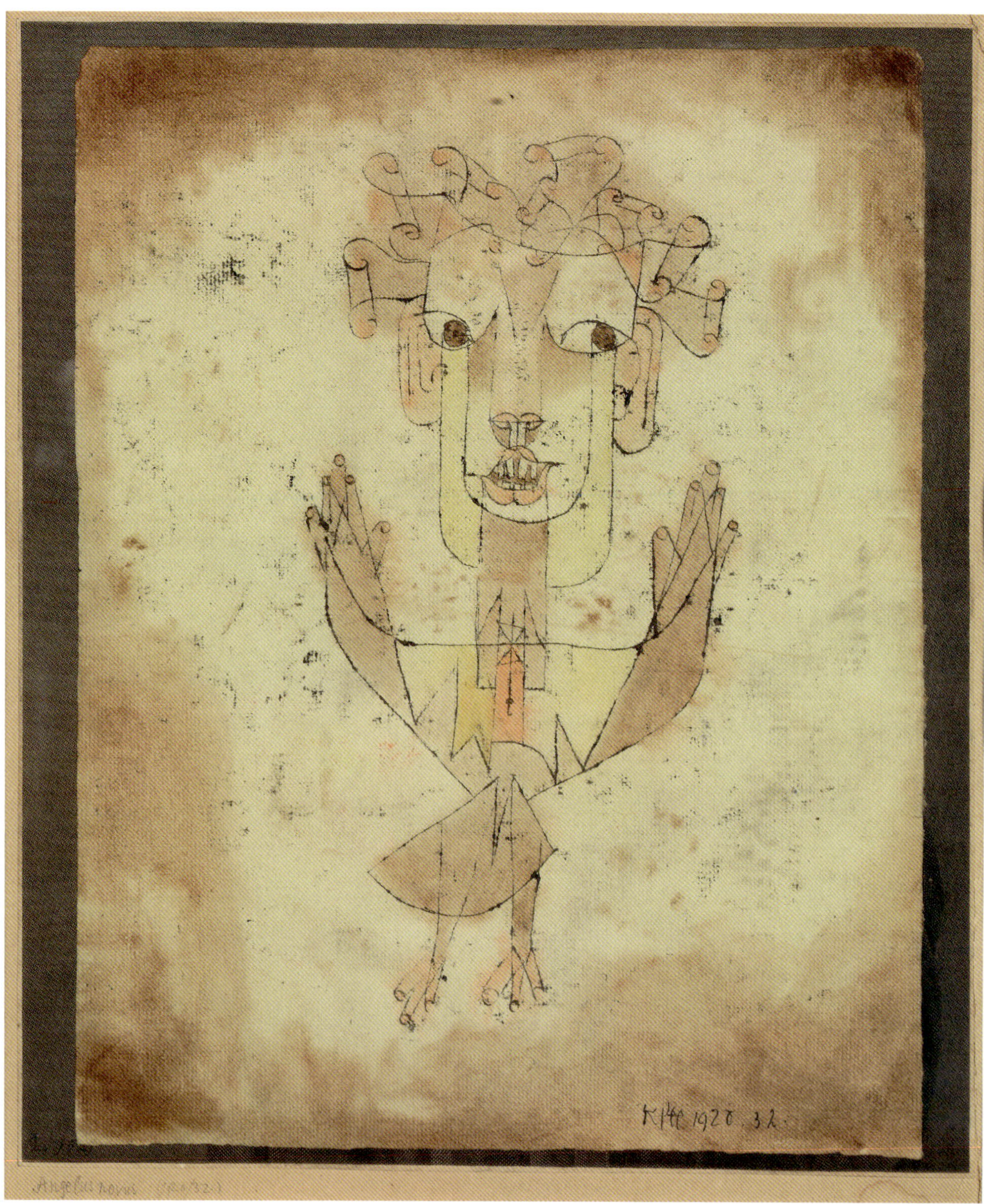

Fig. 4. Paul Klee. *Angelus Novus*, 1920, India ink, colored chalk, and brown wash on paper, 12 ½ x 9 ½ inches (31.8 x 24.2 cm), The Israel Museum, Jerusalem, Gift of Fania and Gershom Scholem, Jerusalem, John Herring, Marlene and Paul Herring, Jo Carole and Ronald Lauder, New York. B87.994

A Klee painting named "Angelus Novus" shows an angel looking as though he is about to move away from something he is fixedly contemplating. His eyes are staring, his mouth is open, his wings are spread. This is how one pictures the angel of history. His face is turned toward the past. Where we perceive a chain of events, he sees one single catastrophe which keeps piling wreckage upon wreckage and hurls it in front of his feet. The angel would like to stay, awaken the dead, and make whole what has been smashed. But a storm is blowing from Paradise; it has got caught in his wings with such violence that the angel can no longer close them. The storm irresistibly propels him into the future to which his back is turned, while the pile of debris before him grows skyward. This storm is what we call progress.[19]

19. Walter Benjamin, "Theses on the Philosophy of History" (1940), in *Illuminations*, ed. Hannah Arendt and trans. Harry Zohn (New York: Schocken Books, 1968), 249.

Later in the "Theses," Benjamin restates his sense of progress as a storm leaving the past as an undifferentiated pile of rubble. In this second passage he argues that the imperative of history is to sift the wreckage in order to alter the course of that storm called progress. The urgency of thinking-historically-in-the-present prevents the debasement of real struggles achieved in the past to be treated as mere wreckage. He argues that a faithful articulation of history must always contest the ease of forgetting. It is therefore necessary to:

> retain that image of the past which unexpectedly appears to man singled out by history at a moment of danger. The danger affects both the content of the tradition and its receivers. The same threat hangs over both: that of becoming a tool of the ruling class. In every era the attempt must be made anew to wrest tradition away from a conformism that is about to overpower it.[20]

For Benjamin, revitalizing traditions under threat of ever-encroaching revisionism can awaken alternatives obscured by the dominant culture. The reproduction of circumscribed possibilities as "history" has been termed the "selective tradition" by Raymond Williams: "The way in which from a whole possible arena of past and present, certain meanings and practices are chosen for emphasis, certain other meanings and practices are neglected and excluded."[21] The process of refining the objects of historical interest and cultural transmission to a rehearsed and often static canon or tradition serves to regulate and diminish the capacity for social and cultural change. Reconsidering the past requires vigilance, avoiding the power of repetition of the selective tradition that is in effect the violence of history. History is a battleground, a field of conflict from which we must constantly rearticulate lost practices. The helpless movement of the Angelus away from this as-yet-sifted wreckage is the "progress" we must arrest, if only contingently, to find new arrangements of what we call "the past" in this pile of discarded remnants. This may be what Althusser meant by the "fact of contingency." That is to say, the order of the world is fraught with radical instability, and though there is a *fact* of order, that order is provisional and from a medley of various contingent possibilities comes the necessity of any one particular order. It is therefore important, as he wrote, to "think the openness of the world to the event, [to] the as-yet-unimaginable."[22]

In the case of her work on Eshkol, Lockhart asks what Eshkol's modernism—itself a reception of early twentieth-century precedents in the study of movement—can do for us in our present. What can be done today to recover the lost potentials of modernist practices that, for a variety of reasons, can be understood only belatedly? In revisiting these overlooked, and in the case of Eshkol, largely forgotten, practices, a new look at the charge of modernism's strikingly "modern" ambitions can be undertaken. What Lockhart is proposing is a model of continuity for concerns such as attention to form and interdisciplinary hybridity, rather than a model of rupture and rejection. This is a collaboration between individuals and objects, but also between individuals and our collective history. It is historical choreography: the process of writing history into our time, recovering and reinterpreting the objects and experiences "progress" leaves behind.

20. Ibid., 255.
21. Raymond Williams, "Base and Superstructure in Marxist Cultural Theory," in *Problems in Materialism and Culture* (London: Verso Press, 1974), 39.
22. Althusser, 264.

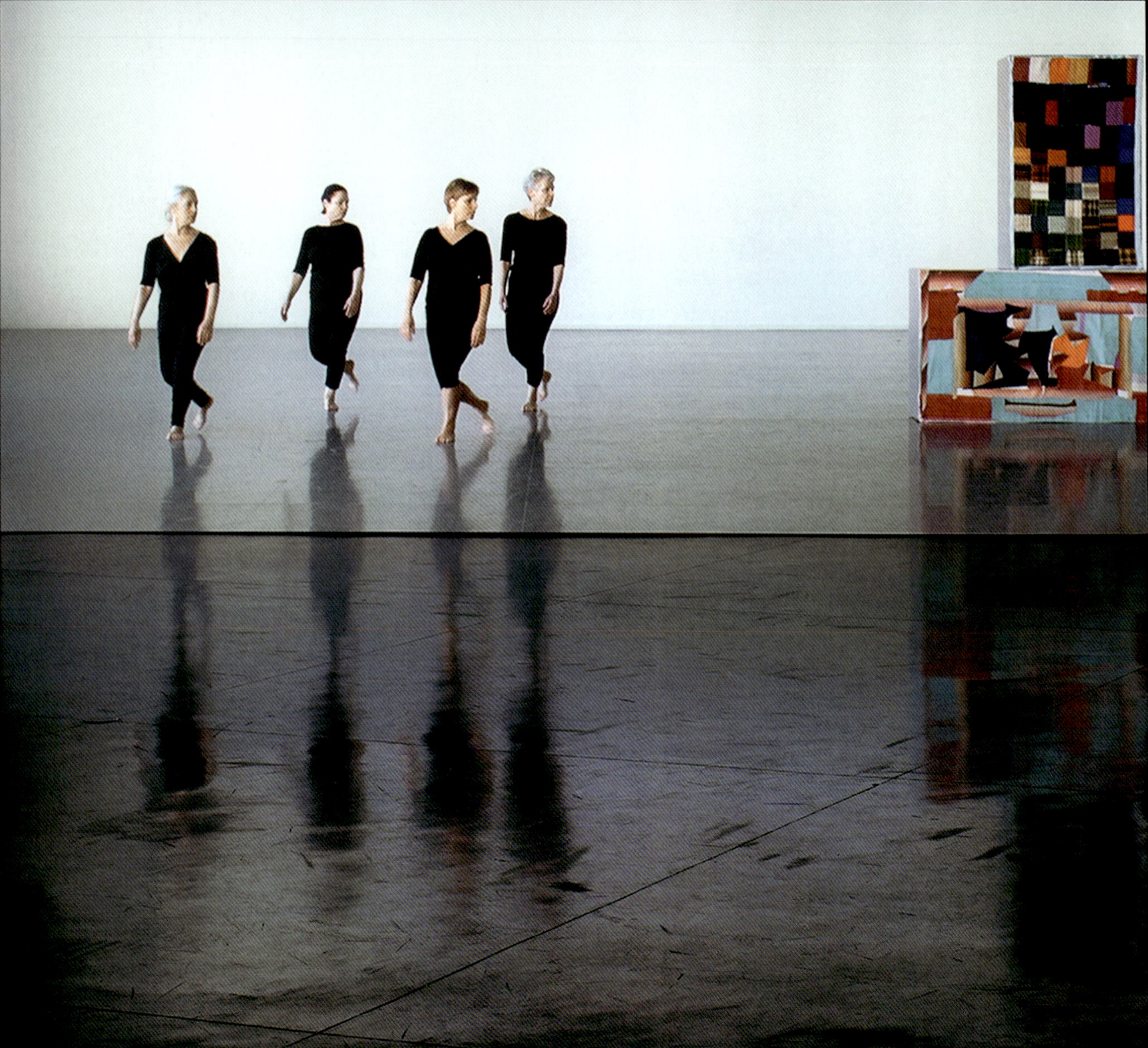

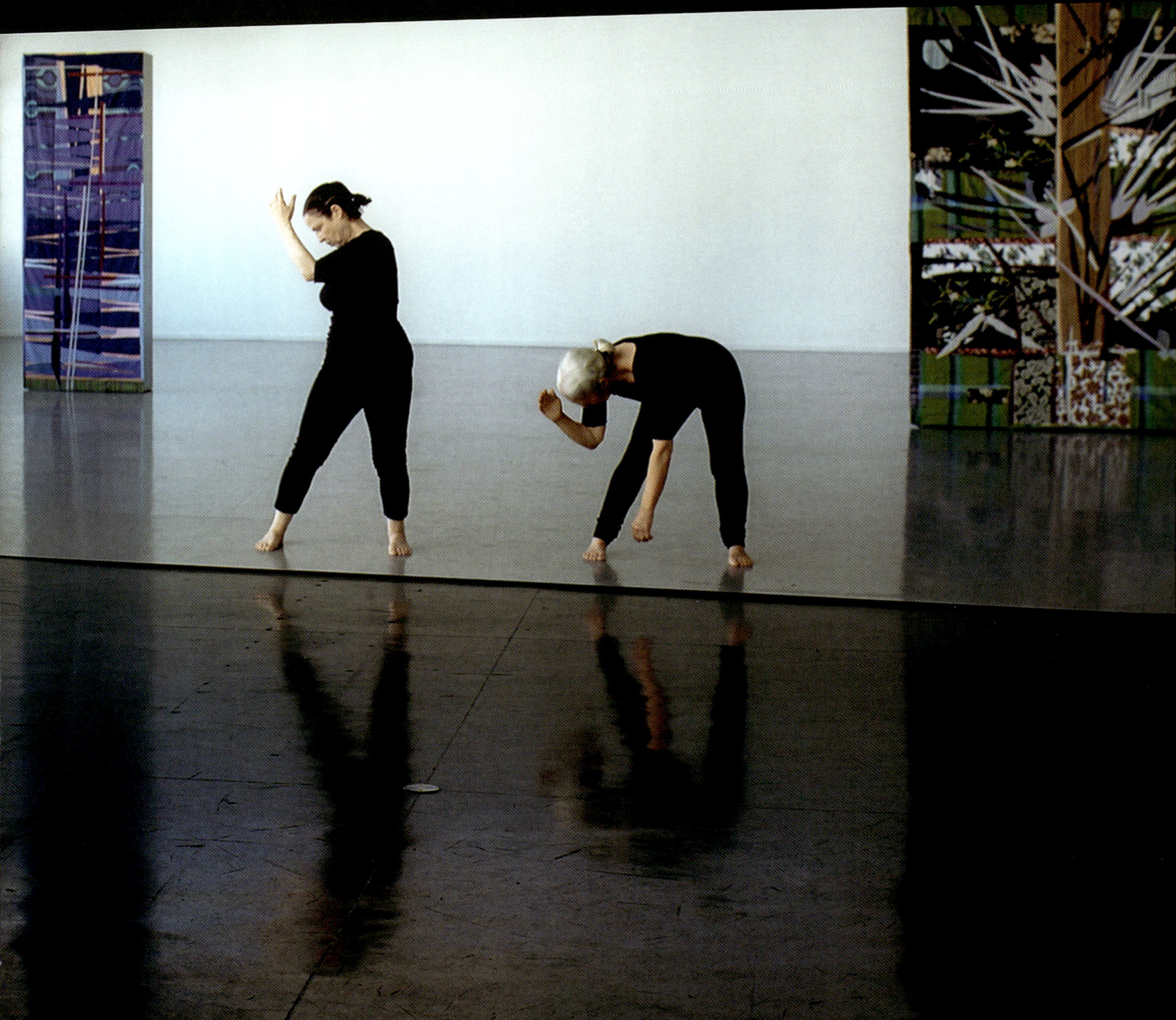

Sharon Lockhart, frames from *Five Dances and Nine Wall Carpets by Noa Eshkol*, 2011
Left to right: Racheli Nul-Kahana and Ruti Sela performing Noa Eshkol's *Duet*

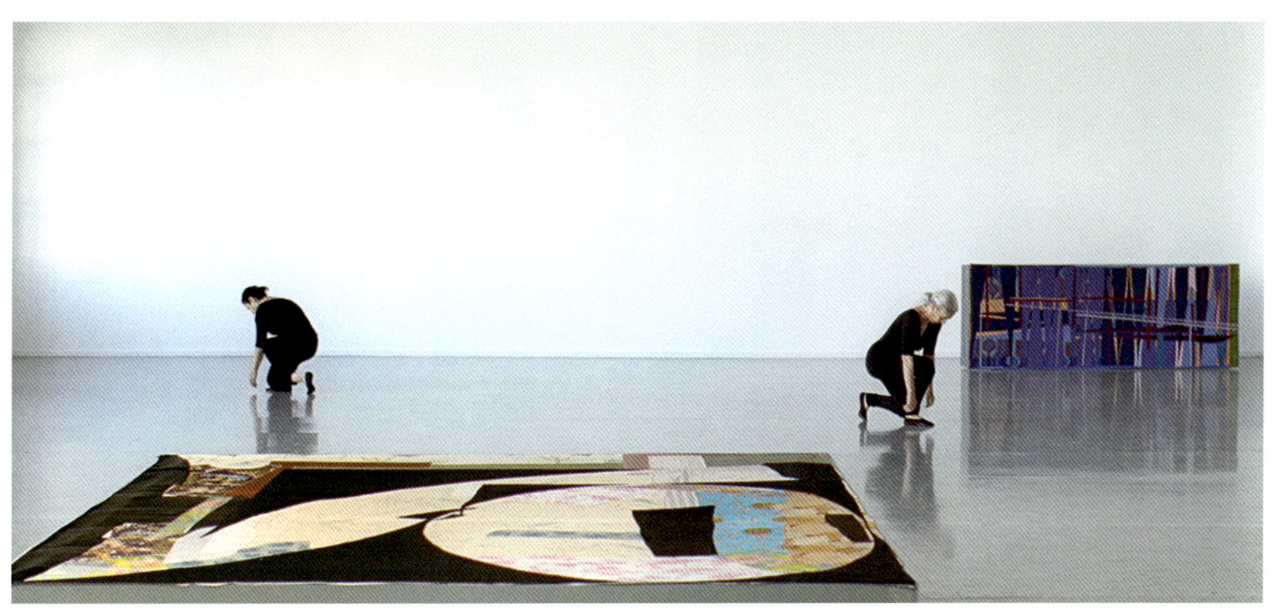

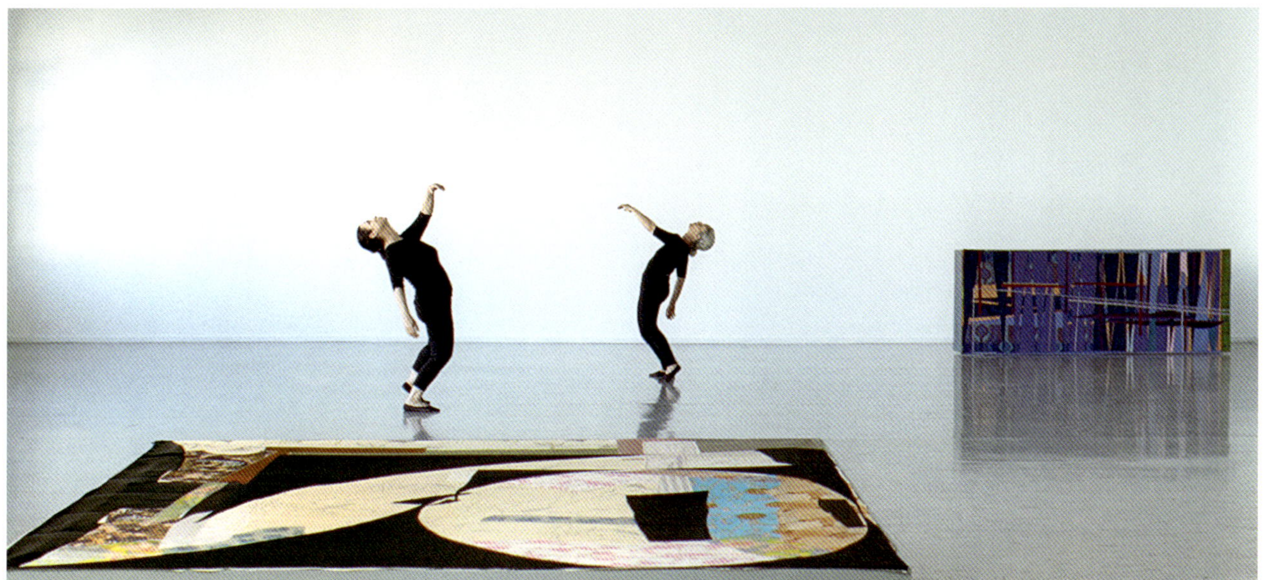

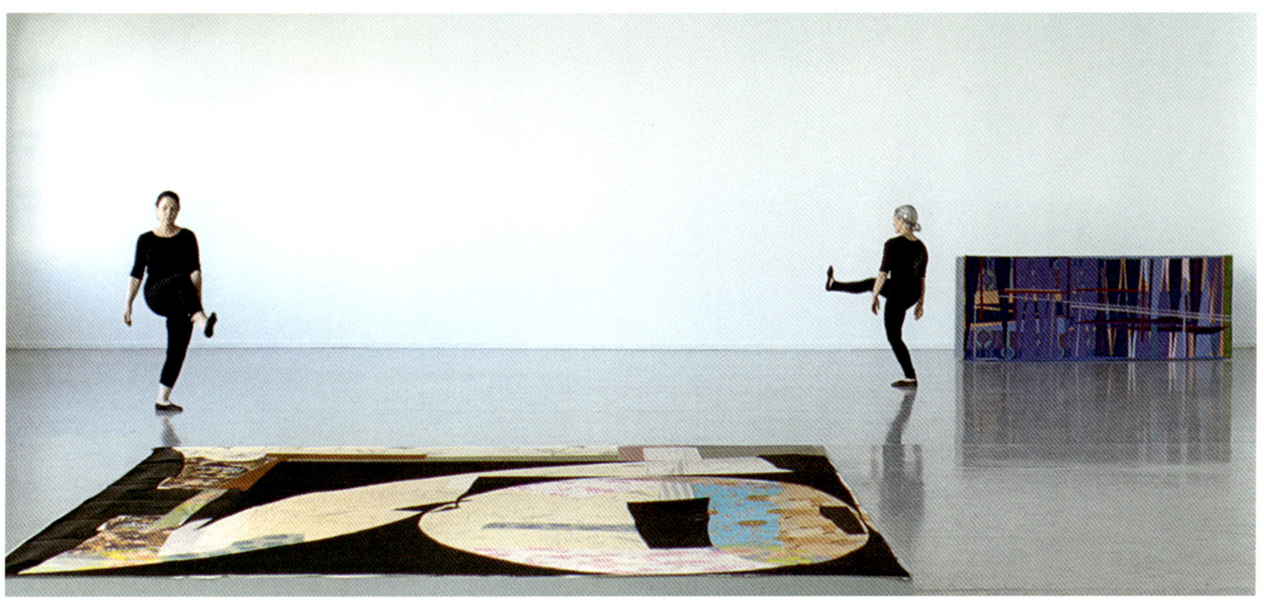

Sharon Lockhart, frames from *Five Dances and Nine Wall Carpets by Noa Eshkol*, 2011
Left to right: Racheli Nul-Kahana and Ruti Sela performing Noa Eshkol's *Fugue*

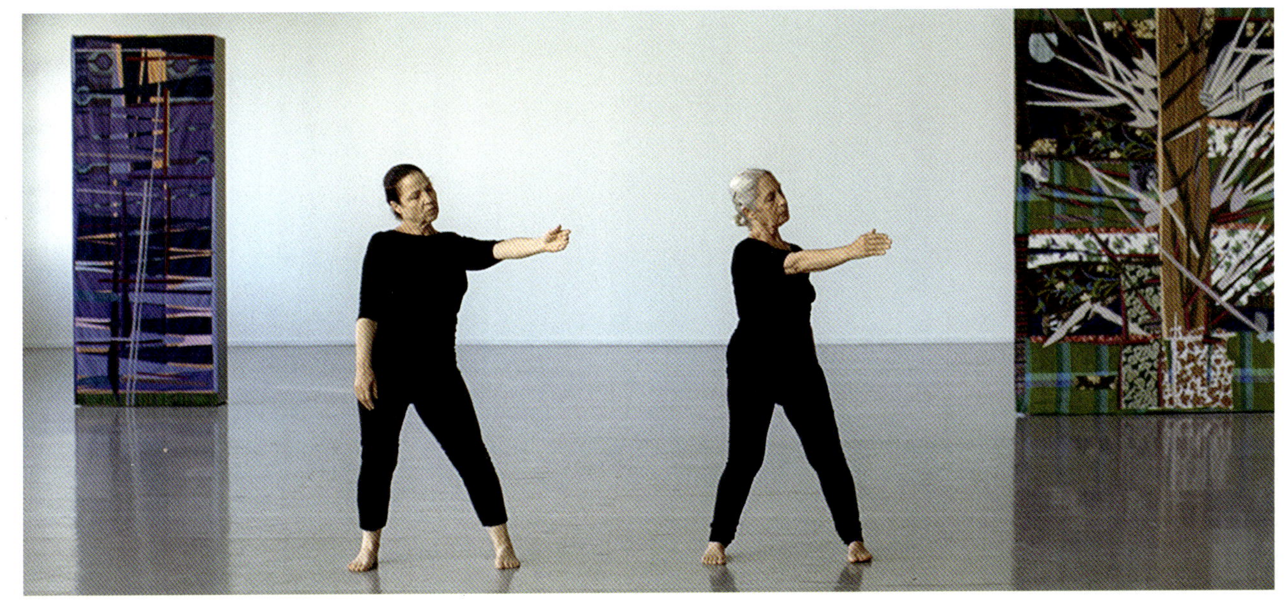

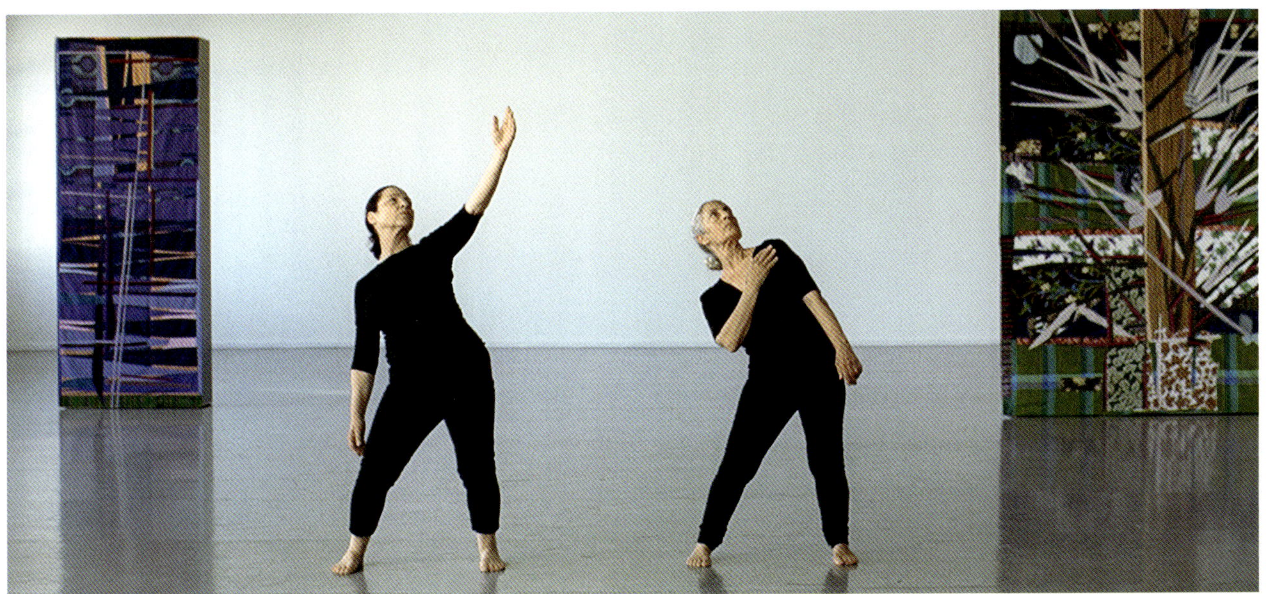

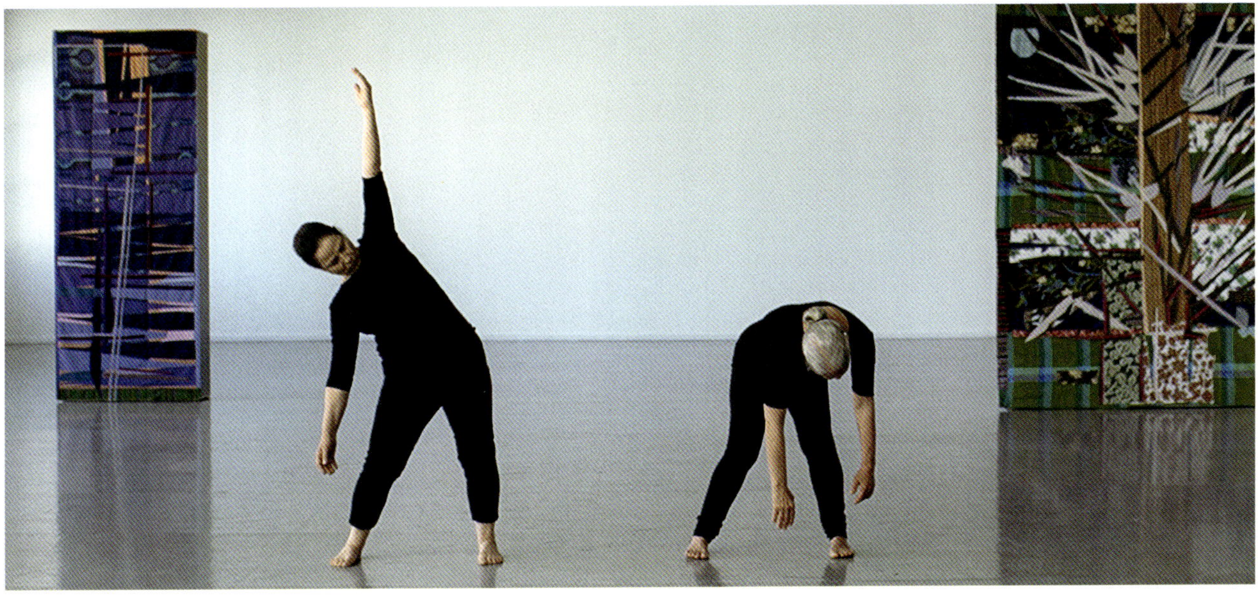

Sharon Lockhart, frames from *Five Dances and Nine Wall Carpets by Noa Eshkol*, 2011
Left to right: Noga Goral, Mor Bashan, Ruti Sela, and Or Gal-Or performing Noa Eshkol's *Ländler*

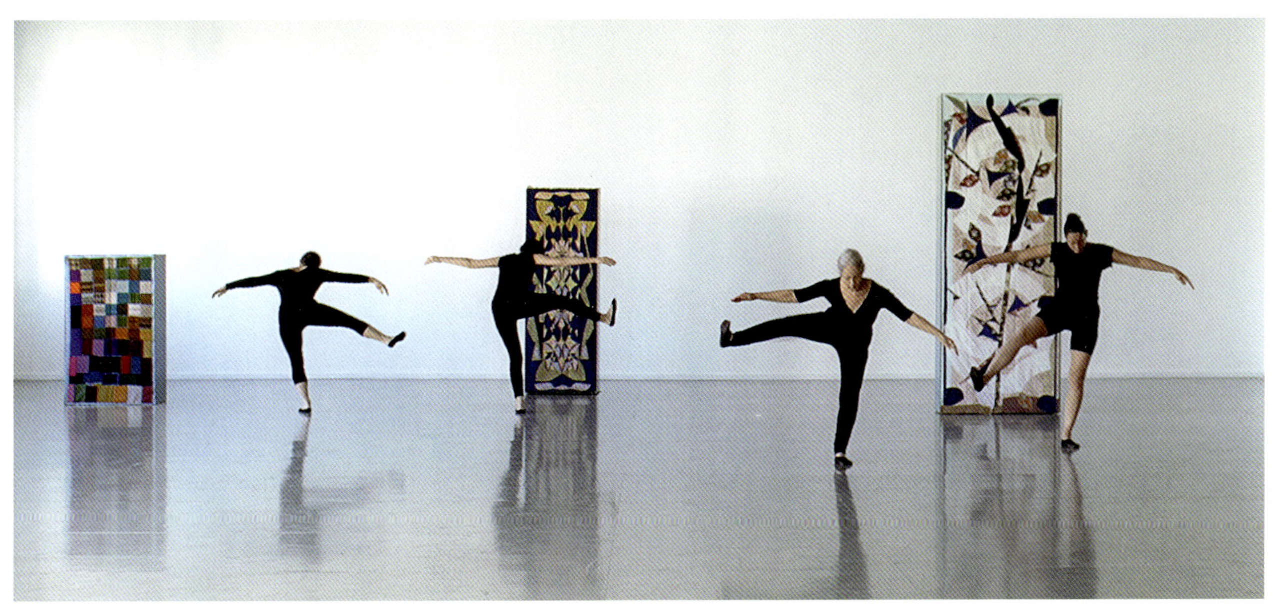

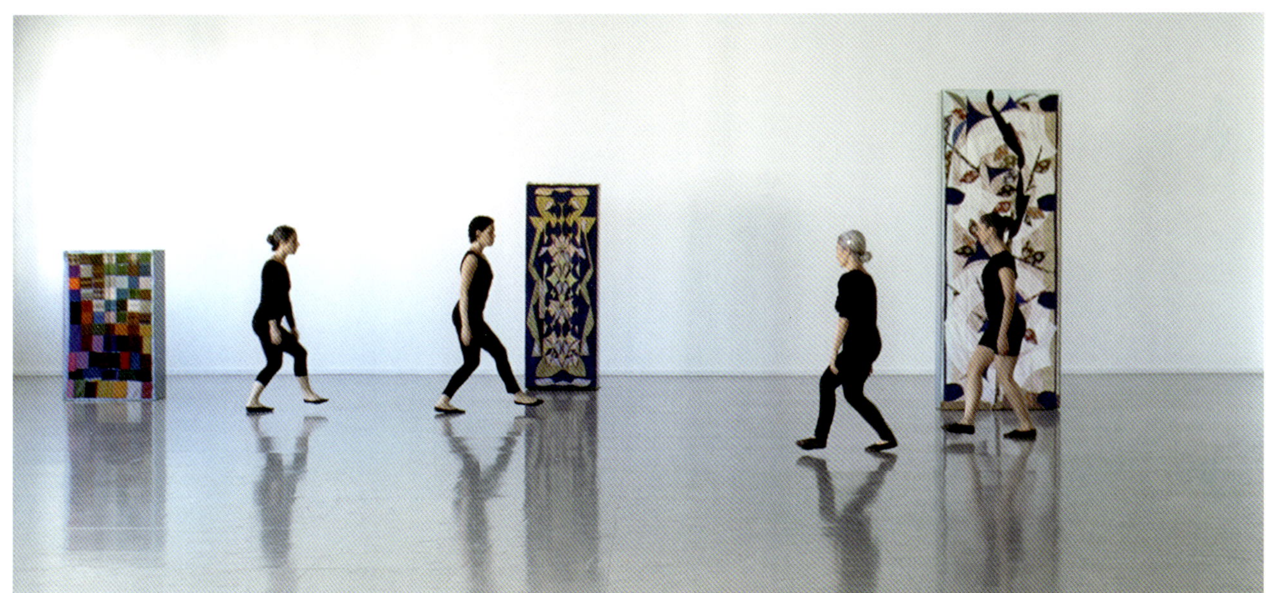

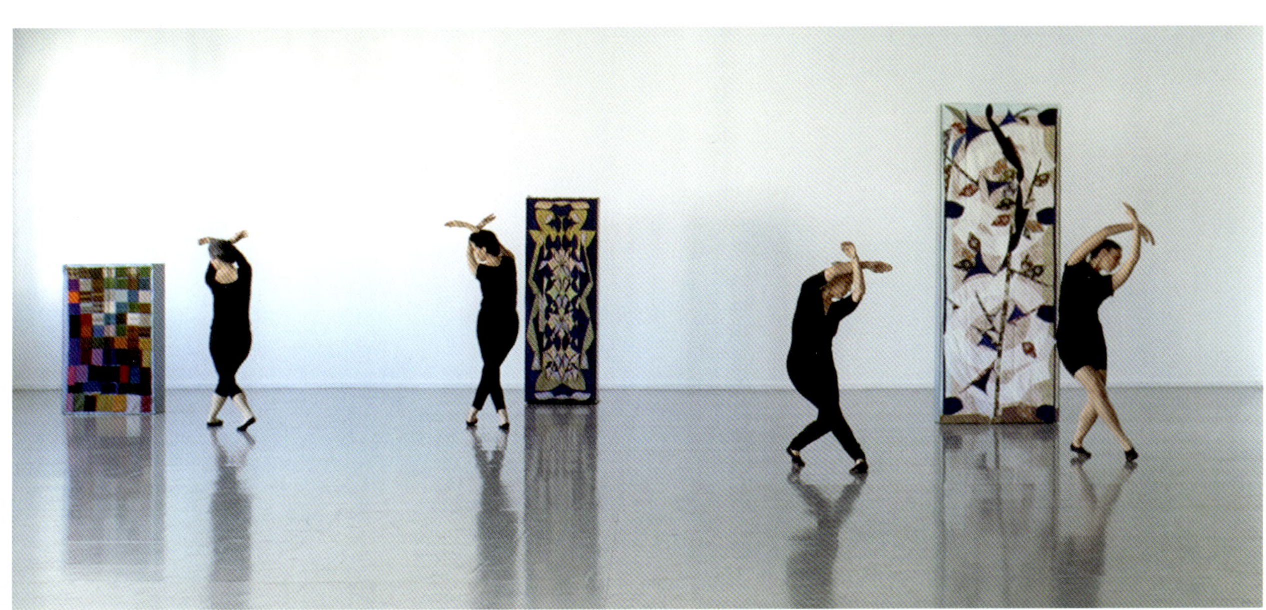

Sharon Lockhart, frames from *Five Dances and Nine Wall Carpets by Noa Eshkol*, 2011
Left to right: Ruti Sela, Racheli Nul-Kahana, Hamutal Peled, and Sara Sheffi performing Noa Eshkol's *Strolling (Promenade)*

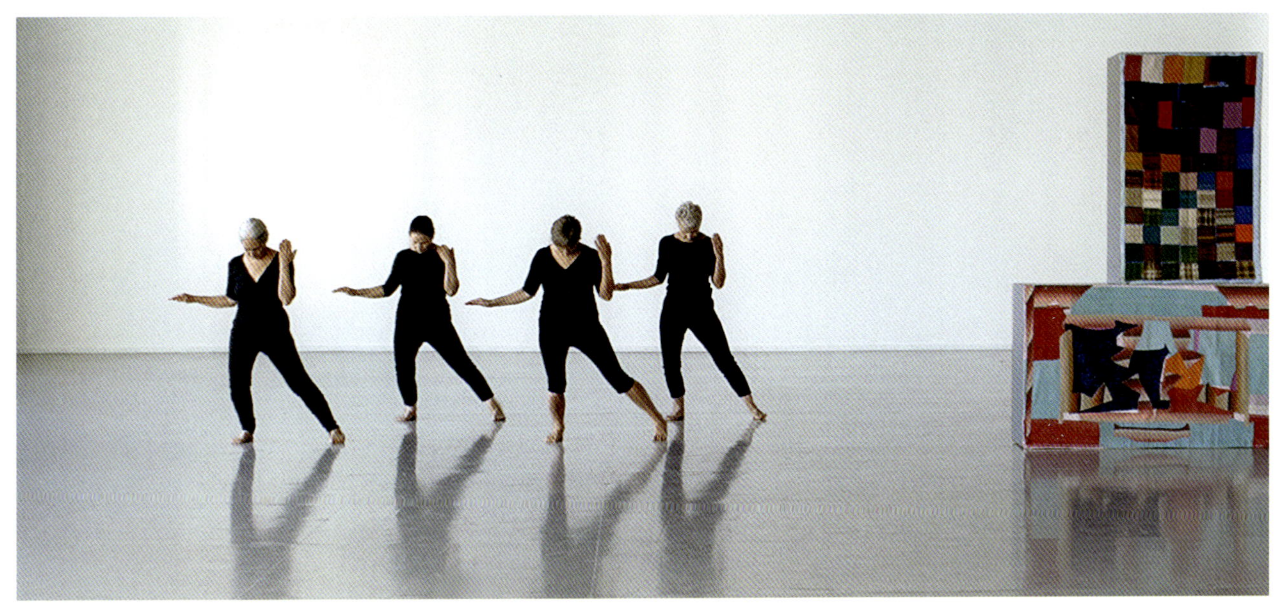

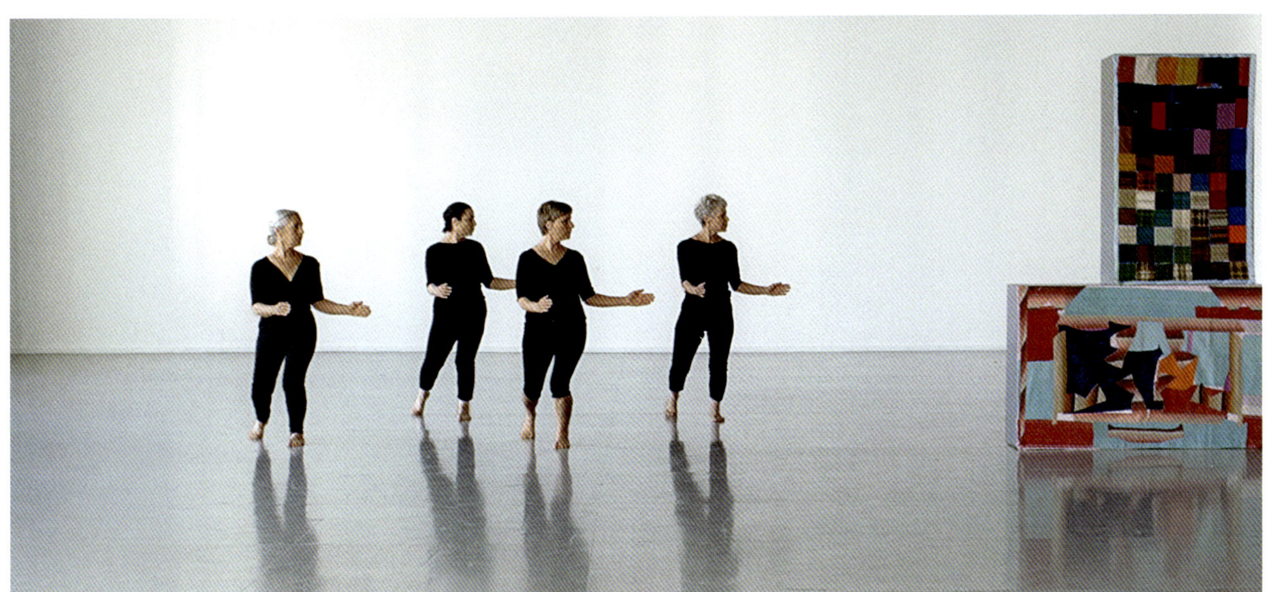

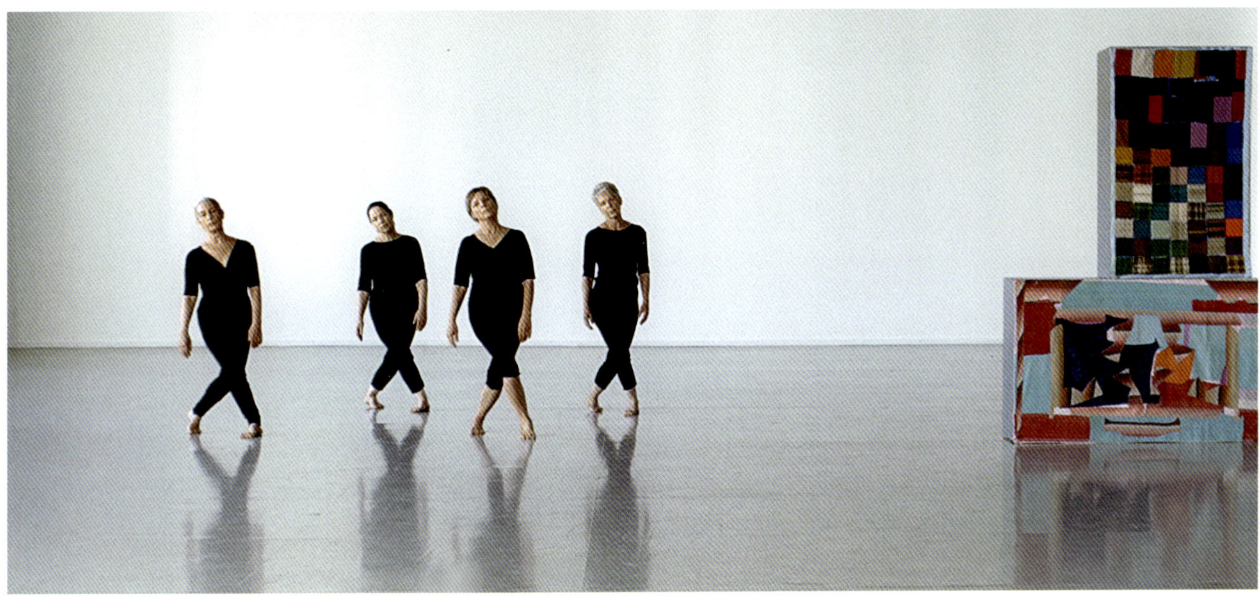

Sharon Lockhart, frames from *Five Dances and Nine Wall Carpets by Noa Eshkol*, 2011
Left to right: Racheli Nul-Kahana, Shmulik Zaidel, and Ruti Sela performing Noa Eshkol's *War Dance (Heraldic)*

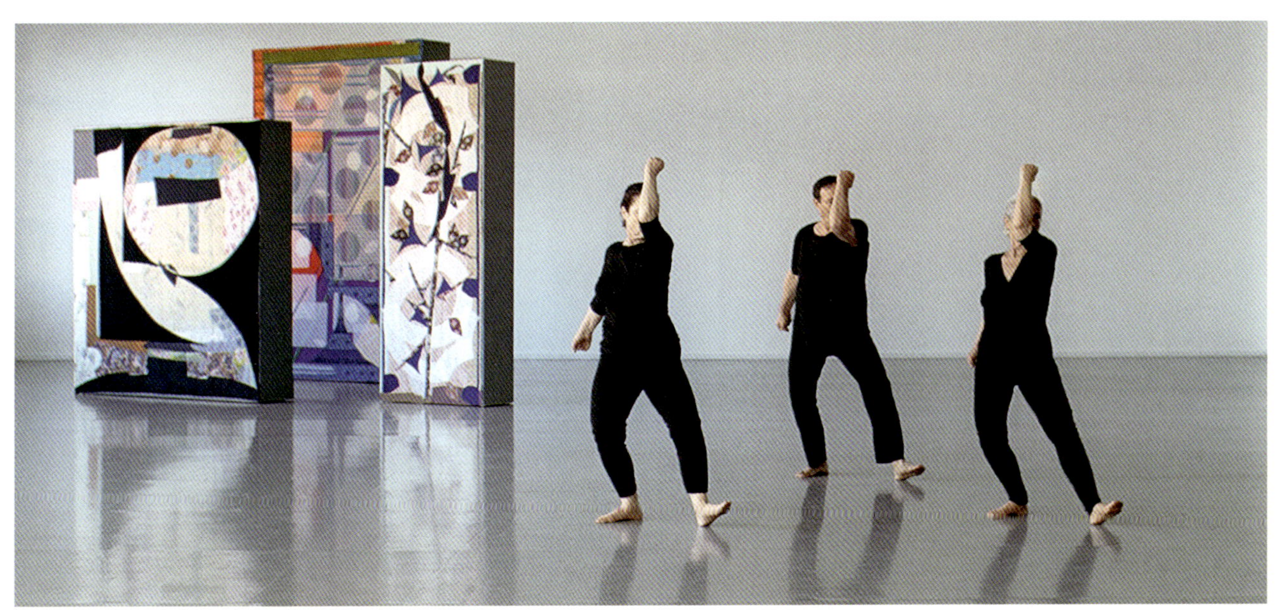
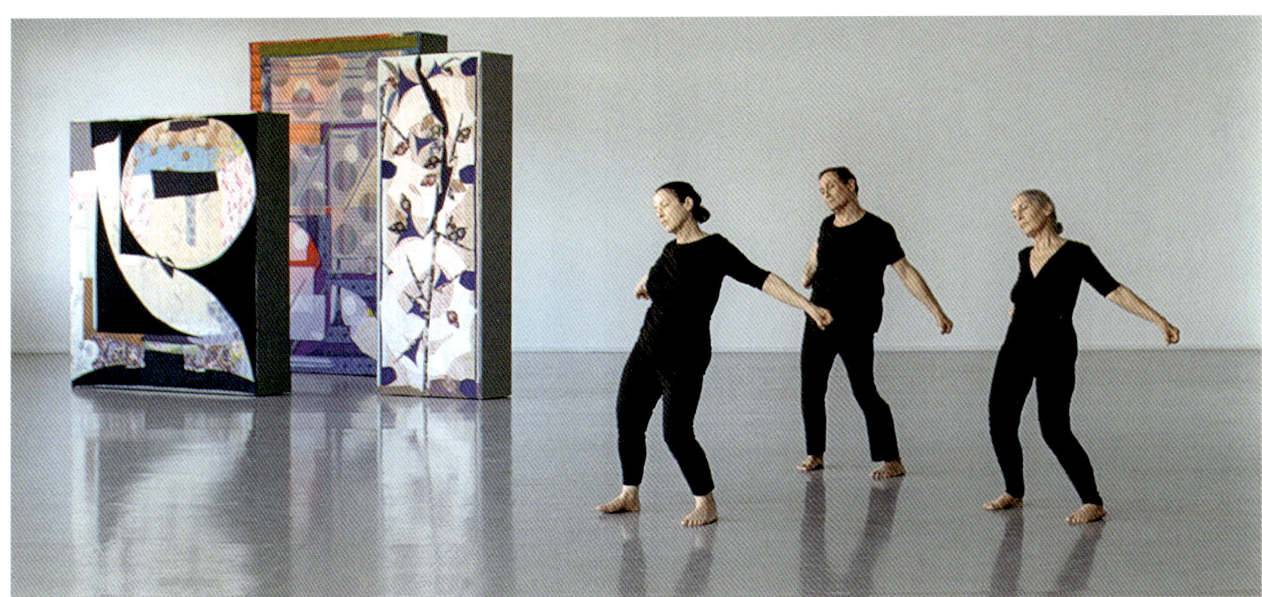
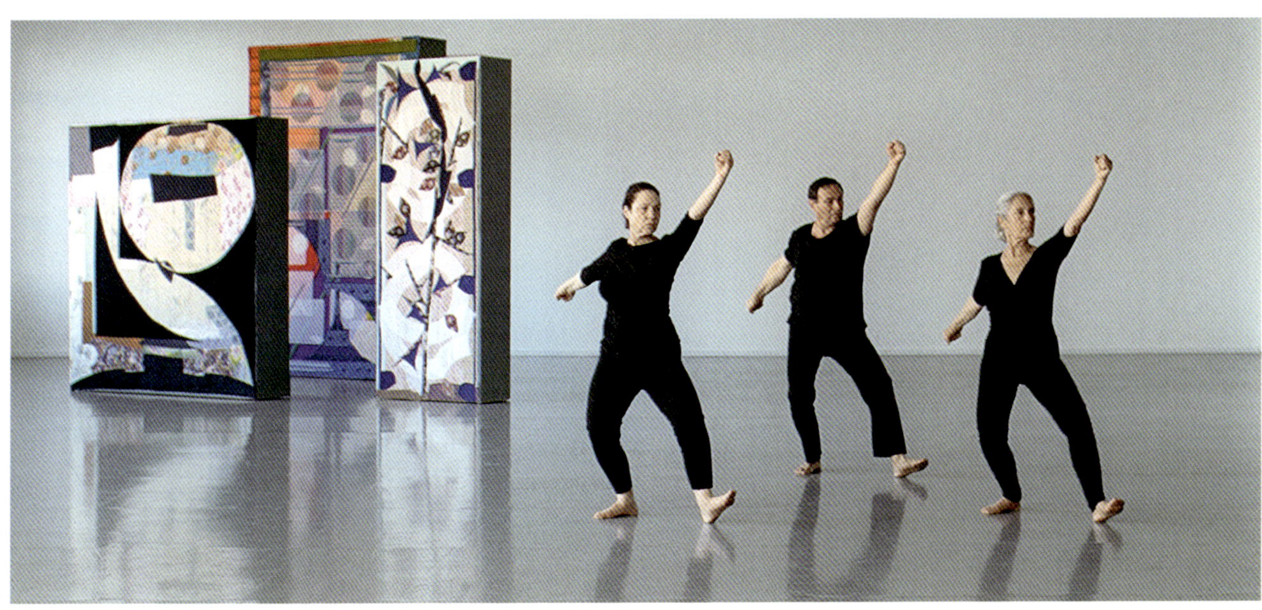

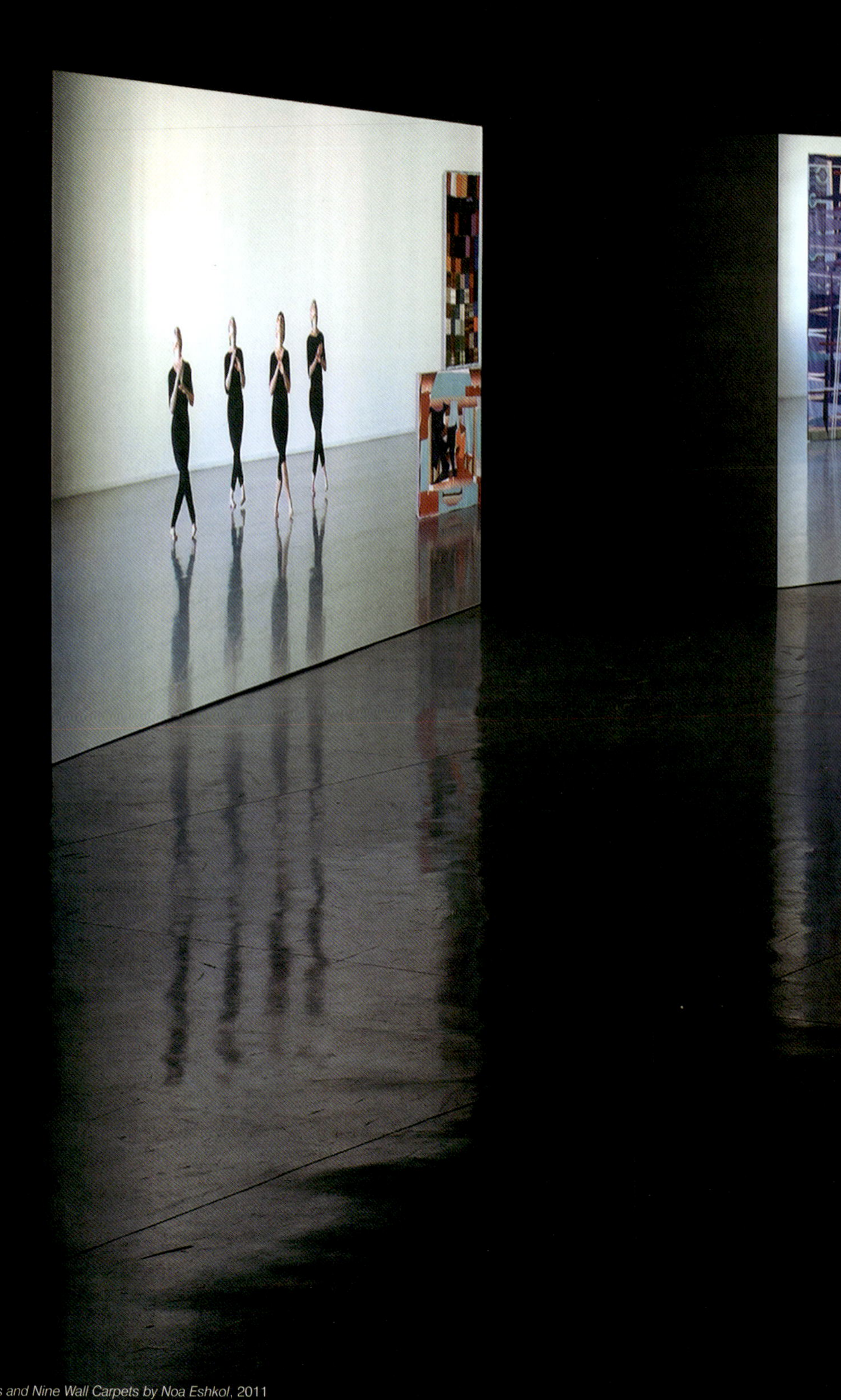

Installation view of exhibition at The Israel Museum, Jerusalem, showing Sharon Lockhart's *Five Dances and Nine Wall Carpets by Noa Eshkol*, 2011

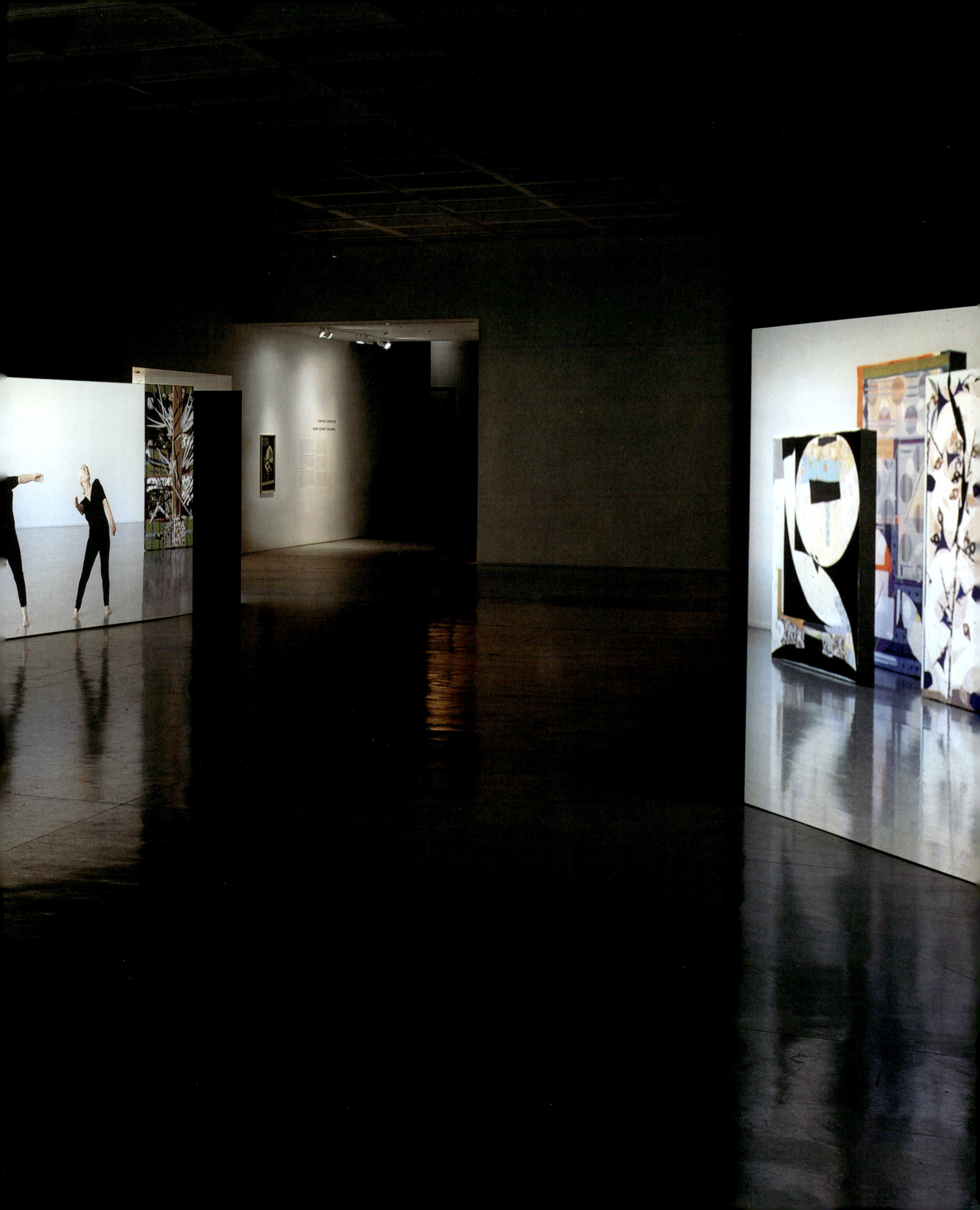

“Summer Wind in the Thistles”

Talia Amar

The year is 1953. The place is Kibbutz Lohamei Haghetaot, Israel. A memorial assembly featuring a large-scale performance with numerous participants is underway to mark the tenth anniversary of the ghetto uprisings that took place during the Second World War. Dancing on the ancient stone aqueduct in the vicinity of the kibbutz are several of Noa Eshkol’s first students. Among them is Avraham Wachman, who would collaborate with her on the development of the Eshkol-Wachman Movement Notation method. Some of the other dancers would shortly join her in establishing the Movement Quartet—the first incarnation of the Chamber Dance Group, whose subsequent incarnations continued to perform the dances Noa composed using her method. Below them, on a low stage, youth from nearby kibbutzim are also dancing, wearing identical khaki outfits. The dancers alternately merge and separate, forming interplays between a single dancer, small groups, and one large, monolithic group moving as a single being. A large crowd arrives from the surrounding kibbutzim and agricultural communities on foot, in horse-drawn carts, and in trucks. Musicians perform. In the intervals between different parts of the ceremony, the country’s leaders deliver pathos-infused speeches. These scenes unfold in a silent film shot that day, which has been preserved in the archive of the Noa Eshkol Foundation for Movement Notation.

Noa had been invited by the kibbutz to create a movement-based performance—a format frequently used during those years for festive ceremonies and holidays, and typically combining dance, singing, and recitations. The performance she created, however, differed in both appearance and style from the realist theatrical performances characteristic of this era. The theme, as expected, was national and heroic—emphasizing courage and valor in those years of turmoil, as well as remembrance and hope. The “scenes” moved between the group and the individual—the courageous ghetto fighter or the partisan in the forests—while creating an affinity between these figures and the New Jew, symbol of the young Israeli state’s promising future. These compositions, which feature large numbers of participants, are reminiscent of the “movement choirs” developed by Rudolf Laban (1879–1958) that performed in Germany during the 1920s and ’30s. Yet the compositional forms are more minimalist and are joined with a dance resembling a hora circle dance stripped of its ecstatic characteristics. Together, these elements produce an abstract, succinct form of movement whose powerful effect lies in its restraint. Although this performance was a singular event within Noa’s wide-ranging oeuvre, it seems to embody several important elements of the social, historical, and cultural context in which her artistic vision grew and

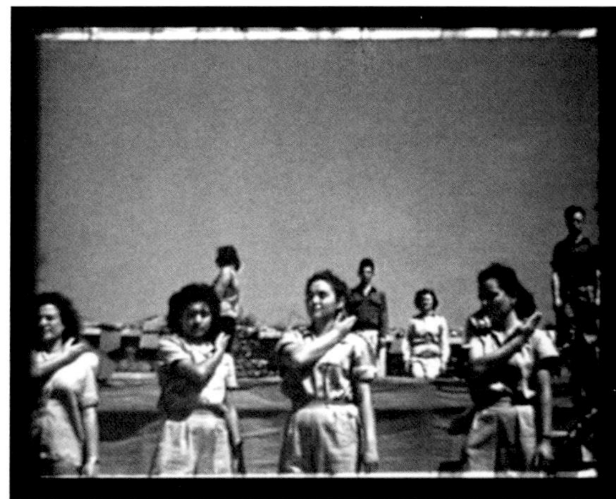

Fig. 1. Unknown filmmaker, memorial assembly at Kibbutz Lohamei Haghetaot, Israel
Still from a silent film, 1953, the Noa Eshkol Foundation for Movement Notation

evolved, as well as her rebelliousness, while revealing the first signs of her pioneering and groundbreaking work (fig. 1).

The 1950s were a decade of transition from the Yishuv—the Jewish community of the British Mandate for Palestine—to an independent state, the first decade in which Israel's national institutions were consolidated. These same years were also marked by a search for new forms of expression in dance, after a long period shaped by the influence of German Expressionist dance (*Ausdruckstanz*). This strain of dance, which had dominated the European dance world between the two world wars, was characterized by an emphasis on expressive movement, on the relations between body and soul and between human beings and nature, and on social involvement. It was part of a larger "body culture" (*Körperkultur*) that had developed during a period marked by growing nationalism and the rise of the cult of the healthy body—based on the ideal of a physically fit body living a morally upright lifestyle in nature, close to the earth, while combining gymnastics and various types of dance. The conception of this "New Man" and of the modern body attempted to transcend the rational aspects of modernity in search of ecstatic experience. In this context, the body dancing freely on the earth of the German fatherland manifested a mysterious inner experience, freedom, and national identity. *Ausdruckstanz* was perceived as a way of restoring to the body its role in creating a harmony between human beings and the universe that had been disrupted by the age of industrialization.

Laban, the influential founder of *Ausdruckstanz* and the creator of a movement-notation system called Labanotation, believed that one of the functions of modern dance was to serve society. The mass movement choirs he developed played a central role in the processions and outdoor performances organized by labor unions and other groups. His complex dance compositions were based on simple movements that could also be performed by amateurs and underscored the importance of movement as a means of communicating ideological messages.

A balance of creative individualism and group work also characterized the approach of Mary Wigman (1886–1973), a student of Laban's who was the most important dancer of her time in Europe and who founded a dance school in Dresden, the largest of its era.[1] Her personal vision of "absolute dance" was liberated of dependence on music or narrative. It was concerned with the components of movement and with novel, personal, expressive forms as a means of creating abstract images, which give external expression to internal, subjective, and metaphysical experience. In her work with groups, speaking and moving choirs emphasized the moral significance given to human beings by belonging to a community.

1. Mary Wigman was associated with the prominent German Expressionist art group Die Brücke and especially with Emil Nolde and Ernst Ludwig Kirchner, who both created paintings inspired by her and her dances.

As the Second World War progressed, the further development of *Ausdruckstanz* in Germany was stemmed; in prestate Israel, by contrast, this style, which combined primeval associations and revolutionary ideas, found fertile ground thanks to a number of Jewish choreographers and dancers who immigrated to the country from Central Europe in the 1930s. They were all former students or assistants of one or several of the great European "masters," such as Laban, Wigman, Gret Palucca, and Kurt Joos. The absence of any Western dance tradition, and especially of classical ballet, together with the desire to express the excitement and dynamism of the revived land and nation, facilitated the rapid absorption of this style and its flourishing in the years prior to Israeli independence. The country soon became "the only place in the world where modern dance—European, of course—rather than classical ballet, was the dominant form of artistic dance."[2] Creativity, musical talent, and personal expression were the main characteristics required of the dancers who affiliated themselves with this style, while technique was viewed as secondary in importance. These dancers performed, taught dance and gymnastics, participated in the creation of various ceremonies, and played an important role in laying the basis for the country's artistic dance world.

One of these dancers was Tille Rössler, a former student of Wigman's and a principal teacher at the dance school of Gret Palucca in Dresden who emigrated to Tel Aviv in 1933. Rössler was known for her more structural and systematic approach to teaching dance composition and also for her emphasis on physical education, which led her to establish the country's first course for teachers of physical education. Rössler inspired many students—one of whom was Noa Eshkol. She introduced Noa to the foundations that came to serve her later on: anatomy and a profound understanding of the body and methodical dance work. Noa ultimately concluded, from her extensive background in the study of music during her youth, that what was missing in dance was notation. At the time she was not aware of the existence of any form of dance notation. Rössler told her about Labanotation. Moreover, she recognized Noa's analytic orientation and suggested that she pursue her studies at Laban's school in Manchester, England, where Noa enrolled in 1946.

Ausdruckstanz was integrated into movement-based performances presented within the framework of public ceremonies and agricultural celebrations. These performances typically took place in the open fields of the agricultural communities and were staged by these dance pioneers, who resided, for the most part, in the country's urban centers. As described above, they included singing and movement choirs, music, and dance. Often related to biblical themes, they combined ancient Jewish history and symbolism with the Zionist history of that era, and they served to cement the connections between the individual and the *kevutza*, or communal group; between the group and nature, the earth, and agriculture; and between the Jewish people and the ancient land, the Hebrew language, and the new, modern, secular state, which was founded upon quintessentially socialist principles. Dance, in this context, was perceived as an agent for transmitting these messages and as a tool for strengthening a sense of connection to the place, to a unified collective, and to shared ideas (fig. 2).

•

The desire to instill Zionist ideals by creating an emotional connection to local landscapes was also related to the New Jew that the Zionist revolution sought to create. This antithesis to the persecuted Diaspora Jew was a person who lived close to nature and who worked the land as a substitute for religious ritual, an idealist revolutionary or even a world-reformer, a warrior and a pioneer committed to national and social goals. Strong and radiant with health, this "Sabra"—like the prickly-pear plant after which the New

2. For a discussion of the development of artistic dance in Israel, see Ruth Eshel, *Dancing with the Dream* (Tel Aviv: Sifriyat Hapoalim, 1991), 113 (in Hebrew).

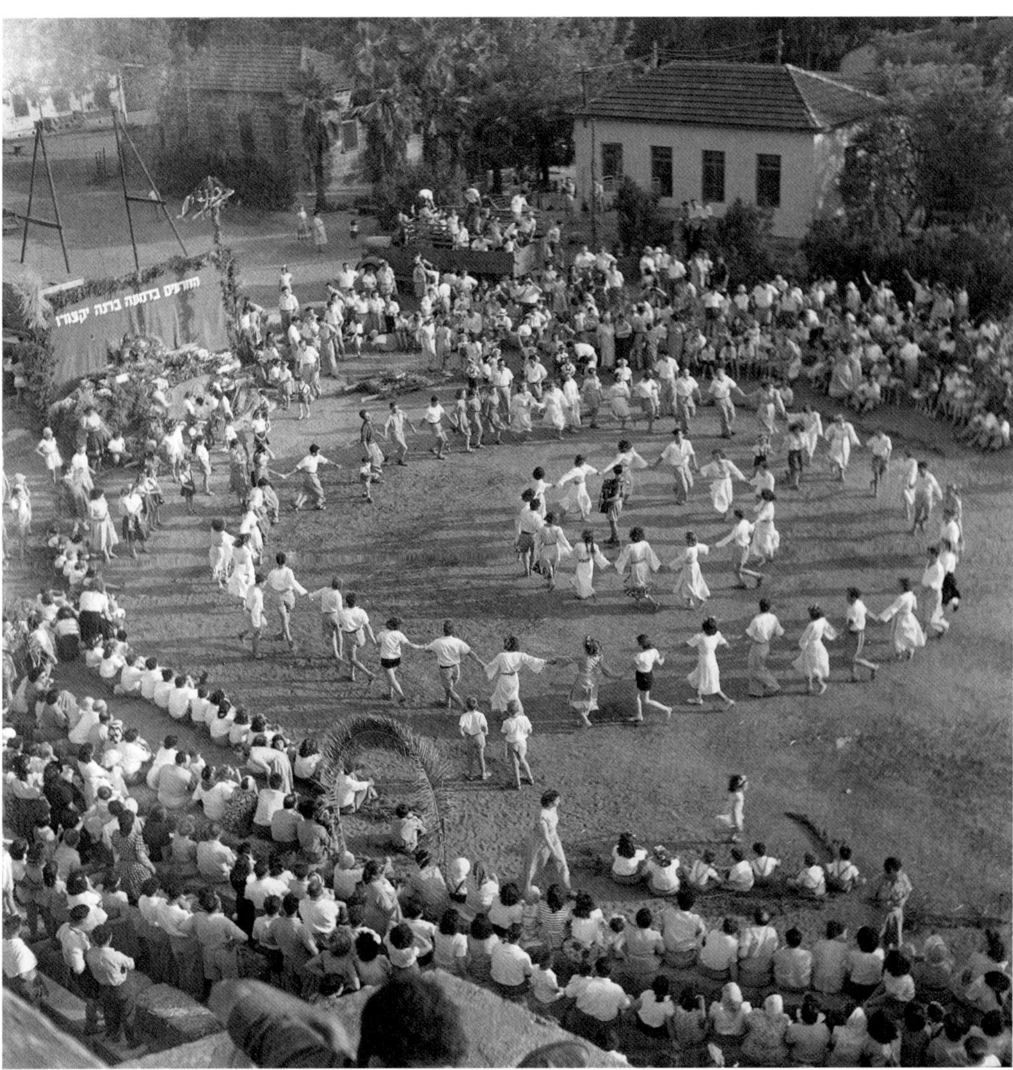

Fig. 2. Dr. Jacob (Jack) Rosner, Israeli, born Germany, 1902–1950, *Festival of Shavuot (Harvest Celebration) in the Kibbutz*, 1949, printed from the original negative, The Israel Museum, Jerusalem, Gift of Naomi Schwartz

Jew was named—was rough and thorny on the outside and soft on the inside. The ideal embodiment of this persona was the sunburned kibbutz member Uri, the mythological protagonist of Moshe Shamir's 1947 novel, *He Walked in the Fields*. Most Israeli leaders and thinkers during this period had participated in founding the first kibbutzim. This original and unique creation of the Zionist movement was viewed as an avant-garde destined to lead the entire people into the world of tomorrow. Indeed, the kibbutzim, together with other socialist settlements and institutions, had a decisive impact on the entire Yishuv, far beyond their relative numbers.

In his highly influential book *Paths in Utopia*, Martin Buber defined the kibbutz as a "signal non-failure" and characterized utopianism as a socialist vision that presents a different, high-quality human society created through the inner transformation of human beings.[3] The communal way of life promoted by the pioneers identified the personal destiny of individuals with the collective destiny of the *kevutza*,[4] whose members were united by a sense of fraternity and a shared commitment and interests. The group's devotion to this "experimental laboratory," and the various challenges it faced, were central to its mythologization within local society (fig. 3). The experience of physical labor and training, personal challenges, and collective rituals instilled in the group strength of character, a sense of commitment, and a strong work ethic that amounted in its eyes to a form of

3. Martin Buber, "Epilogue: An Experiment That Did Not Fail," in *Paths in Utopia* (Syracuse, N.Y.: Syracuse University Press, 1996), 148.
4. The *kevutza* is a type of small collective agricultural settlement developed in the first two decades of the twentieth century. The idea of the *kevutza* was followed by the idea of a larger group—the kibbutz. The differences between the earlier *kevutza* and the kibbutzim were gradually erased over the following years.

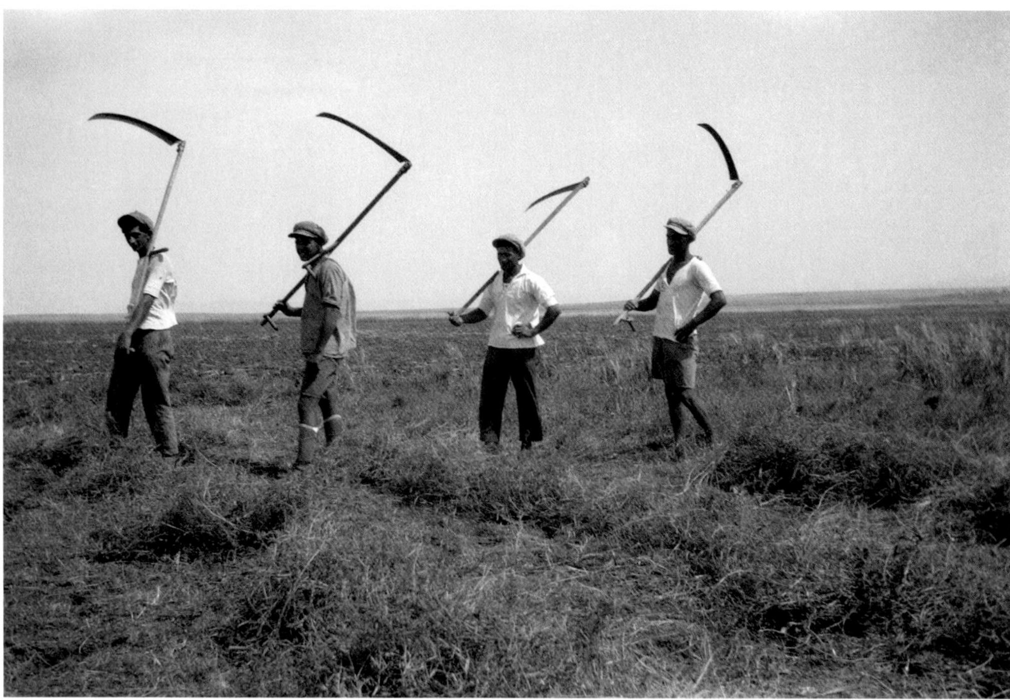

Fig. 3. Yaacov Ben-Dov, Israeli, born Russia, 1882–1968, *Field Workers*, 1920s, printed from the original negative, The Israel Museum, Jerusalem, Gift of Rena (Fisch) and Robert Lewin, London

spiritual transcendence. The first generation of native-born Sabras experienced a natural bond with their homeland, spoke Hebrew as their first language, and were raised on the values formulated by their parents, the pioneers, yet they also grew to attain cultural independence in a society that sought to find the balance between an idealistic, revolutionary spirit and its institutionalization.[5]

Degania Bet, the kibbutz on which Noa Eshkol was born, and which her parents had participated in founding, was the younger offshoot of Degania, the country's first communal group. Although Noa and her mother left it while she was still a child, she seems to have assimilated some of the underlying characteristics of life within this framework, later implementing them in her work with her own groups. These groups were also a kind of experimental laboratory for the study, analysis, definition, and implementation of her new "creed."

Most of Noa's students and dancers were born or raised on kibbutzim, and their shared background contributed to their work as a group and their integration into the various frameworks created around her activities. ". . . And then I came to Noa" is how many of them sum up their experience of working and studying with their teacher,[6] hinting at the sense of intimate belonging and collaborative outlook that could—and in fact did—serve as an alternative to the kibbutzim they were constrained to leave in order to realize their individual dreams of studying and dancing professionally. Even if this idealistic, demanding framework required hard work, persistence, and great precision, and involved overcoming numerous challenges to win the approval of "the founding mother and group ideologist," many of them viewed it as a "home" whose character and daily routines are revealed by the daily entries they wrote in the work diaries for the house. This home provided a distinct identity, while positing rules and principles and requiring a methodical work process, constant practice, and meticulous concern with details to achieve the required level of perfection.

Within this ethos of teamwork, the focus was on the intimate chamber group rather than on the individual; there were no soloists, and the emphasis was on research, practice, and the creation of compositions, rather than on public exposure. The devotion to the

5. For a discussion of the Israeli Sabra, see Oz Almog, *The Sabra: The Creation of the New Jew*, trans. Haim Watzman (Berkeley: University of California Press, 2000).
6. See the texts by the dancers in "The School of Eshkol," in this book.

group and its leader, the commitment to an idea, and the willingness to engage in physically challenging work—values on which the members had been raised as children—found their ideal fulfillment in the context of this pioneering, revolutionary group. Even today, in Noa's absence, the house in which she lived, and where the reconstituted Chamber Dance Group continues to meet and work, is the center of a daily routine of practice, rehearsals, and work with the notation method and the archive, while its small dining area—like the communal dining room that was once the pulsating heart of every kibbutz—remains the core of its everyday activities.

•

The 1950s, a period of transition from the generation of the state's founders to those who came of age during the first decade following the declaration of Israeli independence in 1948, were years marked by massive waves of immigration, attempts to create a social melting pot, and security-related struggles. During this era, the kibbutz gradually lost its prominent status in Israeli society, and most of the tasks it had previously fulfilled came under the responsibility of the state. But although this period is remembered as one of ideological conformism, it was in fact one of significant intellectual and political ferment. A range of critical voices during those years argued that the new Israeli society and culture should be allowed to develop spontaneously, rather than being dictated from above by the authorities.[7] The last years of that "first decade," when conventions had yet to become fixed and the creation of an establishment culture was still in process, were dominated not by conservatism, but rather by receptivity to novel and original ideas.

Feeling that it did not provide answers to the problems that concerned her, Noa quit the Laban school and transferred to the Sigurd Leeder School of Modern Dance in London. This was where she met John Harries, who became her first student.[8] In 1951 she returned from her studies in England to Israel. She had grown disappointed with Laban's movement-notation system. "The central system of symbols in Labanotation represents a limited and fixed number of static positions (referred to as 'directions'). Movement is referred to as a 'transition' that is more or less known . . . and taken for granted. As if there was only one known, 'natural' route between two points. This is, in our opinion, the essence of the erroneous approach of a positional system. A movement-notation method must center on movement. The task of the movement notation is to describe, as precisely as possible, that 'transition' or orbit created by the moving limbs." Whereas the system of symbols that constitutes Labanotation is still partially metaphorical, and describes movement by means of words and signs related to external referents, Noa Eshkol aspired to create an abstract, analytical system. Like other notation systems, Labanotation was, as she put it, a "literary notation system"—that is, one that copies the words used to describe actions "from life." "A word used to describe an action implicitly describes a typical, characteristic form of movement . . . we fall downward; soar upward; stand vertically and die horizontally. Life unfolds within endless frameworks of action . . . [Eshkol-Wachman] movement notation does not at all attempt to describe actions; rather, it describes that primal thing from which actions are created . . . i.e., movement."[9]

In Holon, Noa turned to inventing and developing her own notation method with her former student Avraham Wachman.[10] Their method, which is distinguished from other systems that serve merely for the notation of dance,[11] is based on the understanding that every movement of the limbs is circular. It received official recognition in 1958 in conjunction with the publication of their book *Movement Notation*, when it was presented as a uniquely Israeli invention at Expo '58 in Brussels. It had been presented a year earlier in an exhibition at the Royal Festival Hall in London.

7. See Yaacov Shavit, "Messianism, Utopia, and Pessimism in the 1950s," in *A Restless Mind: Essays in Honor of Amos Perlmutter*, ed. Benjamin Frankel (Portland, Ore.: Frank Cass, 1996), 23–48.
8. John Harries participated in the preparation of the first book on EWMN, as well as in the composition of the texts and the design of the illustrations for many of Noa Eshkol's publications. In the 1960s he began to implement movement notation into visual art, including abstract video and animation compositions written in EWMN. He continues to pursue this work and has written articles on the subject.
9. Noa Eshkol, in Dalia Lamdani, "Movement Notation: Invitation to a Revolution," a conversation with Noa Eshkol published in the daily newspaper *Haaretz*, February 2, 1968.
10. On the foundations of this movement-notation system, see Michal Shoshani, "Foundations and Unique Aspects of Eshkol-Wachman Movement Notation," in this volume.
11. "While 'movement' is the name given to the material wherein all dance is wrought, the 'dance' is always the result of a specific way of that material." Noa Eshkol and Abraham [Avraham] Wachman, *Movement Notation* (London: Weidenfeld & Nicolson, 1958), vii.

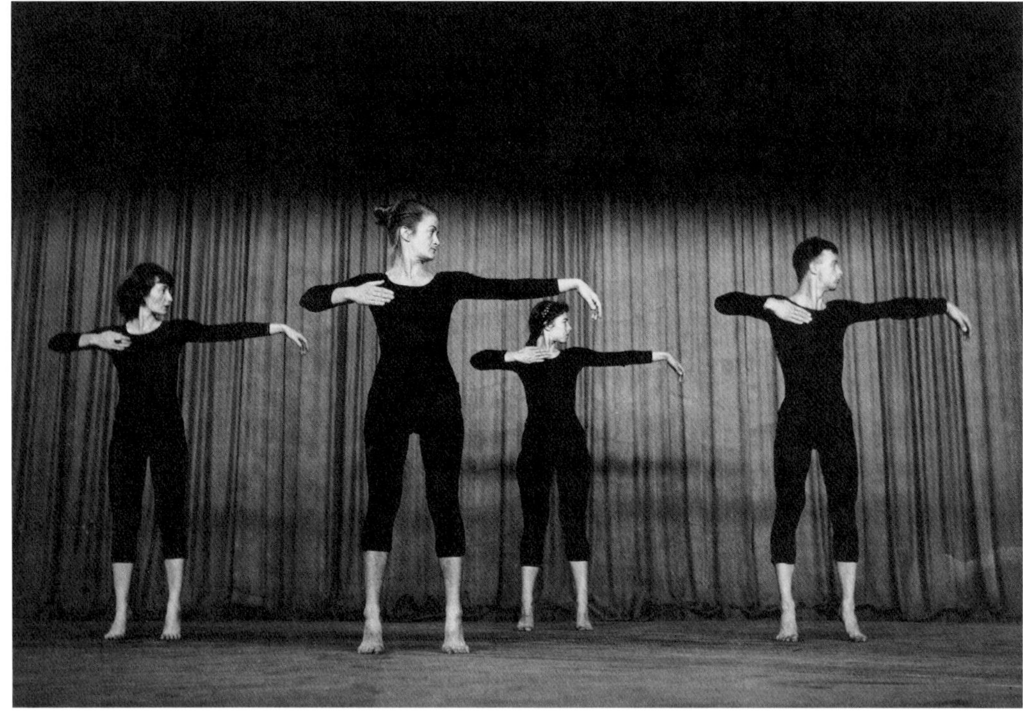

Fig. 4. The Chamber Dance Group 1 (Movement Quartet), *Étude* (Naomi), Ohel Theater, Tel Aviv, 1954–56, performed by: Noa Eshkol, Naomi Polani, Mirale Sharon, and John Harries, the Noa Eshkol Foundation for Movement Notation

Devoted to her path, Noa worked on the notation system in collaboration with her students and dancers, "from each according to his ability."[12] Wachman contributed the mathematical system and geometrical three-dimensional model used to demonstrate the "system of reference"; John Harries used his artistic talent to draw the illustrations and diagrams that accompany the explanations; Amos Hetz helped produce the spherical models and designed the poster for Expo '58,[13] which was also used to publicize the performances given by Noa's nascent dance group; and all the dancers performed the compositions, études, and dances based on the new notation symbols and signs to the sound of a ticking metronome. Naomi Polani, a member of the original group, described that early period in the following words:

> Noa's heart is wide open to her students! With full intention for each and every person . . . pure intention is also expected from the student toward the material and toward his fellow students, and here there is no leniency whatsoever! There are "commandments"!! = thou shalt, and thou shalt not (and the notation, meanwhile, is "ripening") . . . and here we are—three—who have persisted, already a dance group. We dance with pleasure and awe, and Noa dances with us . . . and the notation continues to "ripen" and is consolidated, and there are students and persistent people who have found what they were searching for here.[14]

Between 1954 and 1956, the "Movement Quartet" (Eshkol, Polani, Harries, and Mirale Sharon) performed its first program in Tel Aviv and in various kibbutzim. Noa formulated the principles underlying the stage performances:

> We relinquish the use of all tools that are not inherently related to movement, such as: 1. Stylized or picturesque costumes 2. A division of time based on acoustic means, music . . . 3. Lighting that adds to or changes the essence or character of the movement . . . this program will be performed in one dress under one light. Both having no other purpose but to help the spectator to see. . . . The works show the stories of movement. No other story is intended. No tale to be looked for. . . . A notation of a movement . . . Invented by a member of the group (fig. 4).[15]

12. In 1951, following her return to Israel, Noa taught movement at the Cameri Theatre Drama School. At the time, the Cameri was a new, innovative theater founded by young actors, which put an emphasis on the production of original Israeli plays. Here Noa met Avraham Wachman and Naomi Polani, who were both acting students at the school. This encounter led to their fruitful collaboration. Additional students in Noa's classes who later became prominent Israeli actors attest to her significant impact on their professional development, and on their ongoing reliance on the methods they studied with her.
13. Amos Hetz is a dancer and choreographer and a teacher; EWMN is the basis of most of his work in composition and teaching, as well as his publications. He was the director of the Movements ensemble, with which he performed in Israel and in Europe; in 1989 he founded and became the artistic director of the Heder (The Room) Festival of Chamber Dance. In 1965 he replaced Noa Eshkol as teacher at the Jerusalem Academy of Music and Dance. At the academy he established the Faculty of Movement and Movement Notation, which he headed until his retirement. Presently, Hetz teaches movement and movement notation, lectures, and performs in and manages dance projects in Israel and Europe.
14. Naomi Polani, "A Small Window onto Noa Eshkol's World," remarks on Assembly Day in Memory of Noa Eshkol, Seminar HaKibbutzim College of Education, Tel Aviv, January 2010 (in Hebrew). Naomi Polani is an actress, musical director, stage director, and choreographer who is associated with Israel's popular musical history from its beginnings during the early years of the state. She is especially known for her work with the successful group Ha'Tarnegolim (The Roosters) in the early 1960s. Songs for the group's shows were specially written by Israel's best songwriters. Using sophisticated structural music and movement compositions influenced by movement notation, Polani's musical and stage direction expressed the spirit of the young "Sabra" culture.
15. From the program printed for the Movement Quartet's performances, 1954–56.

This approach gave rise to a new kind of awareness of the moving body, which did not involve the imposition of extraneous representational patterns or of other elements, such as music, which similarly impose themselves on the viewer's experience. "Noa believed," as Michal Shoshani explains, "that if you work correctly, the body has an ability for self-expression, and is in no need of support. The bare dance and the relinquishment of support from any other medium are the deepest possible expression of a dance composer's faith in the human body."[16] Yet the relationship of the dance to music is given expression through recurrent sequences of movements and seriality, which are hinted at by titles such as *Theme and Variations*, *Preludes*, and *Fugues*. The limbs, which function as "musical instruments" (together with the metronome, which determines the beat), create multivocal, polyphonic movement chords—a "visual music."

Any artistic process is, in essence, a process of searching; Noa's quest focused on the precision and purity of movement. Like a succinct, highly concentrated haiku, the notation she created refines the components of the movement material into a single, pure movement that contains an entire world. Moving in a continuum of precise angles, like pure sounds whose complexity is almost unnoticeable, the dancers return at the end of every dance to its point of origin, to the "zero position." Between "the axis of movement" and the "axis of the limb," the circular movement completes its orbit only in order to retrace it once again.

•

Following Martha Graham's 1957 visit to Israel, which presented her brilliance and professional technique, modern American dance became the dominant strain of dance in the young nation, replacing the declining tradition of *Ausdruckstanz*. Whereas the local language of dance was still concerned with the body as a tool for representing meanings that are external to it, Noa was by contrast already abstracting dance into an analytic system characterized by a minimalist aesthetic. She did away with external context, put the emphasis on the body as an autonomous arena, and directed the gaze inward, to movement-based materials and to the meaning gleaned from pure movement—to the structure disassembled into its individual components, the movement of the limbs, and their location and orbits in space and time.

As structuralism rose to the fore in the context of linguistic theory, and Minimalism burst into the arena of visual art in the United States, Noa Eshkol appears to have been several steps ahead of her time in the field of dance. Her work may thus be affiliated with late modernism in dance, whose characteristics developed and matured in the United States in the mid-1960s and '70s—with the style that dance scholar Sally Banes has defined as "analytical post-modernism."[17]

In 1965, Yvonne Rainer described in her well-known "No Manifesto" the principles that guided her and her colleagues at the Judson Dance Theater, considered to be the cornerstone of postmodern dance in the United States: "No to spectacle. . . . No to transformations and magic and make-believe. . . . No to the heroic. No to the anti-heroic. . . . No to involvement of performer or spectator. No to style. . . . No to moving or being moved."[18] These principles are reminiscent of those defined and followed by Noa a decade earlier, which appear in her performance program from the mid-1950s.

Original thinking, nonconformism, a critical, curious stance, and an attempt to probe limits and shatter conventions were characteristic of Noa's work and art. Her notation method and the nature of the dance to which it gave rise were groundbreaking and revolutionary. Her method was created and developed on the cultural periphery but is universal and has served as a creative and analytic tool. It is capable of describing every potential

16. Michal Shoshani, in conversation with the author, January 2012.
17. The term "postmodern," in this context, was used in the chronological sense and not in the current sense of the term "postmodernism." See Sally Banes, *Terpischore in Sneakers: Post-modern Dance* (Middletown, Conn.: Wesleyan University Press, 1987).
18. Ibid. Historical modern dance never was truly modernist. Analytic postmodern dance was the main representative of modernist approaches such as Minimalism.

combination of movements produced by the body or any movement-based discipline, independently of any specific style, genre, or field.

Over the years, Noa collaborated with local and international institutions, colleagues, and scholars in a range of different fields. For example, at the drama school affiliated with the Cameri Theatre in Tel Aviv, she created the movement for one of the theater's first plays. With Moshe Feldenkreis, the founder of the Feldenkreis Method, she established a long-standing collaboration and a dialogue. Her notation method is studied at the Jerusalem Academy of Music and Dance, Seminar HaKibbutzim College of Education, and elsewhere. She herself taught in a range of frameworks, published research-based books and scores in collaboration with the members of her groups, and organized an international congress on movement notation methods in Tel Aviv. The movement notation continued to evolve; over time, it was used by several of her students and dancers as the basis for their own independent creative work, which developed in different directions.

Much like the kibbutz, Noa is a short or long chapter in the lives of many—those who continued to live within the existing framework, those who left and returned, and those who left never to return again. As Amos Hetz put it, "Noa's voices filters through the personal prism of each and every one."[19]

•

In the 1970s, a new, additional chapter in Noa's artistic output began with the creation of "wall carpets" composed of scraps of fabric—leftovers collected for her in sewing workshops and fashion studios, and donated by those around her. This development was related to a traumatic turning point in the history of Israel—the Yom Kippur War of 1973. Noa created the first carpet during the course of the war itself, when work with her dancers was temporarily suspended.[20] Its colors—black and off-white—do not yet hint at the rich combinations of textures and colors that would characterize the 1,800 carpets she went on to create over the next three decades.

Whereas her movement-notation method and dance compositions are carefully planned, structured, monochromatic, minimalist, and innovative, her carpets are spontaneous, colorful, and almost chaotic. Nevertheless, the connection between these two artistic mediums is noticeable: the formal and geometric motifs of the carpets are reminiscent of the principles of movement notation and their visual expression both in her dances and in the illustrations and drawings accompanying related explanations.

Utilitarian fabrics served as the backings for the carpets: military blankets and practice targets, bedspreads, blankets, and curtains from different kibbutzim. Noa treated the scraps she placed on these supports as readymades and did not cut them or change their form before integrating them into her compositions. The reason was ideological: form had to be found within existing limitations, and challenges had to be met and overcome in a creative manner. This was the approach that guided her dance compositions, and this was also what she taught. In order to create compositions—and Noa saw herself as a creator of dance compositions rather than a choreographer—one must set a limit and search for the solution within this limit. Just as she chose the titles of her dances only after their composition had been completed, so she chose titles for her wall carpets only after she had completed each composition, from which a form and an image miraculously emerged: a bird, a leaf, a lotus flower, or an abstract image that triggered a certain association.

Noa "painted" with these pieces of fabric, and her dancers and friends then handsewed them on to the cloth backings, "performing" the compositions she created. Here, too, the work had a collaborative aspect to it, and each participant had a clearly defined role. The arrangements of expensive and cheap fabrics, ethnic patterns and simple lace created

19. Amos Hetz, in conversation with the author, January 2012.

20. For an account of these developments, see the texts by the dancers in "The School of Eshkol," in this book.

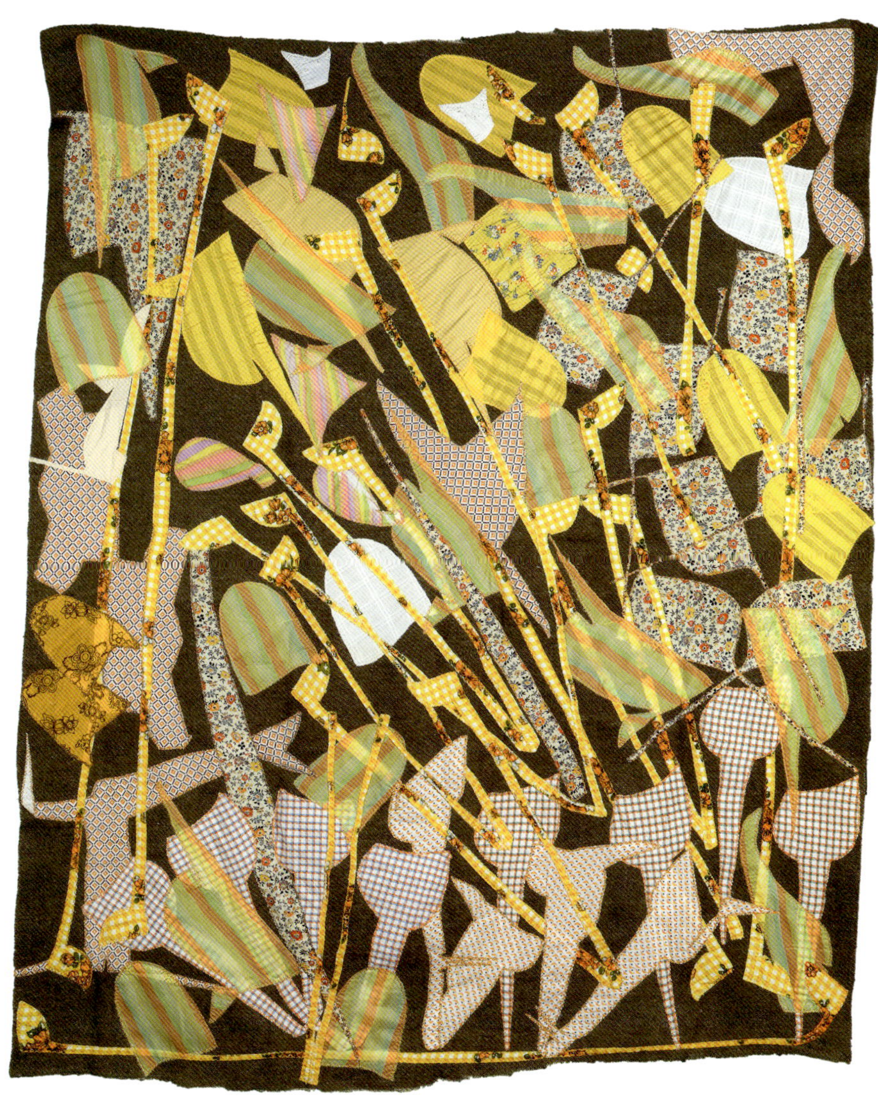

Fig. 5. Noa Eshkol, *Summer Wind in the Thistles*, 1970s, cotton, wool, and polyester, 62 1/4 x 55 1/8 inches (176 x 140 cm), the Noa Eshkol Foundation for Movement Notation

surprisingly stunning harmonies. The carpet titles and the materials from which they were made—upholstery fabrics and patterns popular during the 1970s, as well as the famous Israeli Maskit designs—lead one's imagination to a particular era or event, to personal or collective memories. Despite their abstract thrust, this variety of carpets bespeaks a profound connection to local landscapes and colors, to nature and to the seasons of the year.

Summer Wind in the Thistles is a carpet "depicting" the landscape of the Jordan Valley in summer (fig. 5). On a support made of an olive-green military blanket, windblown thistles gradually overtake the field and the few flowers that have survived in the summer heat. The print of small, delicate flowers Noa integrated into the carpet is perhaps nothing but a dream, or metaphor—for Israel's summer fields do not sprout flowers, but only thorns, nettles, and thistles. The shades of yellow in this carpet, as in many others, allude to the blazing sun, blinding light, desert colors, and long Israeli summer. In the Bible, thistles are related to images of abandoned human settlements or uncultivated land. The flowers that stubbornly bloom beneath the blanket of thistles on Noa's carpet are an expression of longing, like the hope of those first pioneers to create the New Jew, the native Sabra naturally rooted in the earth, and like the yearning that became a reality—to stick to the hardened, desiccated, sun-scorched land, and turn it into a homeland.

Translated from the Hebrew by Talya Halkin

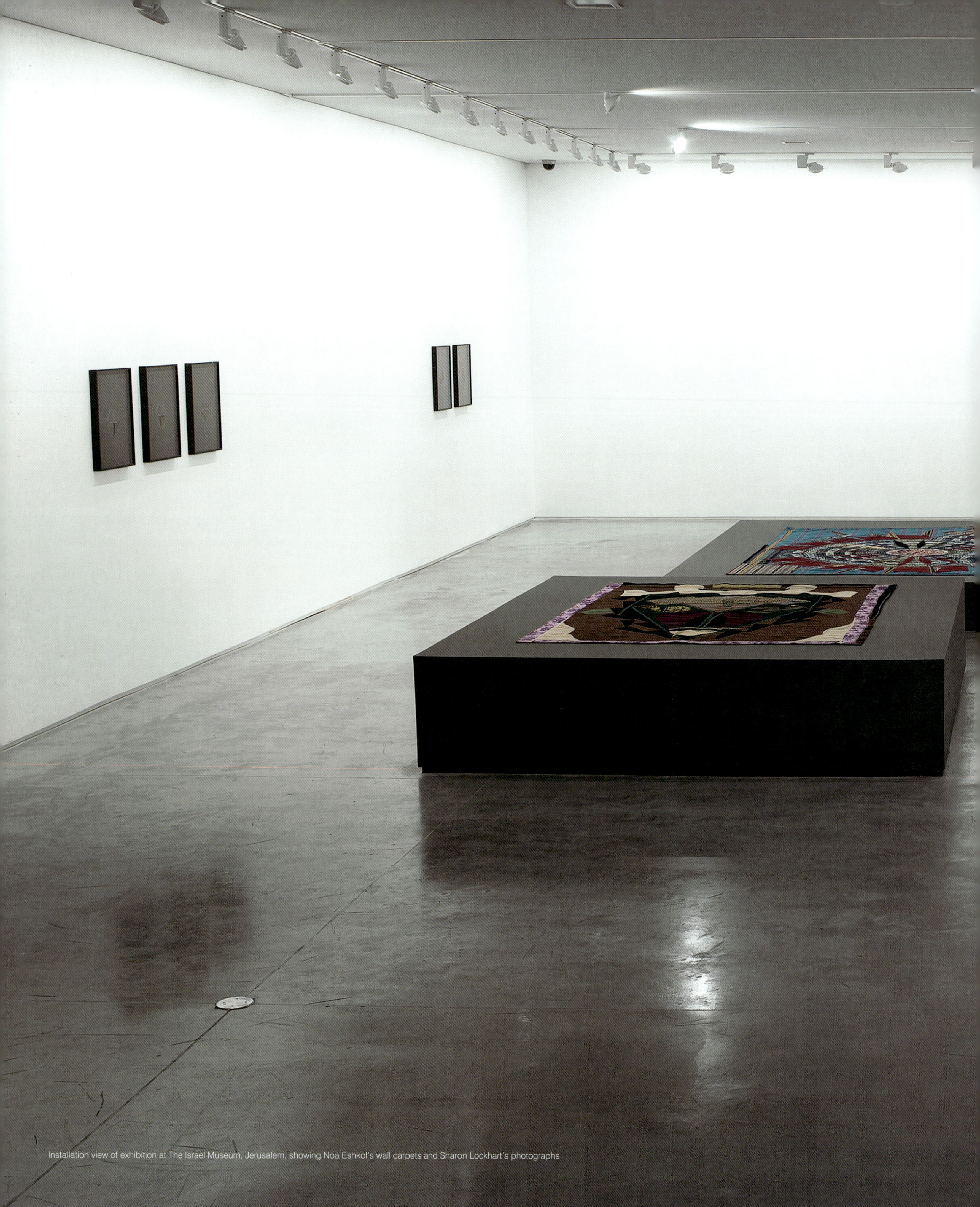

Installation view of exhibition at The Israel Museum, Jerusalem, showing Noa Eshkol's wall carpets and Sharon Lockhart's photographs

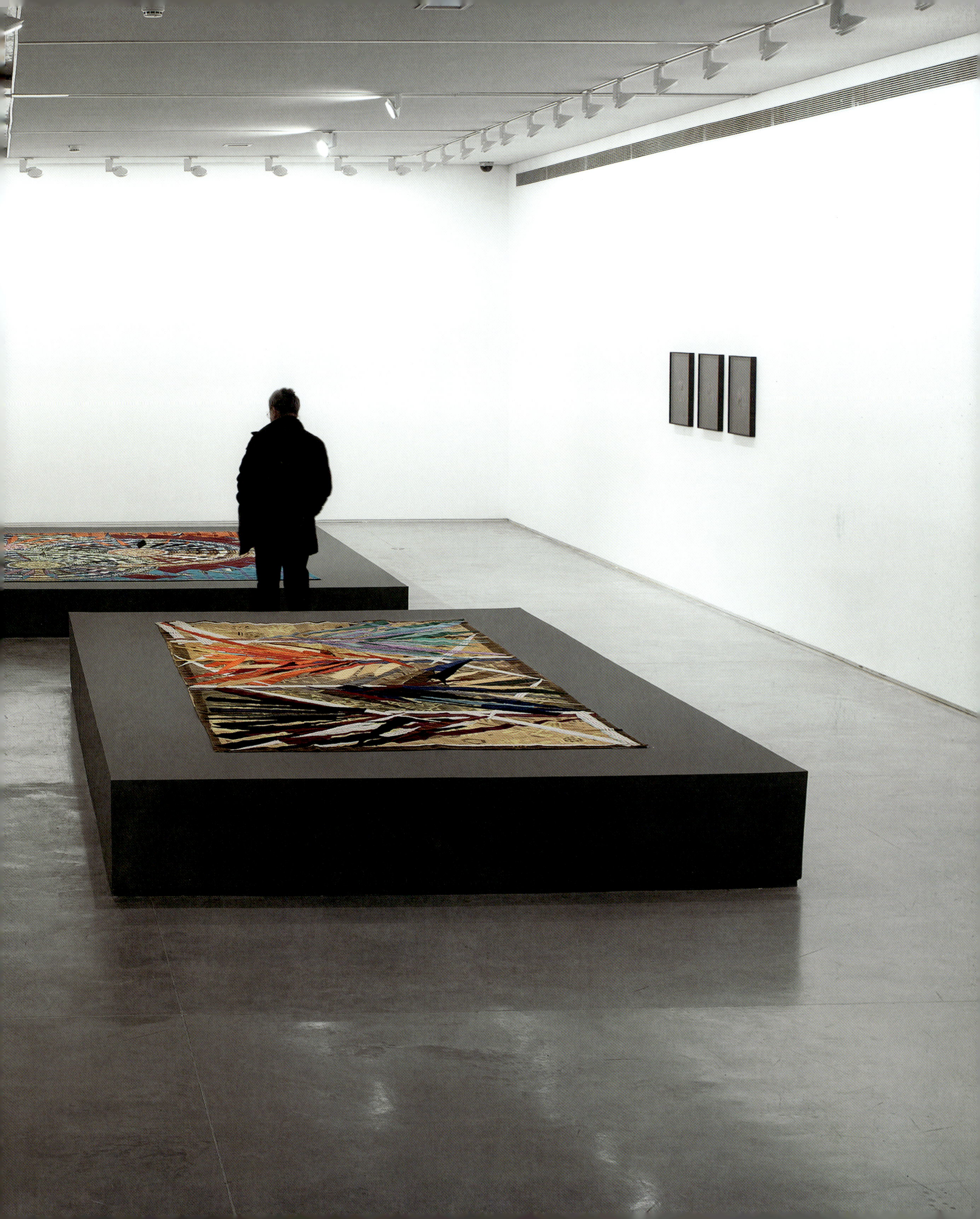

Wall carpets by Noa Eshkol
Opposite: *King Mooky I*, 1980s; pp. 46–47: *Chinese Circus*, 1990s; p. 48: *Umbrella Flower*, 1970s; p. 49: *Plane Tree*, 2000; pp. 50–51: *The Four Seasons*, 1970s; pp. 52–53: *Celebrating Circle (Wedding)*, 1980s

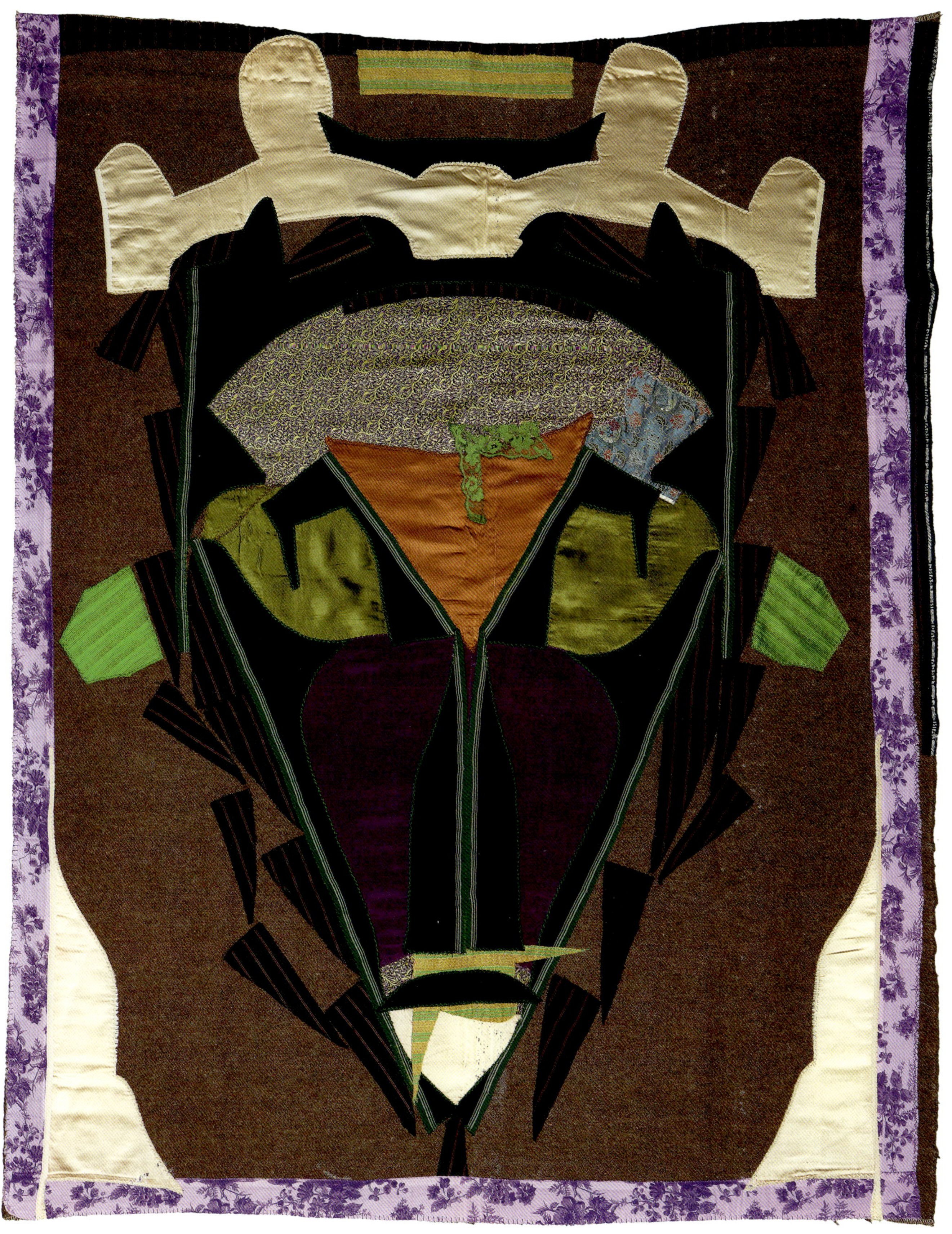

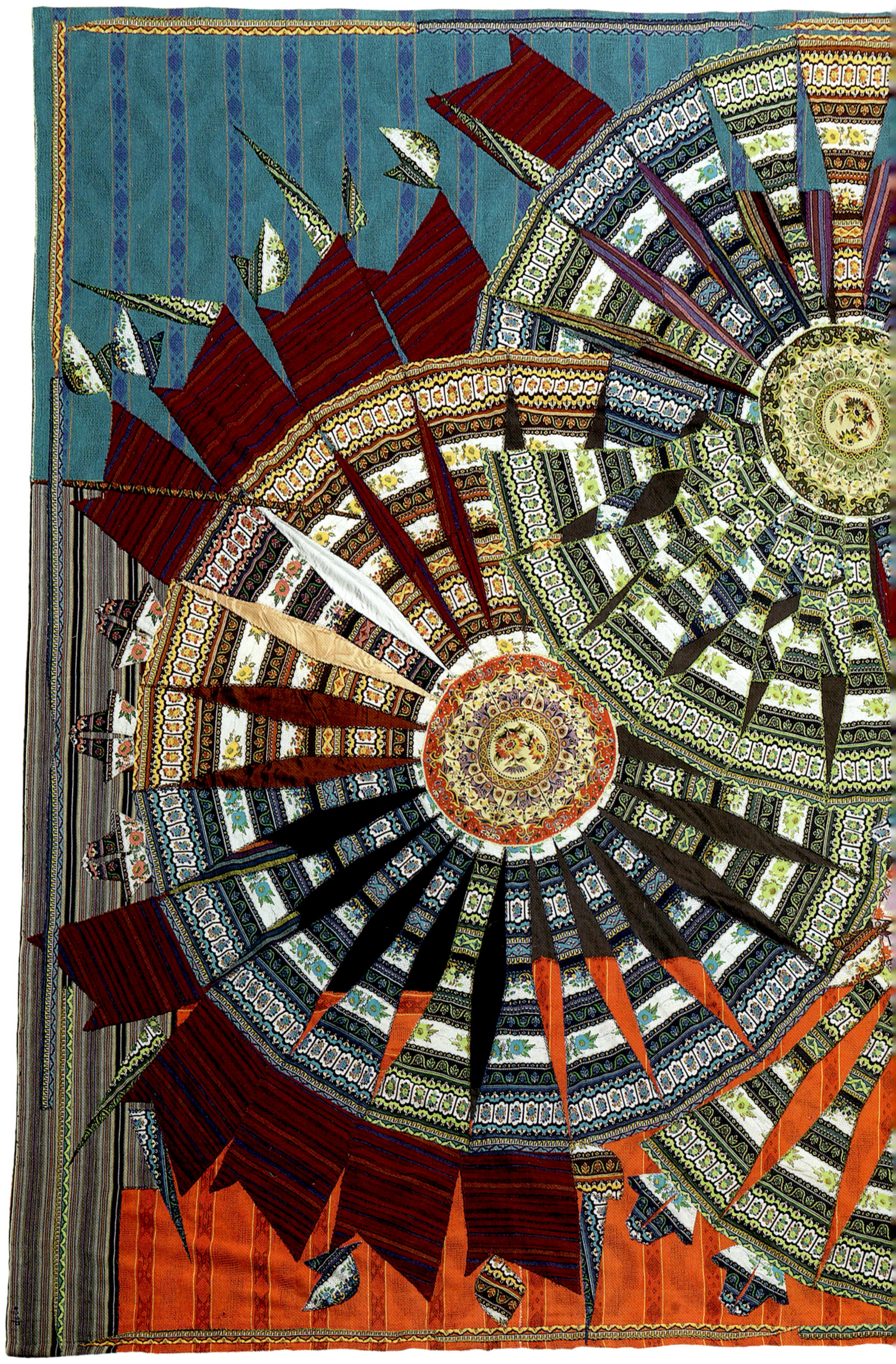

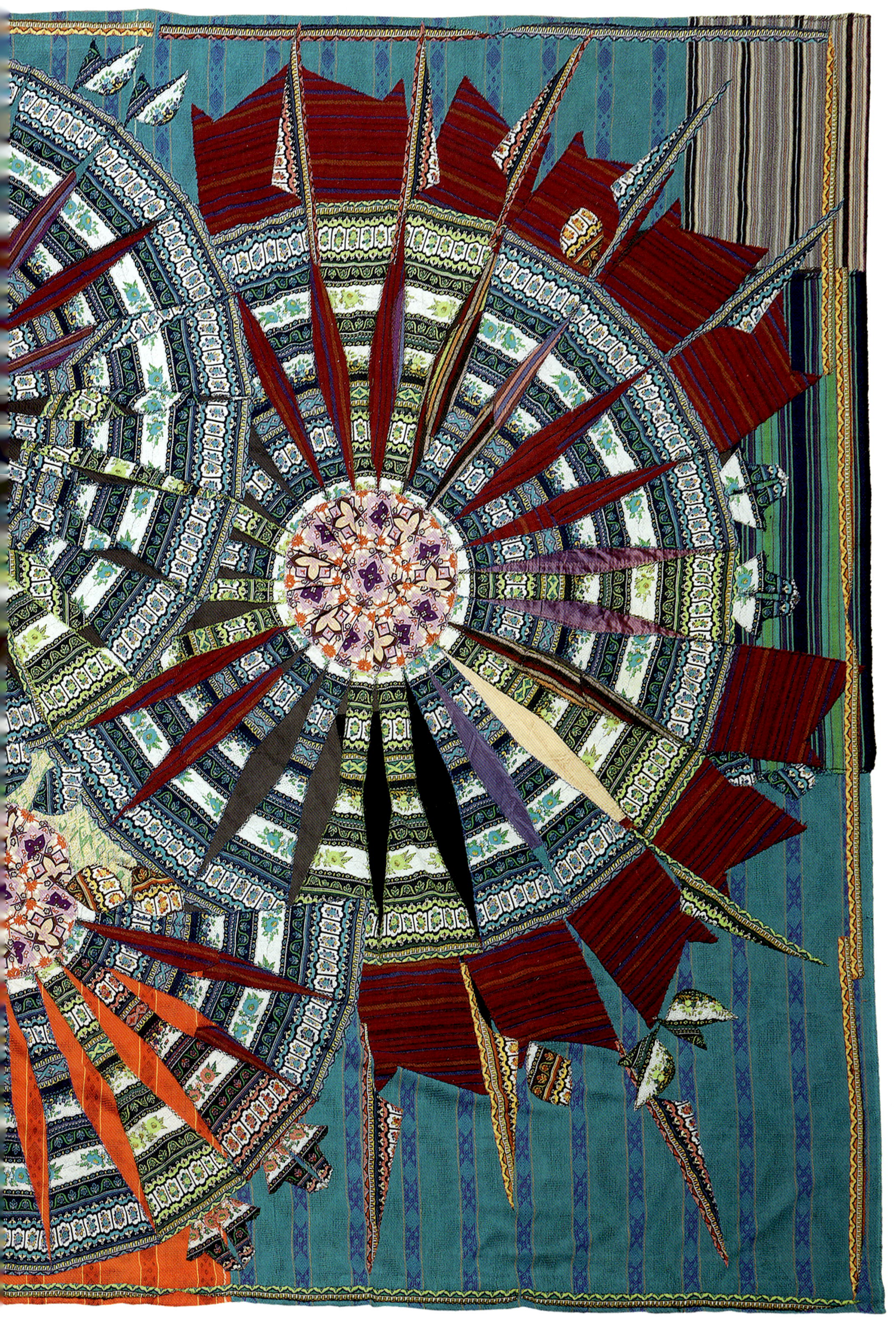

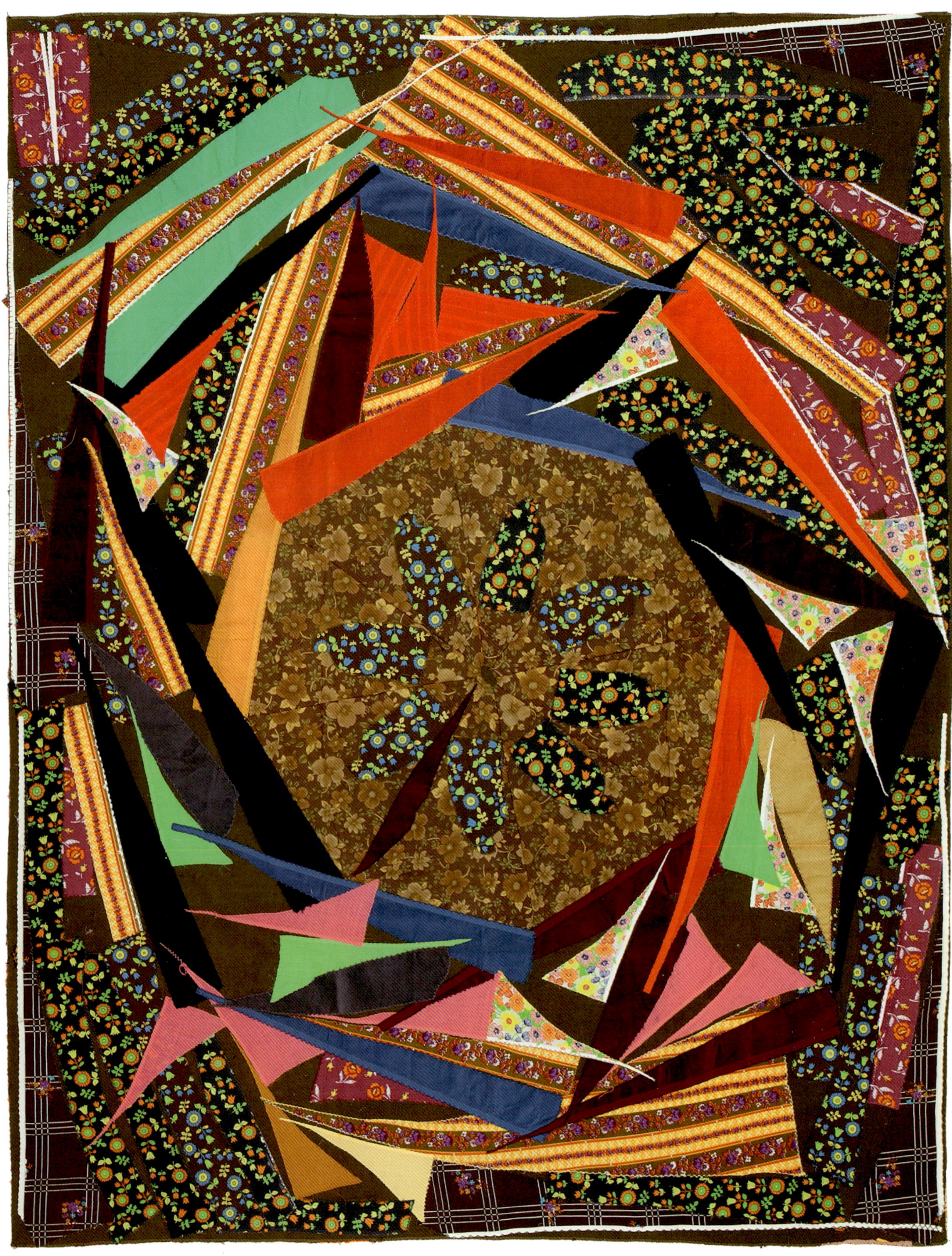

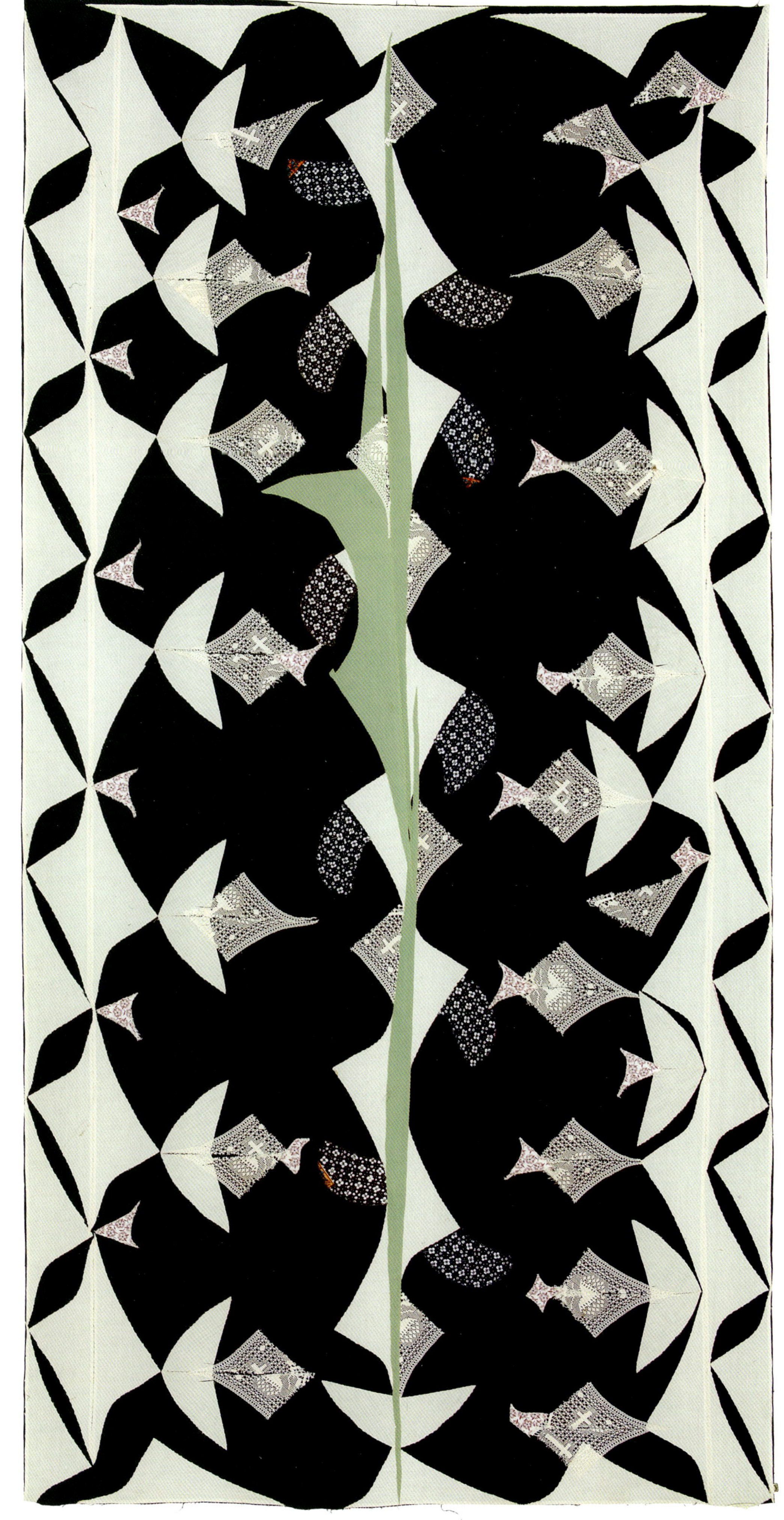

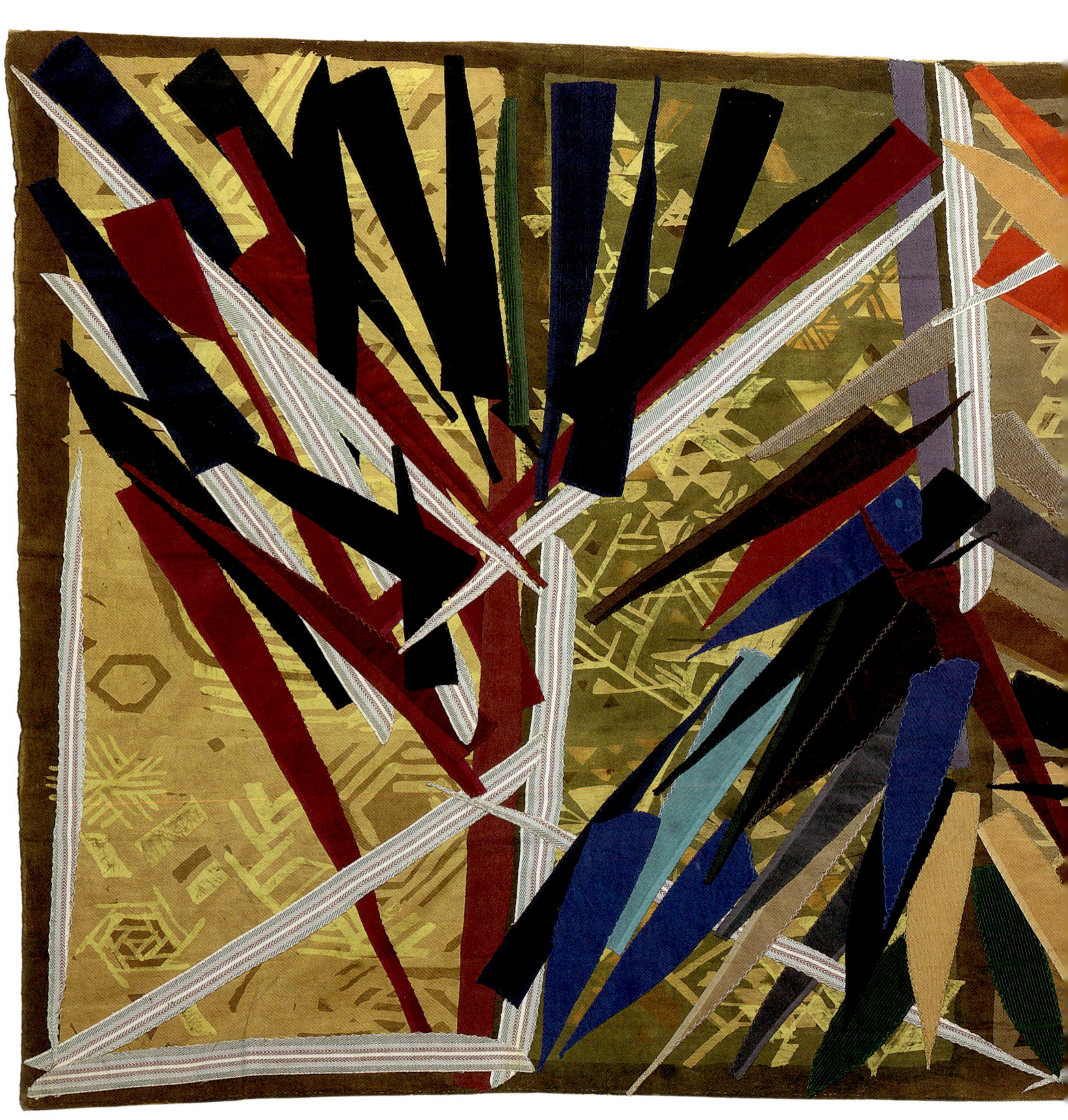

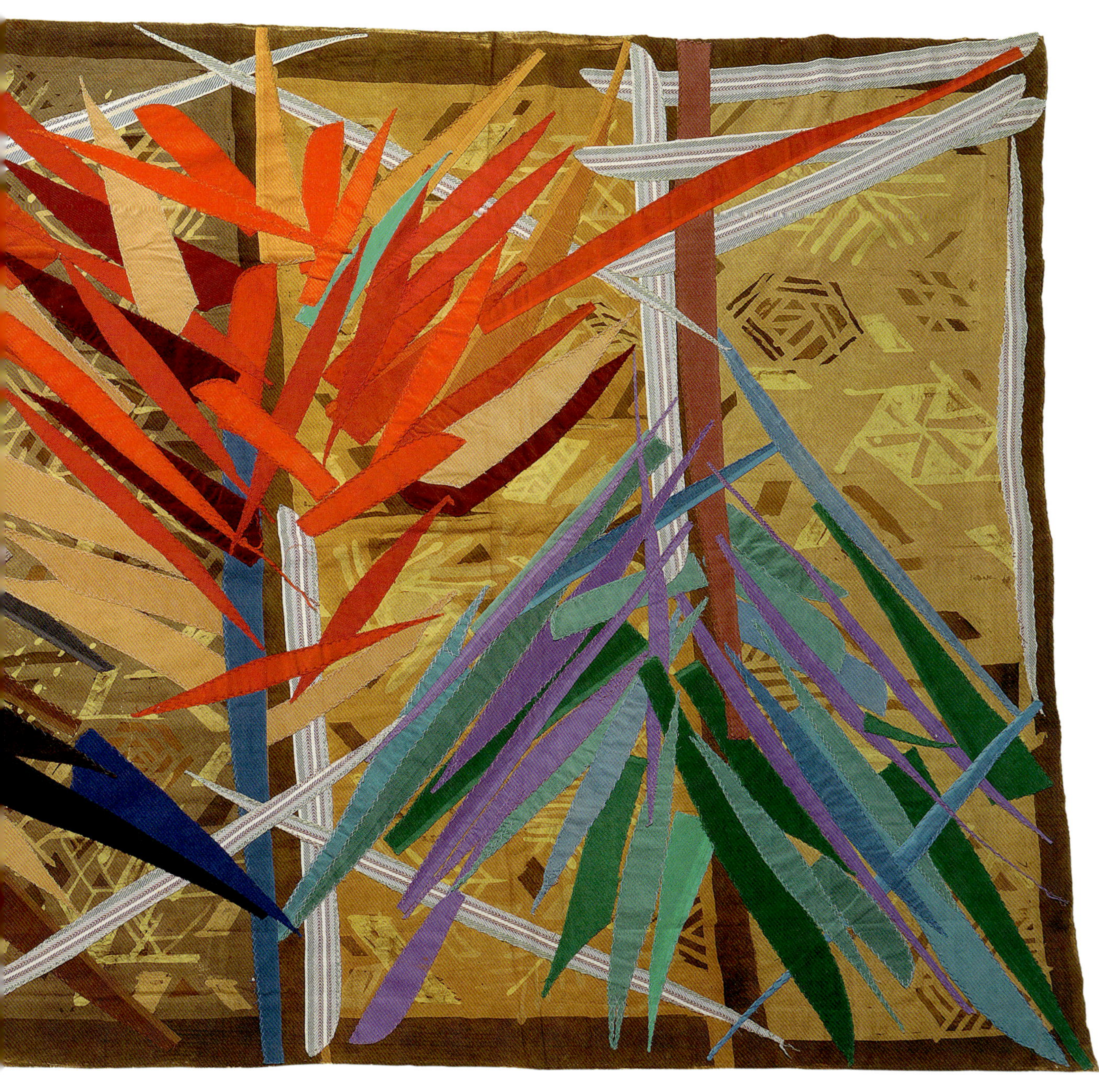

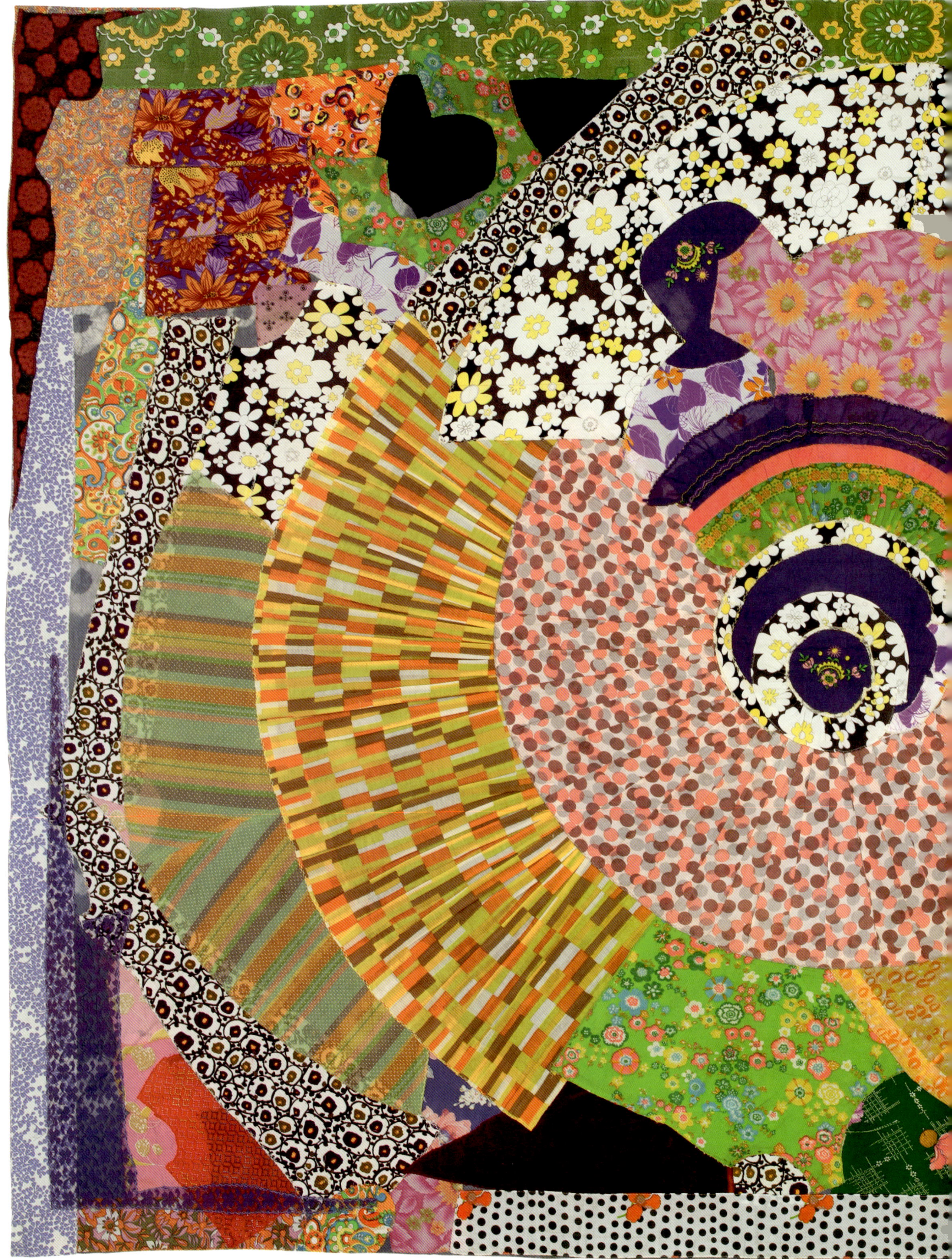

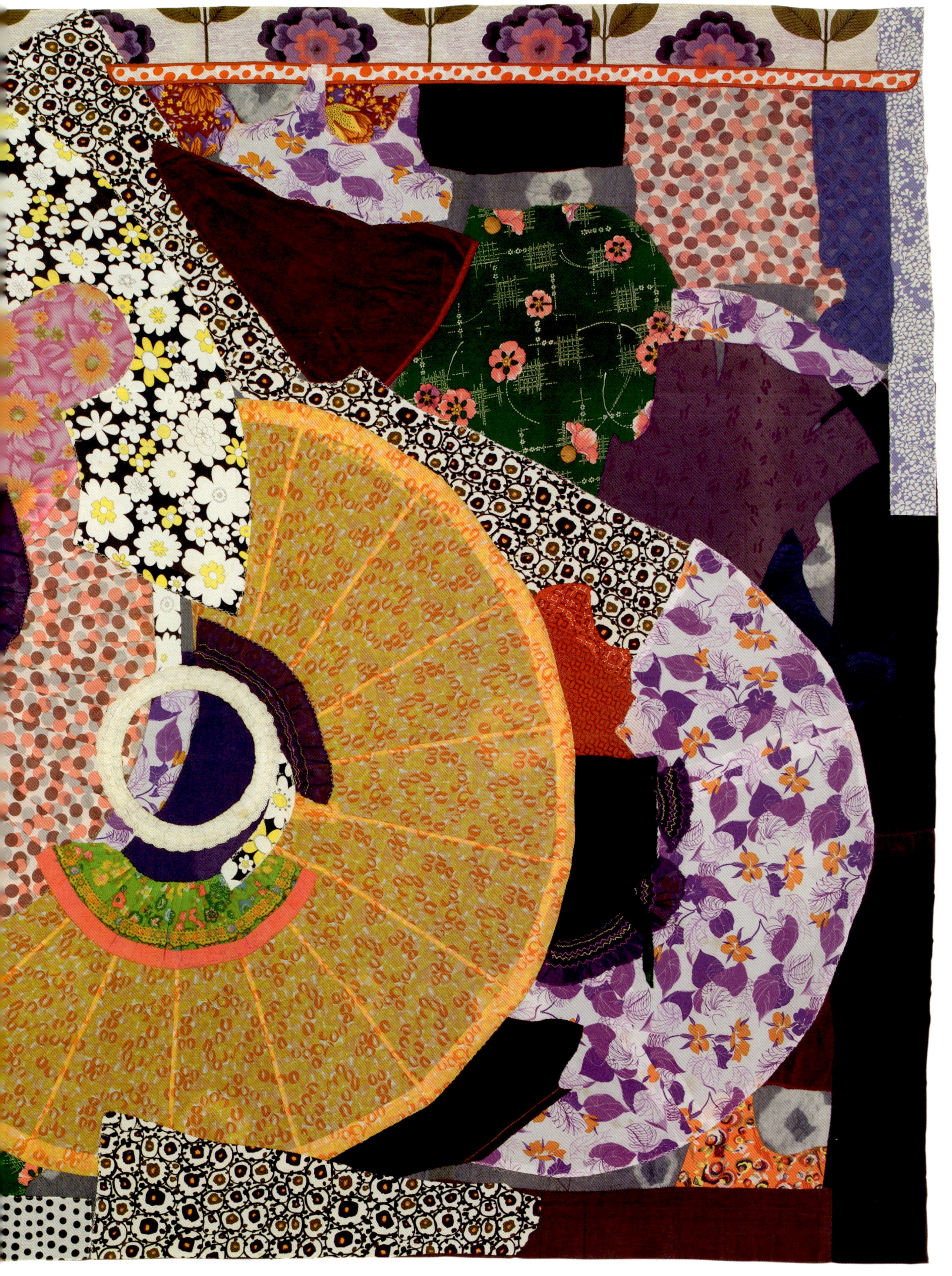

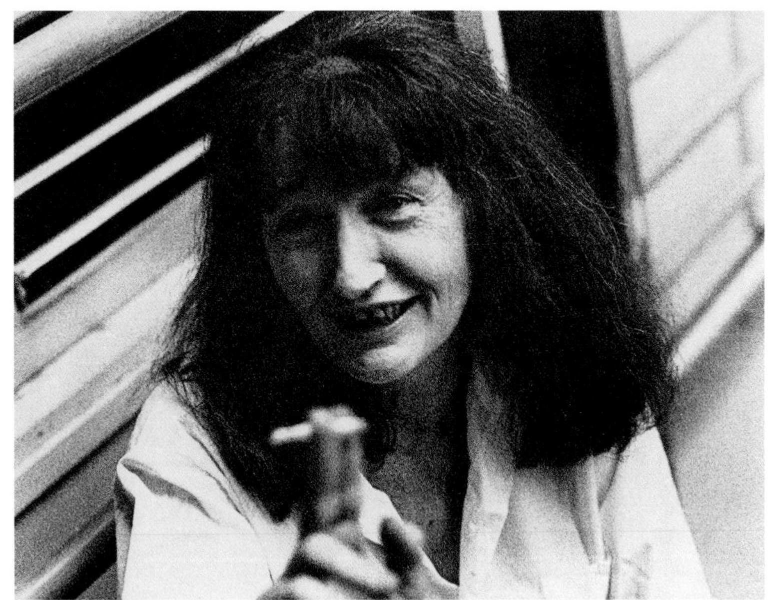

Noa Eshkol, 1980s

The School of Eshkol

Racheli Nul-Kahana, Shmulik Zaidel, Ruti Sela, Mooky Dagan, Mor Bashan

Noa Eshkol's former home-studio is located in Holon, a city in the Tel Aviv metropolitan area. When Eshkol moved there in the 1940s with her mother, Holon was a brand-new development rising from the arid sand dunes outside of Tel Aviv, a bus ride away. Tel Aviv itself was a new city, founded in 1909 primarily by European immigrants like Eshkol's parents. A center of modern culture, it became known as the "White City" because of its concentration of International Style architecture. It was a place where the modernist imperative to "make it new" flourished, which the young Eshkol must have absorbed.[1]

Eshkol took over the house in Holon after her mother died tragically in a household accident in 1951. It was here that she developed Eshkol-Wachman Movement Notation (EWMN), composed dances, designed wall carpets, and wrote books and articles. Her house became the locus of a creative community—dancers, designers, architects, scientists—attracted by her magnetic persona. Over the years she enlarged the house from one story to three so that it could accommodate her constantly growing library, which ranged from literature, including poetry, to philosophy, dance theory, science, and art; the vast collection of fabric scraps from which she created her wall carpets; and, of course, the dancers who practiced there daily.

Like Eshkol herself, who was born in Kvutzat Degania Bet, one of the first kibbutzim in Israel, most of her dancers were born and raised on kibbutzim.[2] But they all left the collective communities of their childhood as they struggled to find their paths in life. One by one they encountered Eshkol—many through a class in movement and EWMN she taught at Seminar HaKibbutzim College of Education in Tel Aviv. As the texts that follow show, these encounters transformed their lives. Some made great personal sacrifices to work with her, which was not easy: she expected only the best from her dancers and could be notoriously difficult. But as a teacher she was nonetheless acclaimed for her clarity and her capacity to inspire.

If the community that Eshkol established at her home in Holon did not display the egalitarian ideals to which the kibbutzim aspired, it did manifest the value the kibbutzim placed on hard work, mutual assistance, and radical utopianism. Eshkol's utopianism, however, was dedicated to the perfection of EWMN, rather than to socialism, Zionism, or other ideologies. Indeed, in 1993 she described EWMN as "a thinking tool that can teach people the art of observation, i.e. encourage them to aspire for the ultimate level of seeing, . . . by organizing the 'material' known as movements of the human body in relatively simple categories, thereby allowing us an insight (in-sight) into the complexity of this phenomenon as a whole." In other words, like so many artists of the historical avant-garde, from Mondrian to Malevich, Eshkol believed that her role as a creator was not to produce commodities, but to cultivate the power of perception, to elevate consciousness by teaching people to perceive reality with clear eyes.

The stories of the following individuals, based on interviews that my assistant Meredith Bayse and I conducted in 2011, illuminate aspects of Eshkol's life and work, as well as those of the individuals themselves. I hope that their words offer a glimpse of the "School of Eshkol," whose members have worked so selflessly to keep the vision of their teacher alive. —Sharon Lockhart

I am grateful to John Alan Farmer for sensitively shaping and editing the transcriptions of the many hours of interviews conducted in Israel.

1. See Barbara E. Mann, *A Place in History: Modernism, Tel Aviv, and the Creation of Jewish Urban Space* (Stanford: Stanford University Press, 2006).
2. I owe this observation to Talia Amar, who discusses the role of the kibbutzim in connection with Eshkol and her practice in depth in "Summer Wind in the Thistles," in this book. For more on Kvutzat Degania Bet, see Daniel Gavron, *The Kibbutz: Awakening from Utopia* (Lanham, Md.: Rowman & Littlefield Publishers, 2000), ch. 1.

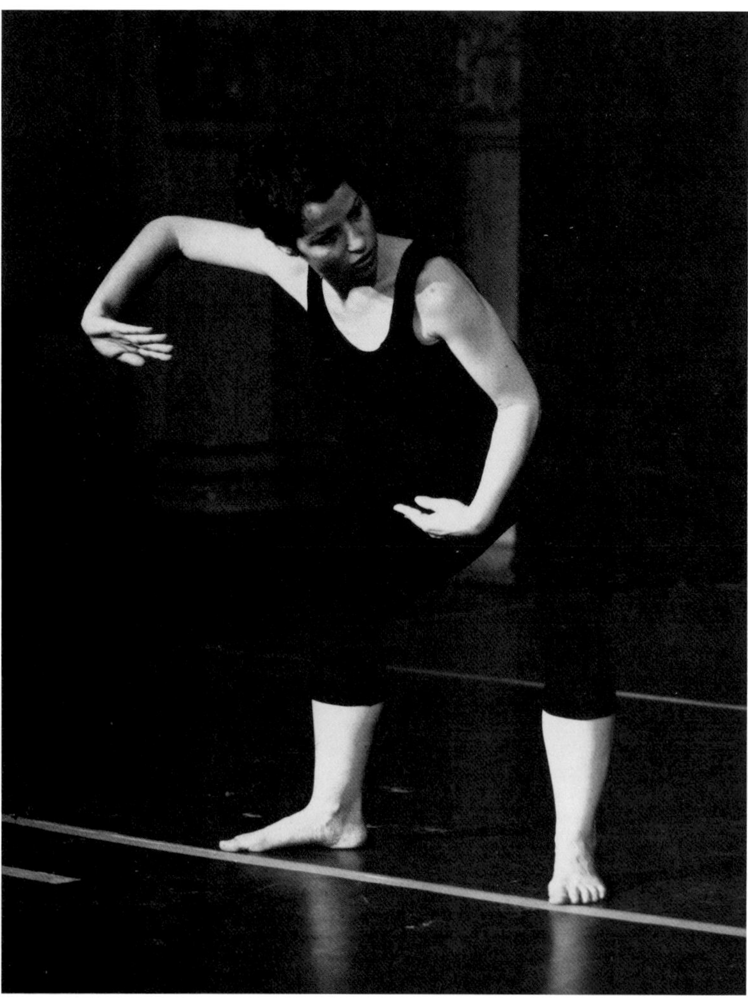

Racheli Nul-Kahana performing in Noa Eshkol's *Long-Necked Birds*, from her dance suite *Right Angled Curves*, performance at the Festival dei Due Mondi (Festival of the Two Worlds), Spoleto, Italy, 1972

Racheli Nul-Kahana
(b. 1942, Kibbutz Degania Aleph)

Noa Eshkol was the daughter of a man who would become the prime minister, but she never wanted to be the "daughter of" anyone: she only wanted to be herself. She never considered herself an artist or a choreographer. Instead, she said that what she did was work—hard work, like that of a coal miner. I was absolutely enchanted by her. She was beautiful, charismatic, and from the big city; and she was the rarest of teachers: one who really knew how to teach. She taught me about both dance and the world.

When I was growing up on the kibbutz, I played the violin. But by the time I was eighteen, I had tired of playing and decided that I wanted to dance, even though I only knew how to perform and teach folk dances. In 1959 a friend of mine who knew I was interested in studying dance arranged for me to meet Noa. People warned me about her: she might throw me down the stairs, they said! So I put on my most beautiful dress and with some trepidation went to her studio. She told me she was planning to begin teaching at the Jerusalem Academy of Music and Dance and suggested that I join her.[1] Because I was an orphan (my father was killed in the Israeli War of Independence in 1948, and my brother was killed in a plane crash while in military service), I was excused from compulsory military service and was able to enroll.

I didn't know if I had any talent, but I knew I had to dance. The government paid for my studies, and I was a good student, though clueless at first—a typical teenager from the kibbutz. I didn't know anything about the big world. For example, I came to my first dance class wearing gym shorts instead of tights.

I studied at the academy for four years, and I dabbled in everything—ballet, Martha Graham, Noa's method. But after a couple of years it became clear that the only thing I liked, and that my body responded to, was Noa's method. Toward the end of my studies, I learned that Noa had a dance group called the Chamber Dance Group, and I asked her if I could join.

In 1964 I met with Noa and Hassia Levy-Agron at Café Kassit in Tel Aviv to discuss joining the group.[2] Both women told me I was too young and didn't know what I wanted yet. Hassia said that if I joined, I wouldn't want to do anything else, and Noa agreed. She suggested I get some experience in musical theater; at the time, musicals like *My Fair Lady* and *Fiddler on the Roof* were popular. Both women thought I'd be perfect for the stage because I could sing, dance, and act. But I disagreed: I wanted to dance with Noa, and I was very persistent. Noa finally agreed to let me work with her for three days a week.

When I joined, the Chamber Dance Group included Ilana Banai, John Harries, Amos Hetz, and Ilana Shaked, among others. The first thing I did was to sit and watch Amos, John, and Ilana Banai perform two dances. I wanted to do exactly what they did. So I started to practice *Ländler*, one of the dances from Noa's dance suite *Theme and Variations*, which Noa wanted us to dance in the spirit of Pieter

Bruegel's paintings.[3] At first I didn't know what I was doing. But the next morning, she told the others to observe how I performed.

From the beginning Noa and I had a symbiotic relationship. All of her students had a special relationship with her, but with me there was something more: I understood what she wanted, and I could do what she wanted. It was as if I could read her mind. But I never saw her dance. She told us she had chosen not to dance herself because her method was so new that someone had to watch and guide the dancers and that person should be herself, the method's inventor. Nevertheless, from time to time she would show us certain movements. She moved like no one I had ever seen.

A turning point in my relationship with Noa came when she took Shmulik Zaidel and me to the United States. In 1968 she was awarded a Fulbright fellowship to conduct research at the University of Illinois at Urbana-Champaign on the analysis of simultaneous movement. Her father, Prime Minister Levi Eshkol, died in February 1969, while she was abroad. She came back to Israel for the funeral. When she returned to the United States, she brought Shmulik and me with her. She arranged performances in various universities, mostly in the Midwest. Each performance was accompanied by a small presentation of models, drawings, and diagrams that explained EWMN, some of which were produced by John Harries. Shmulik and John would install the presentation before each performance and then take it down afterward. The Foreign Office even arranged for us to perform in New York. Merce Cunningham and perhaps George Balanchine were planning to attend, but Noa cancelled the performance. It was a big scandal. In November 1969, on the way back to Israel, we performed in London at a venue called the Place.[4]

Shmulik and I became professional dancers during this trip. We worked with Noa every day, sometimes twice a day, and made great strides. It was an exciting time: the flower children, the moon landing, the demonstrations against the Vietnam War. We even saw a Joan Baez concert. The concert was interesting to me because Noa always believed that performances should be simple, with no manipulation whatsoever. And here was Baez, performing barefoot in a simple dress, but in a huge stadium with dramatic lighting and voice amplification! It was so theatrical. I remember thinking to myself that it was a *show*. By contrast, our performances were more like chamber concerts. We would just execute a dance with no manipulation, but perfectly.

Over the years we worked less and less with Noa. She became impatient with teaching, stopped accepting new dancers and worked only with Ruti Sela and me, and finally ceased composing dances in the 1990s. She began to spend most of her days making the wall carpets and revising EWMN. In the meantime, I established a small dance group of my own, in which I performed my own as well as Noa's dances, and began teaching at Seminar HaKibbutzim. I still wanted and needed a teacher, but I had become too independent for Noa. I wasn't an eighteen-year-old kibbutznik anymore; I was in my fifties and had my own opinions. She didn't like that. She would become angry with me, and she became harder as she got older. I eventually became so troubled that I went to see a psychologist. Ultimately, I told Noa that I had to take care of my own garden, because if I didn't the weeds would destroy it. I left in 2000 and only saw Noa once thereafter.

In spite of the difficulties we had during the later years of our relationship, Noa was by far the best teacher I ever had. She had the ability to inspire her dancers to move in ways that they couldn't imagine. To this day, I've always wanted more than anything to be a dancer who could dance that kind of beauty.

1. The Jerusalem Academy of Music and Dance is a historic and prestigious music and dance academy. Its origins go back to 1932, when the Viennese pianist Yocheved Dostorevsky established a school in Jerusalem for music and the art of movement. In 1958 the academy expanded and was renamed the Rubin Academy of Music. It hosted artists from around the world, including Martha Graham. In 1960 the academy became the Jerusalem Rubin Academy of Music and Dance, and in 1965 Professor Hassia Levy-Agron (1923–2001) founded the dance department, whose curriculum was based on Graham's method. She also cultivated the study of movement and movement notation. The academy is renowned for both its dance and movement departments. The latter offers training in a range of dance and movement styles, including EWMN.

2. Café Kassit was a legendary café located on Dizengoff Street in Tel Aviv. Opened in 1944 by Yehezkel Weinstein (Yehezkel Ish-Kassit), it was a meeting place for generations of artists, writers, actors, dancers, singers, and bohemians. Here they would drink, smoke, gossip, and talk art and politics. See Barry Frylender, *Café Kassit: Photographs* (Jerusalem: Israel Museum, 1985).

3. *Ländler* is the name of a dance by Eshkol inspired by a traditional couple dance of the same name popular in Bavaria and Austria that has roots in medieval German peasant dances and that influenced the development of the waltz. *Ländler* melodies became popular in Vienna in the eighteenth and nineteenth centuries. Composers such as Beethoven, Schubert, and Mahler incorporated such melodies into their work.

4. See John Percival, "Noa Eshkol Group Dances in London, Eschewing Music," *New York Times*, November 10, 1969.

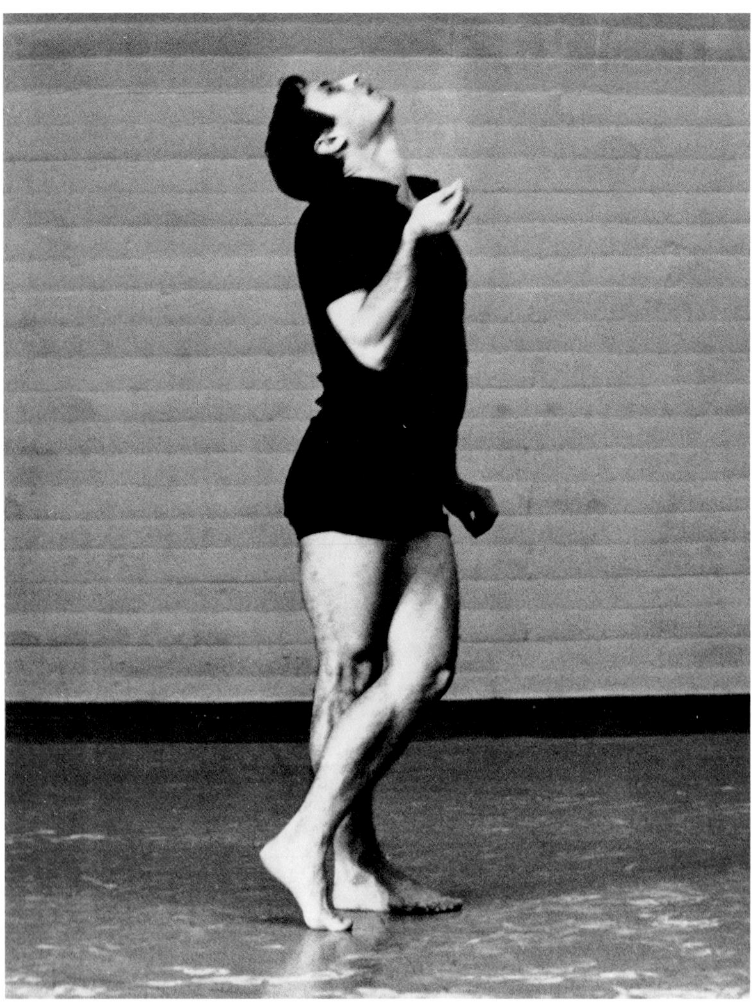

Shmulik Zaidel in rehearsal for Noa Eshkol's *Peacock*, from her dance suite *Theme and Variations*, at Seminar HaKibbutzim College of Education, Tel Aviv, 1970s

Shmulik Zaidel
(b. 1940, Kibbutz Ein Harod)

As a child on the kibbutz, I studied folk dancing. When I was in the fourth grade, I began to work with Rivka Sturman, who lived on my kibbutz and was famous in Israel for composing folk dances.[1] She would try out her dances on me before she premiered them publicly. In 1958 I left the kibbutz to join the army. I was a good soldier, but I danced all the time—especially with the female soldiers and especially on holidays. Although I enjoyed serving, I left in 1961 and returned to the kibbutz. But in 1964 I left for good to study at Seminar HaKibbutzim. My goal was to become a physical-education teacher, which was how I met Noa. She taught just one class, which I had to take for my degree. The class met six days a week; it began at 7:00 p.m. and ended when she said it did. She taught movement, and Amos Hetz taught EWMN. For exercises, she would give us subjects, and we would invent our own short dances.

When I finished my studies in 1966, Noa told me that I had to dance with her Chamber Dance Group. I wasn't planning to be a professional dancer, and I had never earned my living from dance, but I decided to join. Every morning I would go to Noa's home-studio in Holon to practice. At that time Racheli Nul-Kahana would teach us the basic movements, and then Noa would help us perfect them.

My work with Noa was interrupted when the Six-Day War broke out in June 1967.[2] I was called up to fight. After I completed my service, I returned to Holon. At that time we focused on preparing for more performances in Israel, the most important of which were in Tel Aviv.

At the same time that I was working with Noa, I devoted a lot of time to collecting and learning Israeli, Yemenite, and Kurdish folk dances.[3] In 1968 I began working with Ilan Golani, a professor of zoology at Tel Aviv University, who was studying the courting and mating rituals of golden jackals.[4] He came to Holon to consult with Noa on analyzing animal locomotion using EWMN. Noa suggested that he work with me because I was good with animals; I assisted him for eighteen years.

Then in 1973 the Yom Kippur War began.[5] Two hours before I was scheduled to board the bus to the front, I went to say good-bye to Noa. She knew that my journey would be dangerous, but she tried to maintain her composure. She found an old woolen blanket and placed it on the floor. Then she took some buttons and old clothes, which she disassembled, and began to arrange the pieces on the blanket. This was the first wall carpet. She became obsessed and never stopped making them. I served in Syria, near Damascus, for half a year and used to send her materials for the carpets, including old army blankets, which she often used for backings.

When I returned home, Noa was still making the carpets. She would finish one every couple of days. At first she made the arrangements from scraps she had around the house, such as old clothes that she took apart and factory pieces (she never cut the scraps). Then, Ruti Sela, Racheli, and I would collect scraps for her. She used to teach a class on Thursday evenings at Seminar HaKibbutzim, in which we participated. After class, Tirza Sapir, who had a car and served as Noa's driver, would take the three of us to Nachalat Binyamin in Tel Aviv, the main thoroughfare in the textile district.[6] At night the factories would throw away all the scraps they didn't need. Every week we would dig through dumpsters for these discards and bring them to the studio. Later, as Noa focused more intensely on the carpets, anyone who had a connection to us—people from all over Israel—would bring scraps or old clothes to the house.

I finally left the group in 1987, and I didn't speak to Noa for five years. My last performances with Ruti and Racheli took place at Tel Aviv University. They called these performances my "last song." I had to leave because I wanted to start a family, and I needed to have a real job to support my children. I could not do this and be committed to Noa at the same time. It was just too hard.

1. Rivka Sturman (1903–2001) is known as the mother of Israeli folk dance. She moved from Germany to Palestine in 1929 and ultimately settled in Kibbutz Ein Harod, where she taught the kibbutz children new dances she composed as part of her effort to develop a uniquely Israeli folk-dance practice that drew from local, rather than European, traditions and that expressed Jewish ideals. Many of these dances became classics in Israel and the Jewish Diaspora. See Judith Brin Ingber, *Shorashim: The Roots of Israeli Folk Dance* (New York: Dance Perspectives Foundation, 1974); Rina Sharett, *Kumah e'kha* (*The Story of Rivka Sturman: Pioneer of Israeli Folk Dance*) (Tel Aviv: Hakibbutz Hameuchad Publishing House, 1988).

2. The Six-Day War, also known as the June War, the 1967 Arab-Israeli War, and the Third Arab-Israeli War, took place June 5–10, 1967. As a result of the war, Israel gained control of the Gaza Strip and the Sinai Peninsula from Egypt, the West Bank and East Jerusalem from Jordan, and the Golan Heights from Syria. Eshkol's father Levi Eshkol served as prime minister during this war.

3. In 1987 Zaidel published a study of ethnic dances from Israel. See Shmuel [Shmulik] Zaidel, *Ethnic Dances: Variations on "Six"* (Israel: The Movement Notation Society, 1987).

4. Professor Golani helped pioneer the scientific application of EWMN, particularly to the analysis of behavioral patterns common to mammals and invertebrates in the contexts of play, courtship, ritualistic combat, and spatial exploration. His findings for the project that Zaidel references were published in Ilan Golani, *The Golden Jackal: Behaviour Studies by Ilan Golani, Notated by Shmuel Zaidel under the Supervision of Noa Eshkol* (Israel: The Movement Notation Society, 1969).

5. The Yom Kippur War, also known as the 1973 Arab-Israeli War and the Fourth Arab-Israeli War, began on October 6, 1973, when Egypt and Syria launched a surprise attack on Israel. It ended when a cease-fire was declared on October 25.

6. Named after what was once the longest street in Tel Aviv, Nachalat Binyamin is one of the oldest neighborhoods in the city. Today, it is the location not only of fabric shops, but of boutiques and cafés, as well as a lively arts and crafts fair that takes place twice a week on the northern part of the street that has been converted into a pedestrian mall.

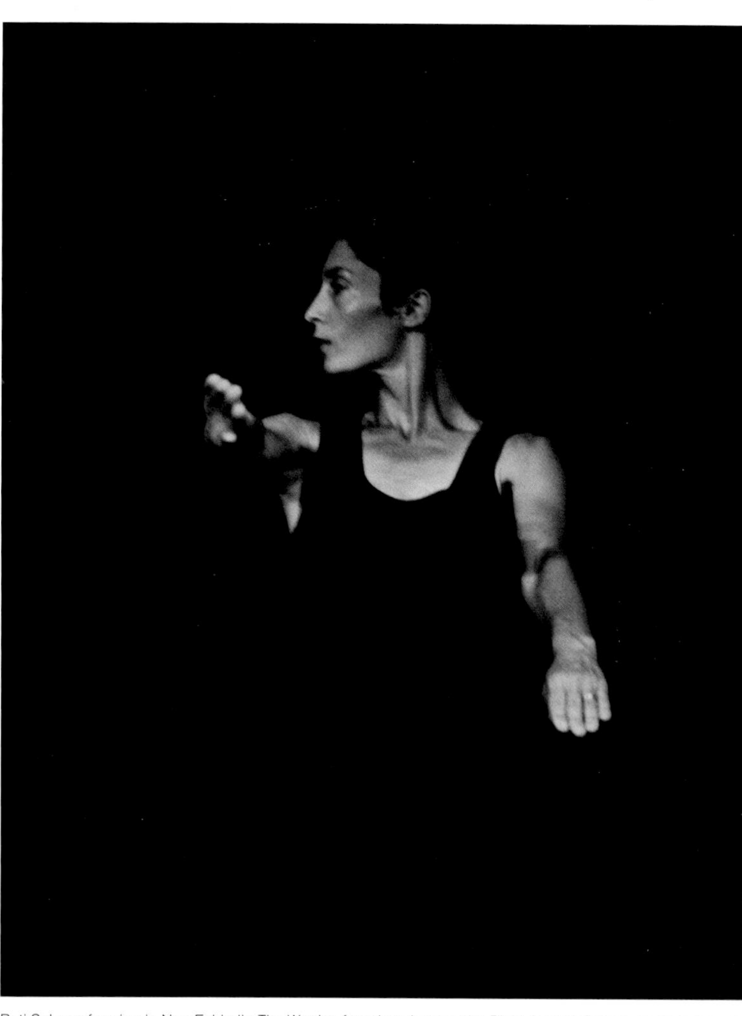

Ruti Sela performing in Noa Eshkol's *The Warrior*, from her dance suite *Right Angled Curves*, performance at the Festival dei Due Mondi (Festival of Two Worlds), Spoleto, Italy, 1972

Ruti Sela
(b. 1939, Kvutzat Kinneret)

I've always known that my talent was dancing, but I didn't decide to pursue dance until I met Noa Eshkol. That decision changed my life. I loved working with Noa—the dancing, the notation, the atmosphere of her home-studio in Holon, where we practiced. Everyone needs a teacher, and she was mine.

My mother didn't want to live on the kibbutz, where I was born. She was from a big city, and the commune lifestyle didn't suit her: she was too independent. She entered the army when I was two and a half years old and died under tragic circumstances when I was four and a half. After my talent for dancing became apparent, the kibbutz's cultural committee decided to send me to Haifa to study dance, but I didn't want to leave. At the time I was sure that the kibbutz was the only place I could live because it was the only place I knew. After I graduated from high school, I worked in the plant nursery, which I loved. Then when I was twenty-one, I married a soldier named Nachik. I gave birth to a son, Gur, about a year later and then to a daughter, Yael, about a year and a half after that. My relationship with Nachik was difficult at that time because he was serving in Iran and was always gone.

In 1966, when I was twenty-five, we moved to Nof Yam, a small residential neighborhood in Herzliya, north of Tel Aviv. I was alone with two young children and was becoming frustrated with my life. Friends told me that I should pursue dance, but I thought that was impossible because of my family obligations. Then a good friend who had studied with Noa told me that if I wanted to dance, I should work with her. So I enrolled in a class she taught at Seminar HaKibbutzim. Racheli Nul-Kahana and Shmulik Zaidel, whom I would come to know very well, were also in the class.

Noa's rich and imagistic language, her phenomenal clarity of thought, and the unique nature of her movements created a physical and intellectual experience that was completely new to me. I finished each lesson floating with joy, but dancing conflicted with my family obligations. I decided to see a psychologist to figure out what to do.[1] We analyzed my dreams, and they revealed to me that I needed to dance.

In 1970 Noa invited me to join her Chamber Dance Group. After much deliberation, I decided to accept, and my life changed. Practicing was hard work, and I also had to take care of my two children, who were in Rishon LeZion. My relationship with Nachik worsened, and he ultimately took the children back to the kibbutz. Yael was very unhappy and wanted to stay with me, but I didn't have enough money to support her. She loved Noa and received all of Noa's wisdom through me, and I feel that she's the wiser for it.

In the 1970s it wasn't "normal" for a mother of two children to make a decision like I did. But the desire to dance was so strong in my body and soul that I couldn't imagine doing anything else. After I made the decision to dance, I couldn't abandon it, no matter how many people told me that I was *meshuga* (crazy), that I wasn't a mother, that

I wasn't a woman. I didn't listen to those people. I only listened to Noa, who could envision the light inside of me, which I couldn't do myself back then. I had no time to think about whether I was a feminist or not, and I don't know if Noa was a feminist, but I believe she felt that if you find your special path in life, you must embrace it. I had to dance because dancing was my *power*.

I learned so much about dance by working with Noa. Her dances represent a new world of movement. They're also difficult, like chamber music. Each time you listen to a piece of chamber music, you hear something you didn't hear before. Similarly, each time you watch one of Noa's dances, you see something you didn't see before. But it takes work, and few people want to make the effort. Specifically, to understand the dances, and to perform them, it is imperative to understand EWMN, which is not easy. Only by notating the dances do you understand what the body needs to do in order to execute the movements as intended.

In addition to dancing, I assisted Noa with making and caring for the wall carpets, which she began to produce in 1973. It took a long time for us to understand that this practice was more than a hobby for her: it was an obsession. She developed a system for categorizing the scraps from which she made the carpets into groups based on color, shape, and size, which she called "themes." First we separated them by color. Then we separated solid colors from patterned ones. Floral prints constituted one theme, stripes another, and square patches yet another. And so on. It was interesting to see how Noa organized the collection of scraps, for which I was responsible.

Noa never referred to the carpets as art. She hated the word "art." Nevertheless, if someone said that the carpets weren't art, she would become furious. She made the carpets until the end of her life. A few days before she died, while she was making one in the studio, she fell and broke her arm. That was the last one. We kept it unfinished, exactly as she left it.

In 2000 Racheli left, and all dancing in the house ceased. I was the only dancer left, and Noa didn't want to work with just one dancer, while I didn't want to dance without Racheli. I didn't dance for seven years. Instead, I continued to come to the house each day to work with Noa on the movement notation and the carpets. I was also responsible for maintaining the house, taking care of Noa, and keeping a diary of our daily activities, which I had done for years. I would arrive at the house each morning at about 6:30 a.m. Most of the time I would come to Noa's room with her tea and speak with her until she got out of bed. Some mornings she was already downstairs, and if she was, we would start working on the carpets. She slept very little: when she wasn't making carpets, she was often reading. She was a voracious reader. I've never known anyone like her. She did everything in excess.

My relationship with Noa deteriorated toward the end of her life. She was diagnosed with lung cancer, and as she became more ill, her behavior became more terrible. She wanted me to stay with her all the time, but I couldn't, and when I would leave, she would feel that I was abandoning her. Eventually we had a difficult conversation about the tension between us. That was the last time I saw her, and it was a tough good-bye. A few days later she was admitted to the hospital and died. I learned of her death when I was at Yael's house in Tel Aviv. I went out on to the street and said to myself, "At last I am free." Yael thought it would be difficult for me to live without Noa, but it wasn't. Working with her had been intense. Now it was really over.

The day after Noa died, Michal Shoshani called Racheli. Shortly thereafter they, Tirza Sapir, and I met at Noa's house. We sat in the kitchen and talked about what would come next. We decided to try to move on. A few days later I danced with Racheli for the first time since she had left, but it was like no time at all had passed. We started with *Homework*. We began to cry because our bodies had been waiting for this moment. I remembered all the movements as if I had done them yesterday. I was shocked to feel what it was like to move at my age. I was also shocked to dance without Noa observing. We couldn't believe that we could work in this wonderful world that she had created, but without her.

Today I am very fortunate to be able to dance and also to have the love and support of my family. For example, Yael now has children of her own, and I have helped care for them since they were born. Everything I couldn't do for her as a mother, I do for her as a grandmother. She tells me that if she had to suffer as she did to have the mother she has today, then it was all worth while.

1. Some of the dancers sought psychotherapy at some point in their lives. On the place of psychotherapy in Israeli culture, see Benjamin Beit-Hallahmi, *Despair and Deliverance: Private Salvation in Contemporary Israel* (Albany: State University Press of New York, 1992), ch. 4 ("The Liberated Self: Developing a Psychotherapy Subculture in Israel").

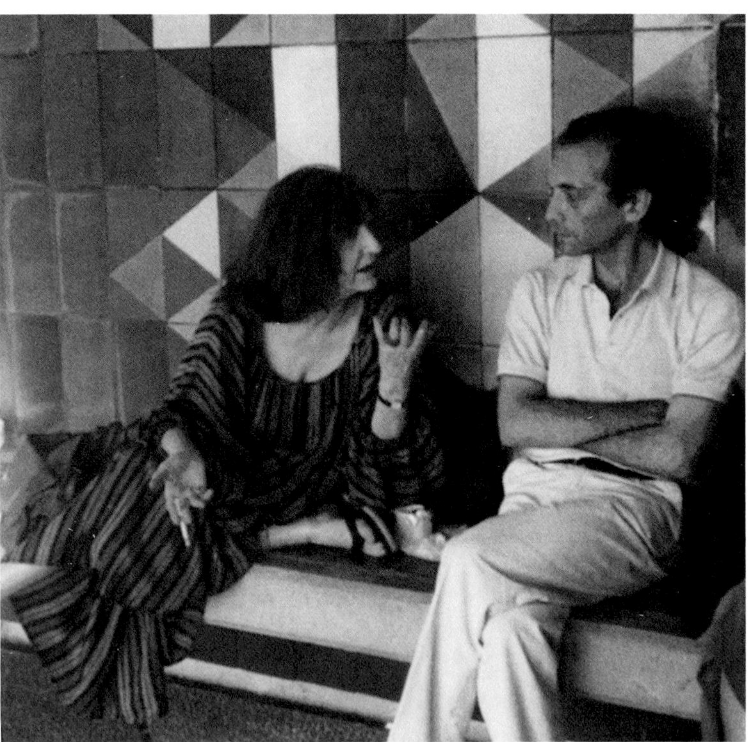

Noa Eshkol and Mooky Dagan at the First International Congress for Movement Notation, Tel Aviv, August 1984

Mooky Dagan
(b. 1946, Tel Aviv)

Noa would say, "I dared to have the nerve to create a language." With EWMN, she created a language to express the phenomenon of movement. She asked herself, "If I start at zero, what do I do from here?" The problem is that movement is natural to everyone, like breathing, so you have to look at your body in a very abstract way. This is exceedingly difficult. The genius of the language she developed is its simplicity: a system indisputable in its principles that she was always striving to make simpler. She originally invented this language with the architect Avraham Wachman, who helped her with the concept of the geometry of the sphere. From the 1950s onward her remarkable practice included the development of EWMN, teaching, and, more rarely, the performance of her dance compositions.

Noa worked incessantly to crystallize EWMN. It was not a static system, but a dynamic one in a state of continuous becoming. Because she was continually investigating new varieties of movement, she was continually discovering new problems that demanded solution in the notation. For example, she was always throwing away symbols because her mode of analysis was quantitative and should theoretically be describable in purely numerical terms. This process of crystallization, however, posed challenges to the dancers, who worked as hard to keep up to date as Noa worked to perfect her language.

For most of her career, teaching was an important part of Noa's practice. Seminar HaKibbutzim became her home, where she taught movement and EWMN. In the 1970s, at the invitation of the Ministry of Education, she designed and taught in a three-year experimental program for future physical-education teachers at the Seminar. By targeting these students, as opposed to ones interested in becoming professional dancers, she thought that she could extend the social impact of EWMN: training physical-education teachers in her approach to movement could revolutionize how physical education was taught in schools, which in turn could transform how the emerging generation conceived the body in movement. Although some of her students left the program right away, others, including myself, thought it was fantastic (I enrolled in the program at Noa's request and then continued studying with her after the program concluded). But because the program required so much work, Noa decided not to continue it after her initial three-year commitment expired. Parallel to this program, she had her own group of students who worked with her exclusively for a longer period of time.

Beyond the Seminar, Noa was also affiliated with other educational institutions. In 1968 she received a Fulbright fellowship to conduct research on simultaneous movement at the University of Illinois at Urbana-Champaign.[1] Then a few years later, in 1972, Tel Aviv University appointed her to a professorship and created for her the Research Center for Movement Notation in the Faculty of Visual and Performing Arts, which published several of the books that she and her colleagues wrote from the 1970s onward. She accepted the professorship on the condition that she not be required to teach at the university, and she conducted all of her research from her home in Holon.[2] The position at Tel Aviv University gave her financial security, which she had until she died.

In addition to developing EWMN and teaching, Noa presented performances of her Chamber Dance Group in Israel, though rarely. International performances were even rarer. One of the Group's most important international performances was at the Festival dei Due Mondi (Festival of the Two Worlds) in Spoleto, Italy, in 1972, which I arranged. I had been introduced to Noa's work by one of her dancers, Ilana Banai, who took me to see a rehearsal of the group in 1965. Having had no great interest in dance or movement at the time, I had what seemed to be an enlightening experience there. I told Noa after the rehearsal that what I saw was probably the most beautiful performance I had ever witnessed in my life, though it had not been explained to me; it was like Bach in movement. We became great friends then and there.

In 1966 I began my first year as the assistant for Gian Carlo Menotti, director of the festival. I told him that he should invite Noa and the group to perform. In August 1969 he staged his opera *The Consul* in Israel. I then arranged for him to meet Noa and see a rehearsal of the group. He was greatly impressed and invited them to perform at Spoleto.

In 1972, after fulfilling all of Noa's requirements for the right conditions for performing (a large, but intimate hall, with no stage, with only the beat of the metronome as sound, and clear, even lighting), Noa and the dancers performed to packed audiences at Spoleto. Years later Menotti told me that in terms of bringing innovative and unique performances to the festival, he was most proud of Noa's dances and Jerzy Grotowski's theater.

Spoleto could have been the launching pad for an international career for Noa, but she didn't want one. All she wanted was to return home to Holon and do her work. She was always interested in two things, which went hand in hand: perfecting EWMN and composing her dances. She was also concerned with the application of the system in areas outside of dance, such as science. For example, the Israeli air force once consulted with her on using EWMN to record the movement of planes. Two officers came to Holon. They explained that they were teaching their pilots about the movement of planes in the air, and they simulated how the planes moved. Noa explained to them that the planes' movement took place on one axis and there was no connection to the ground, and thus no point of reference. "My notation is not for you because you don't need it," she politely said.

In her will, Noa provided for the creation of the Noa Eshkol Foundation for Movement Notation and directed that I serve as the chairman. Established in 2008, the Foundation is dedicated to developing EWMN, maintaining an archive on Noa and her work, and preserving the hundreds of wall carpets she created, with which I have been closely involved from the beginning, having organized all but one of the exhibitions of the carpets to date. Through these activities we strive to preserve her unique legacy.

1. While Eshkol was in the United States, she also became involved in other activities. For example, she was approached by NASA to consult on the application of EWMN to the movement of astronauts. The architect Ifat Finkelman, a former student of Avraham Wachman's at the Technion, has conducted research on this subject.
2. Eshkol inaugurated at the university a program based on the one she taught at the Seminar exclusively for her long-term students. Graduates of this program would earn a diploma in movement and movement notation. All the dancers—Racheli Nul-Kahana, Shmulik Zaidel, and Ruti Sela, among others—enrolled.

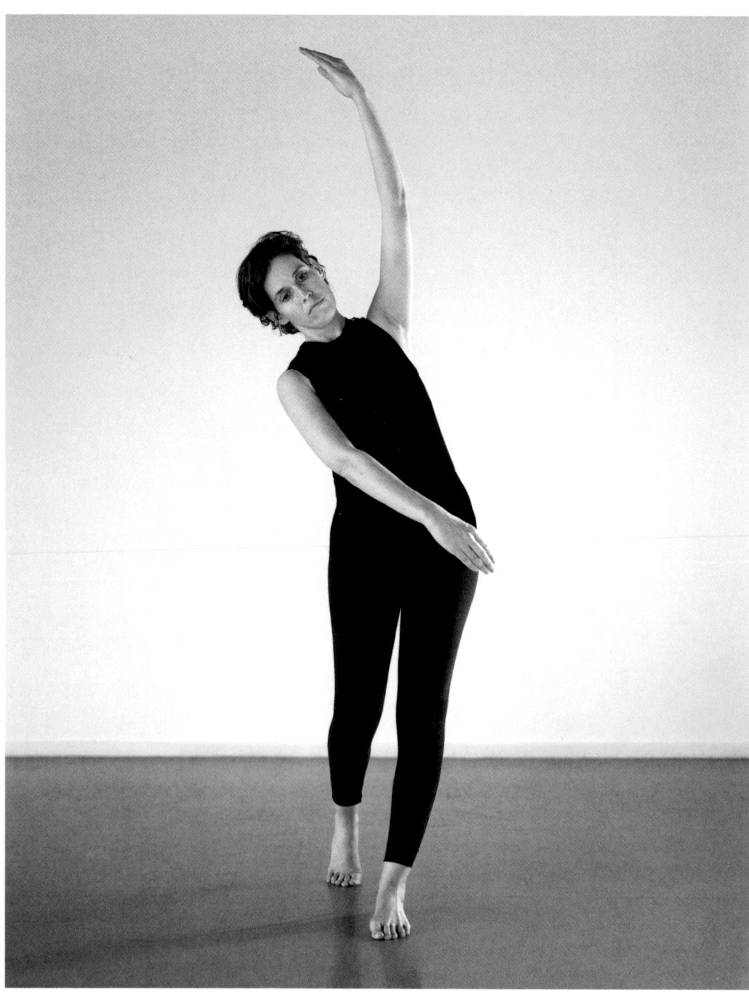

Sharon Lockhart, *"Minuet" Dance from the Suite "Theme and Variations" by Noa Eshkol, Performed by Mor Bashan*, 2010, chromogenic print, 24 ½ x 20 ½ inches (62.2 x 52.1 cm)

Mor Bashan
(b. 1972, Kibbutz Beit Alfa)

As a young girl, I studied classical and modern dance at the kibbutz's regional dance and music center, located in the town of Beit She'an. Besides dancing, I played basketball for the kibbutz's girls team and was considered to be quite talented. Basketball was more popular than dance in those days, and because I didn't want to be the only one riding the bus to dance class anymore, I eventually stopped dancing. When I was sixteen, I moved to the United States with my family and returned to dance, which was taught in a gym class at my high school. After we returned to Israel, I completed my military service. By then, dancing was out of my mind. I traveled around the world for the next four years; for part of that time I lived between Paris and Tel Aviv. But even though those days were exciting, something was missing. I would find that missing piece when I began to study Noa Eshkol's dances with Racheli Nul-Kahana and Ruti Sela.

I first encountered Noa's method through a class in the department of movement and movement notation at the Jerusalem Academy of Music and Dance. My teacher was Amos Hetz, one of Noa's former students. What I saw didn't look like dance as I knew it, and it intrigued me. I saw parallels with Yvonne Rainer and the dancers associated with Judson Dance Theater, whom I love. I don't know if Noa was aware of Rainer, but I find similarities. Both were pioneers who believed in dance as its own medium, separate from music, narrative, and the other theatrical elements usually associated with it—recall Rainer's "No Manifesto" (1965). Both were interested in exploring the three most fundamental components that define dance and movement: body, space, time. Also, one can find in works by both women references to the Minimalist and modernist movements in music and the visual arts. Nevertheless, the results of their experiments are very different. Noa went much further by developing a whole new language: EWMN.

After I graduated from the academy in 2002, Einya Cohen, one of my teachers, invited me to join her dance group. She composed her own dances using Noa's notation. Then I was on the move with my husband for several years: Tokyo, Toronto, New York. In Tokyo I studied at the Kazuo Ohno Dance Studio, founded by the great Butoh master. When we finally returned to Israel, I resumed working with Einya. I also began to teach elementary-school girls jazz dance. But all this time I struggled with the belief that I wasn't really a dancer.

Eventually a friend of mine told me that I might be interested in working with Racheli Nul-Kahana, whom I had known of but had never met. I had first seen Racheli and Ruti Sela in a video screened during a class I had taken with

Michal Shoshani at the academy. They were dancing *The Four Seasons*. I thought, Wow, these woman are *dancing*: they're not just executing movement notations, which is what I had initially thought Noa's method was all about. One day I finally gathered the courage to phone Racheli. I told her I had just given birth and was trying to convince myself that perhaps dance wasn't for me and that I should let it go. I happened to call her a few months after Noa's death. She told me she had decided to commit herself to preserving Noa's legacy and that as part of that project, she was teaching a class of women, all trained teachers in various movement disciplines and Noa's method, that met once a week at Seminar HaKibbutzim.

Racheli suggested I start by taking a few private lessons with her at her house. The first dance she taught me was *Homework*. Soon thereafter I met Ruti. Eventually I asked Racheli if she might be interested in creating a program for younger dancers to ensure that a new generation of professional dancers would continue Noa's work. She replied that if I found some students, she'd be happy to teach them. So I called a few friends and colleagues from school—Dana Bar, Noga Goral, Or Gal-Or, Ayelet Zafrir—and we started to meet with Racheli and Ruti in the evenings. I had no expectations: I just wanted a place to dance.

Usually, Racheli instructs and Ruti practices with us, but when Racheli is absent, Ruti takes over. Racheli is very precise: she knows exactly which instructions to give us to improve our movements. Both women know all of Noa's dances and can perform them perfectly. At the end of each class they show us a complete dance based on what we were practicing. I am astounded by their virtuosity: the head moves in one direction, the hands in another; the legs rise up in the air while the torso rotates.

At first we found it almost impossible to perform and synchronize the different layers constructing each dance. Even though the dances are short (most less than five minutes long), they are difficult because there are so many complexities, both mental and physical. We couldn't dance for more than an hour and a half at a time because it was so exhausting. In fact, it took me more than a year to learn one dance, whose full complexity emerges only when it is performed perfectly.

Working with Racheli and Ruti has transformed my attitude toward Noa's method. Although I had always been interested in its avant-gardism, the fact that it wasn't well-known concerned me: it's difficult to commit yourself so completely to something when you always feel like you have to justify what you're doing. But if I had initially decided to pursue this method as a compromise, consolation for the fact that I couldn't pursue ballet anymore, I gradually began to see it as more of a challenge and to fall in love with it. For the first time I was sure that I was in the right place at the right time: I had found my way of dancing.

When you perform Noa's dances yourself, as we do in class, you understand them in a different way. They are structured like musical scores: a rule generates the composition, and then there are variations of the rule. But producing these compositions in your body is a completely different story. Racheli and Ruti understand that even though the dances are very technical, performing them entails more than simply executing the notation: expression is involved, too. When I dance, each nuanced movement my body produces makes me feel something different. Each formal movement has an expression, which I enjoy trying to find.[1] For example, when we study *Peacock*, Racheli talks about the peacock's attitude and about Noa's private images, which along with the written score, become part of our performing instructions.

The fact that we perform written texts is an unusual practice within the world of dance, a form of art that is delivered and taught only as *toshbah*: from the teacher to her or his student. I'm intrigued by the issues that arise from the encounter between the written text and its performance. As is the case in other performing arts, such as music and theater, Noa's dances provide a comprehensive platform for the performer's interpretation. There is a tension between the written text, to which I'm committed, and the gaps in it—the things that aren't written, which are available for interpretation. As a dancer, I'm challenged to work in that space.

Finally, being in the house where Noa was creating, with the people whom she was surrounded by, has added so much to my experience of her dances. Working in the context of a community of people of different ages, both the previous generation of dancers and the new one, who hold similar ideas and concepts on art and dance, makes it a whole new adventure for me.

1. Expression in this context is not to be confused with emotionalism. In a rare interview with Dalia Lamdani published in the February 9, 1968, issue of the Israeli newspaper *Haaretz*, Eshkol explained why her face doesn't express anything in her dances: "The head, in my use of movement, is not mainly a 'face,' but rather an instrument of movement, and therefore a change in its relationship to other body parts interests me more than theatrical facial expressions. Besides, personally, I don't like the representation of ecstasies that dancers usually add to movement."

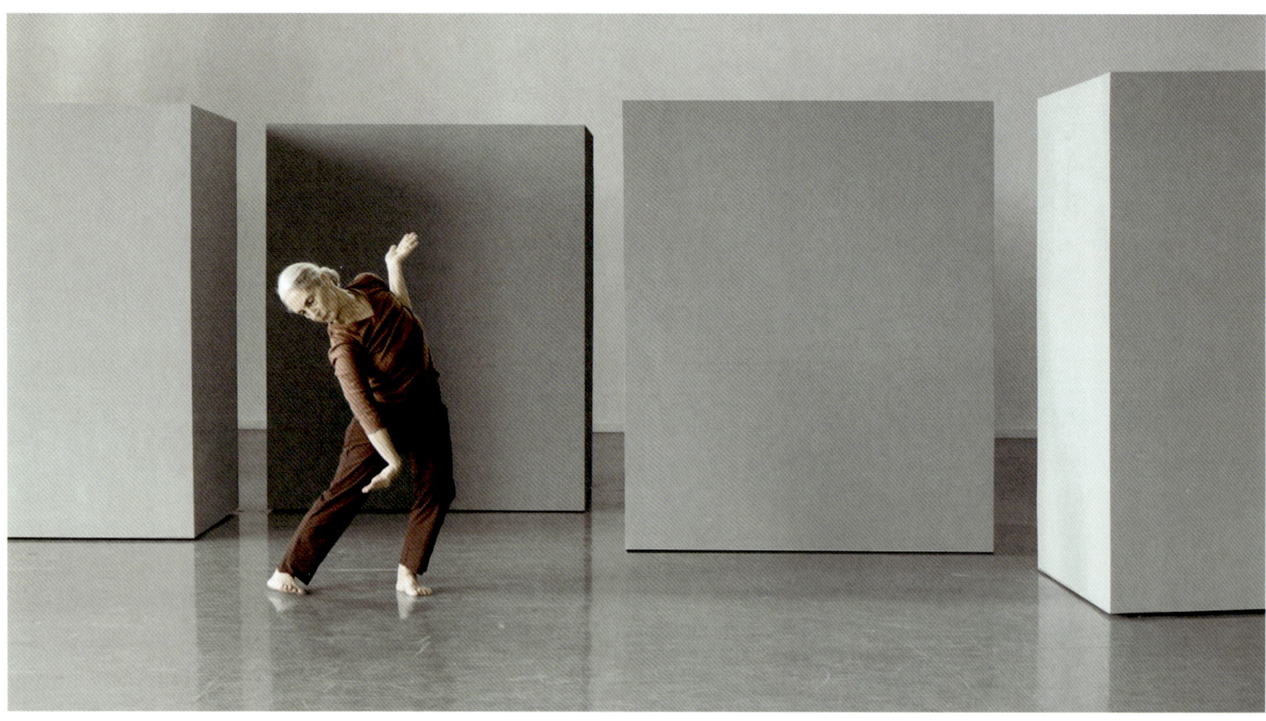

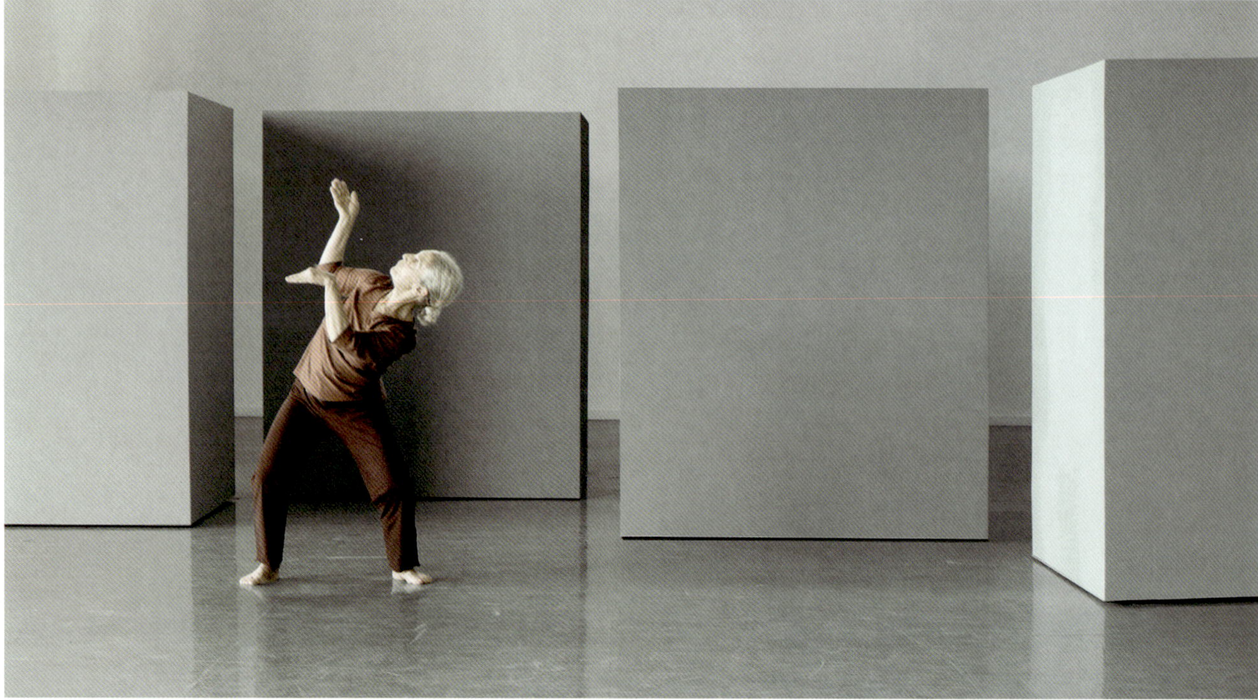

Sharon Lockhart, frames from *Four Exercises in Eshkol-Wachman Movement Notation*, 2011

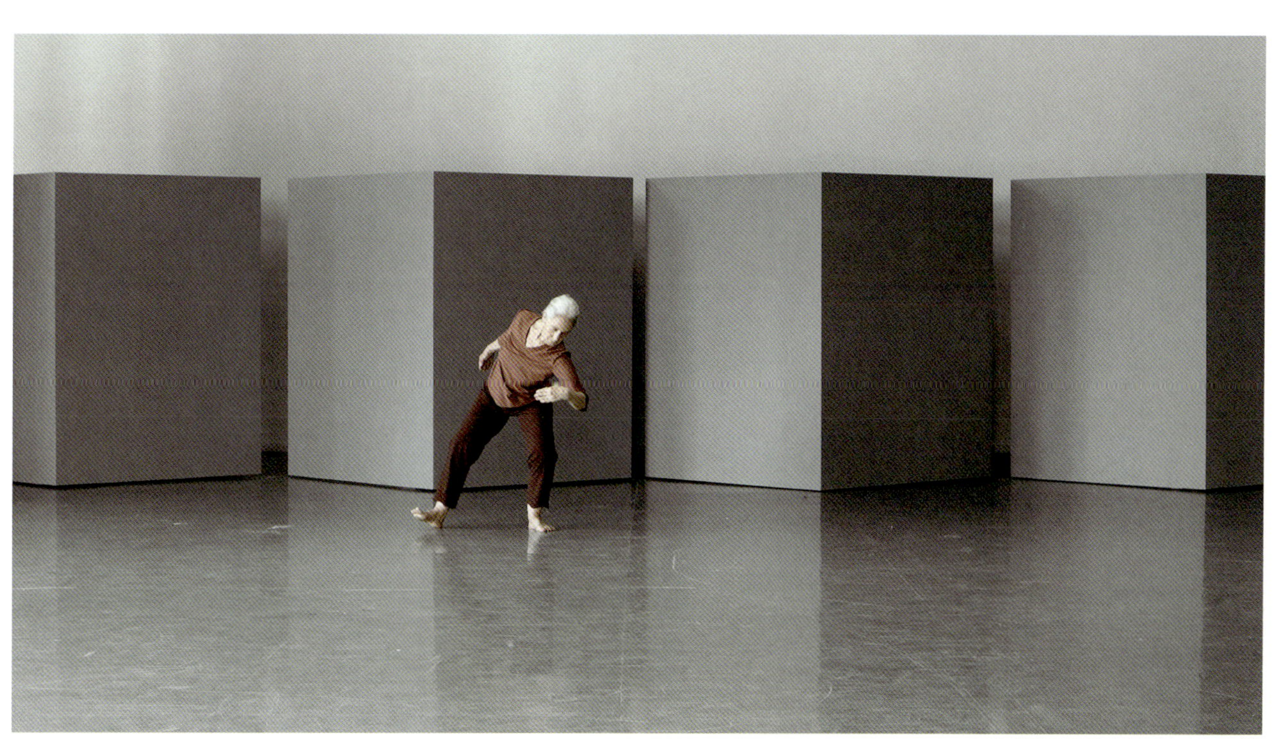

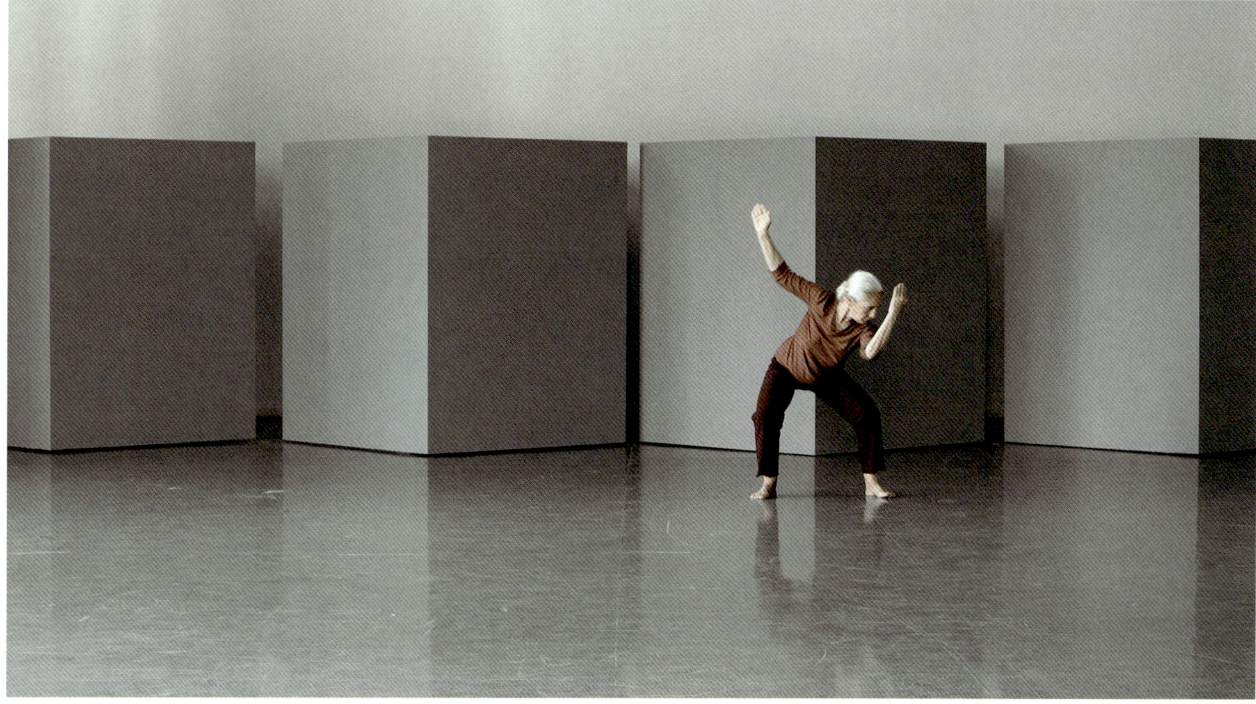

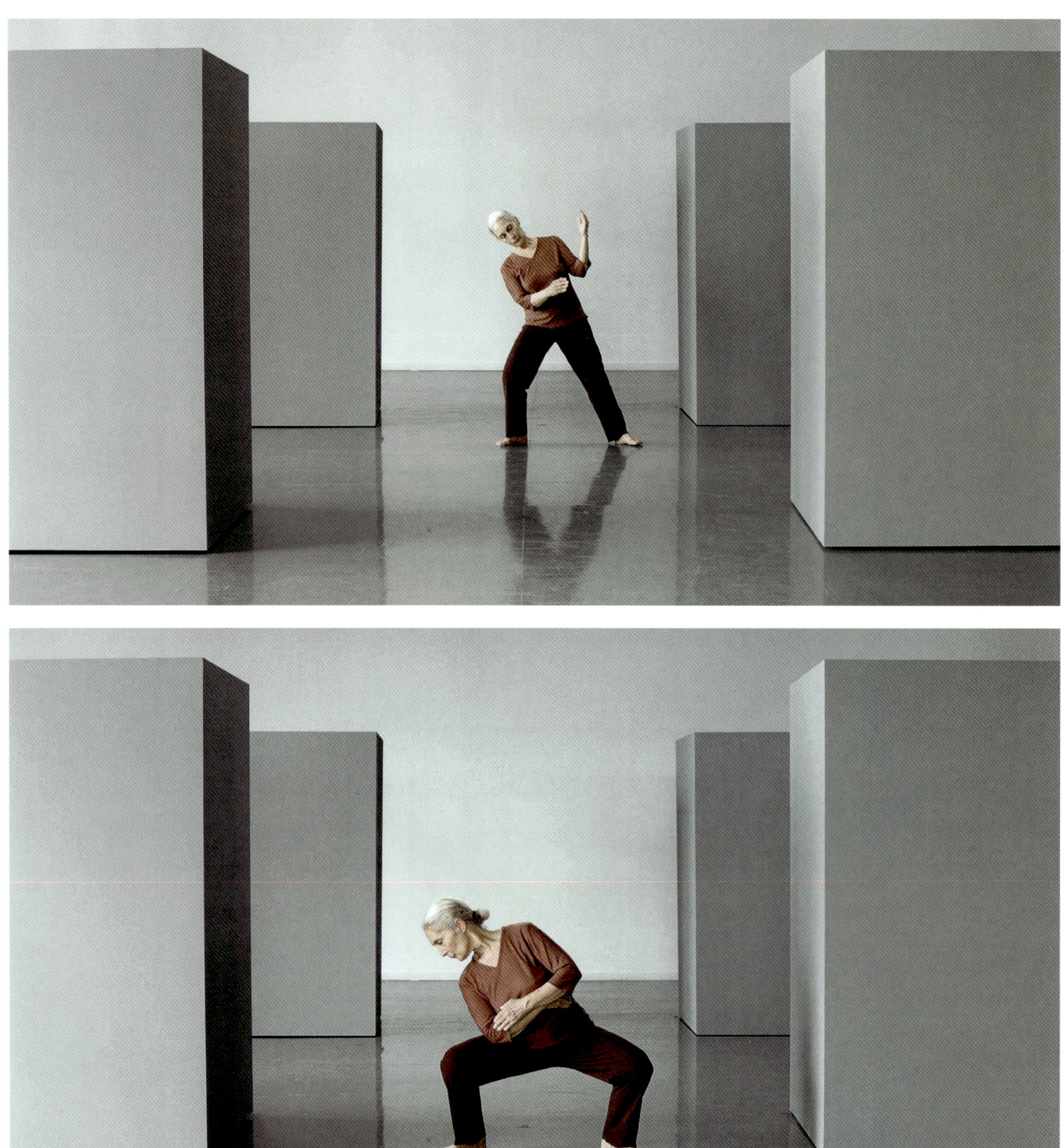

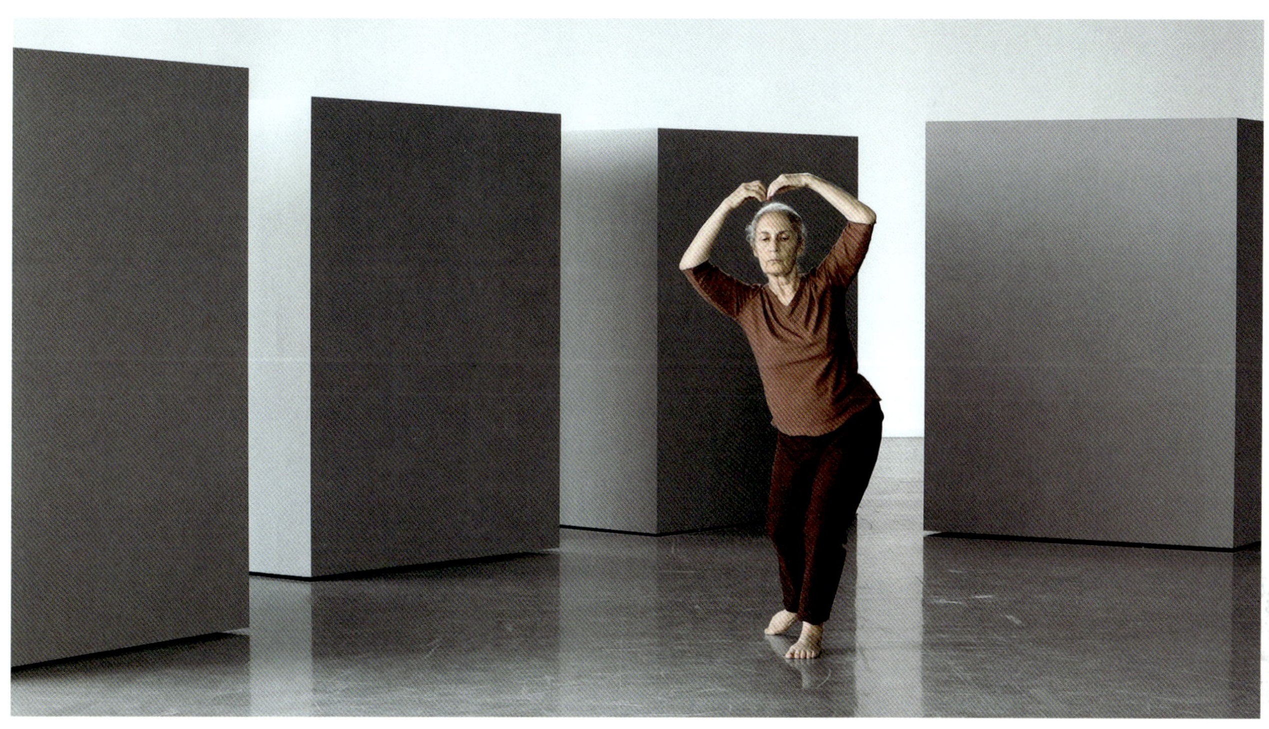

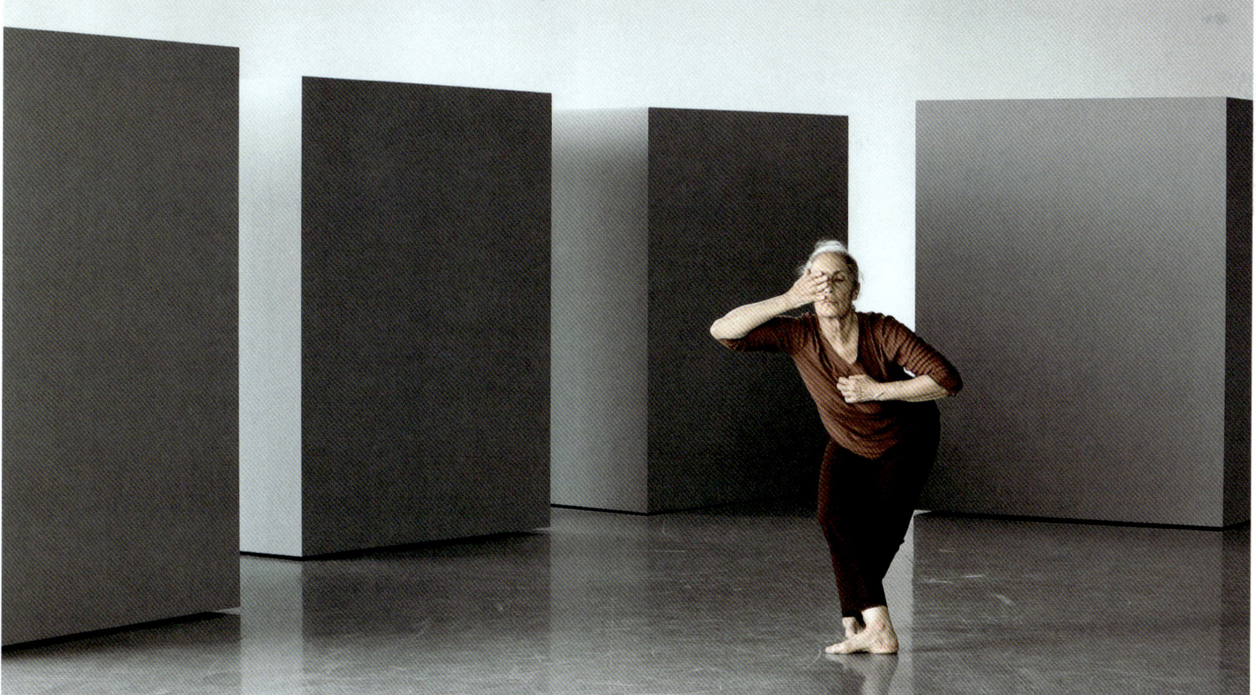

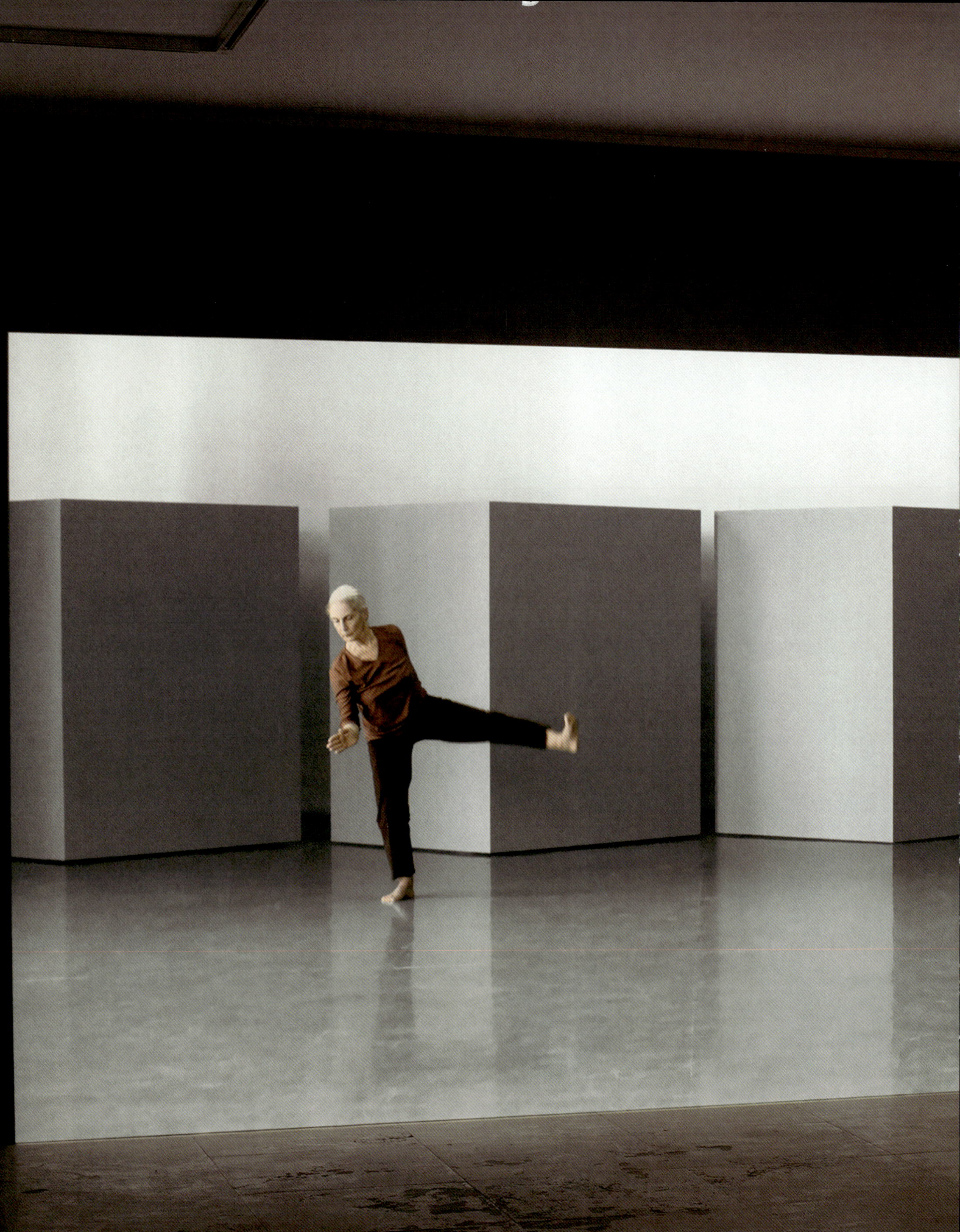

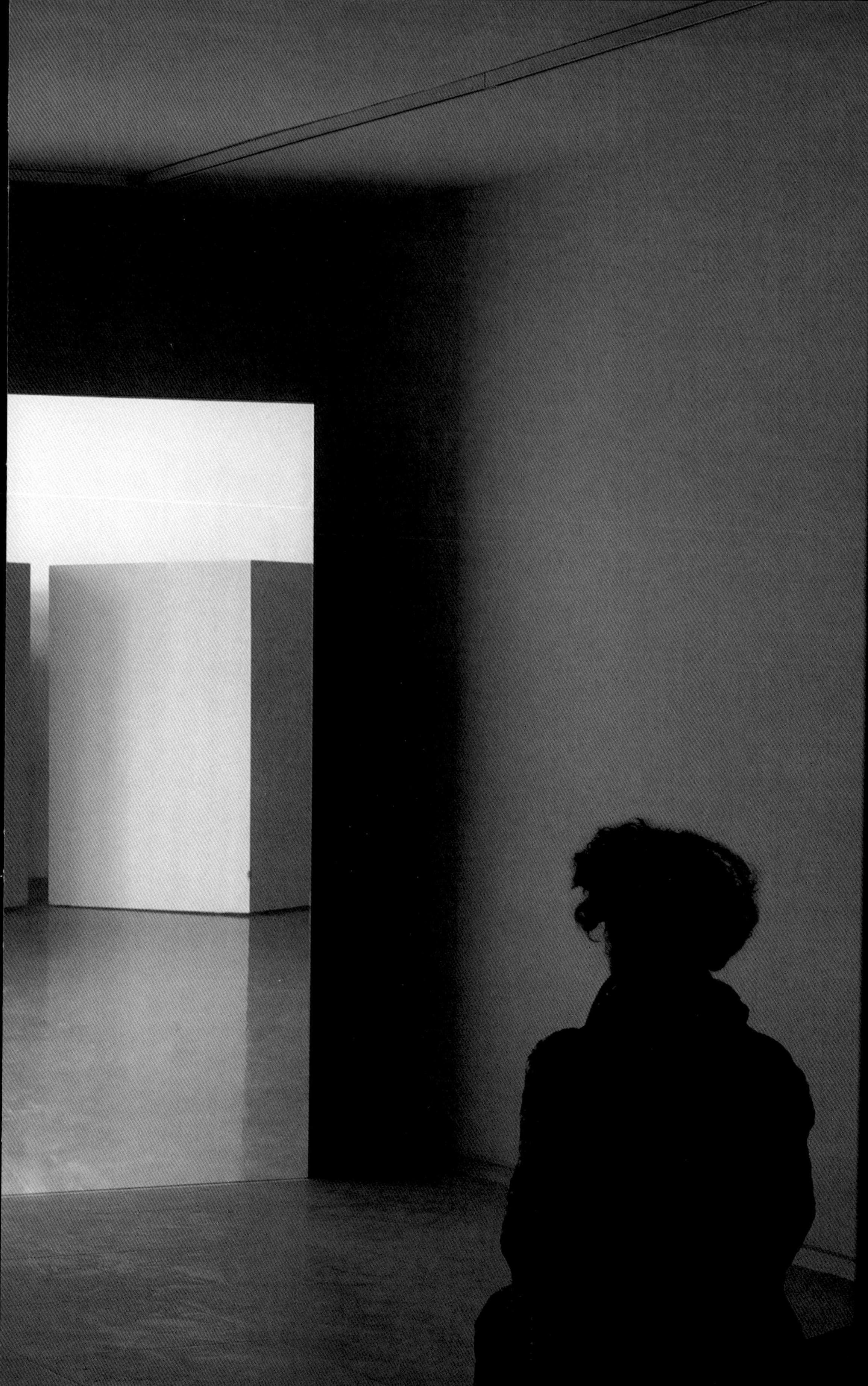

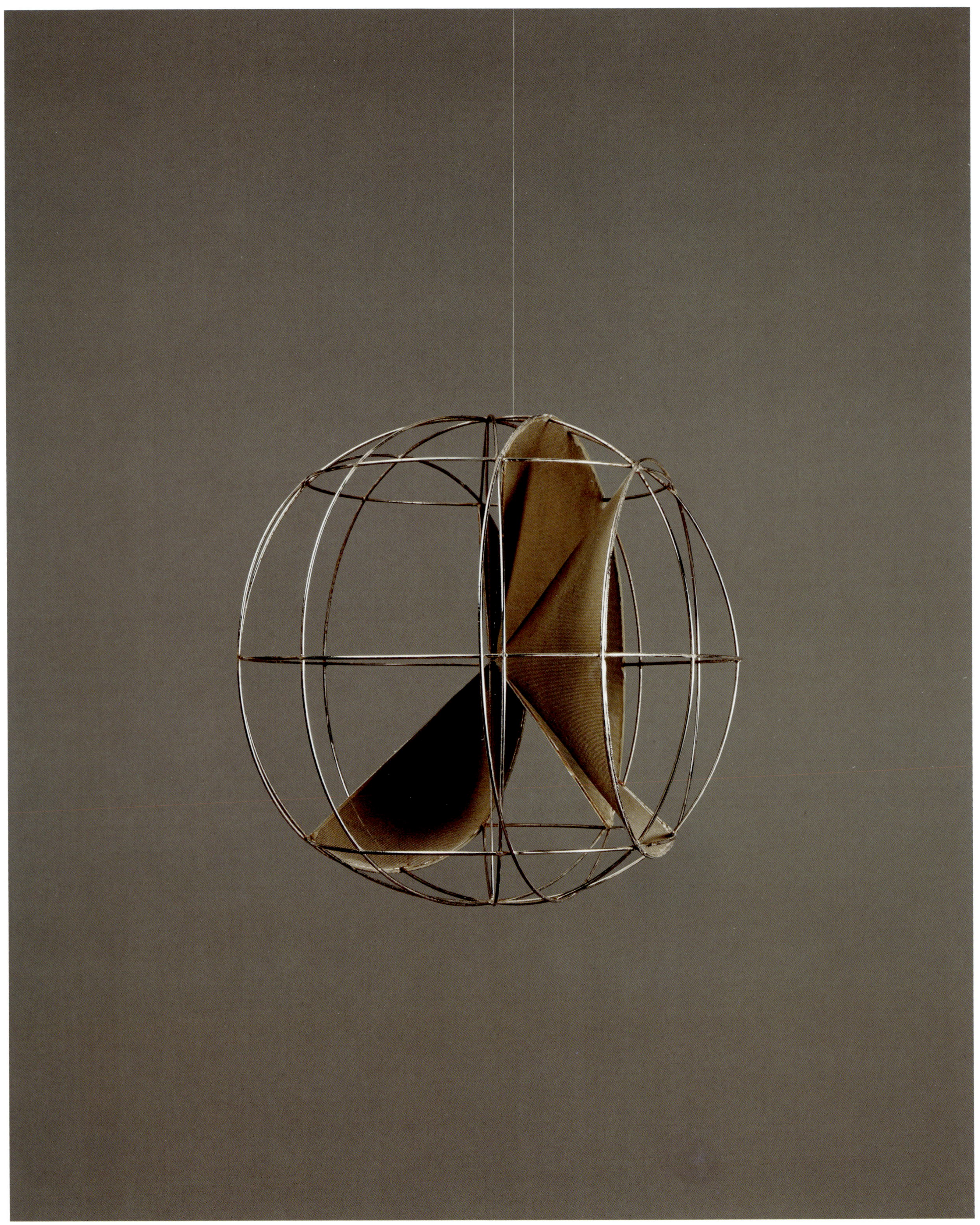

Sharon Lockhart, *Models of Orbits in the System of Reference, Eshkol-Wachman Movement Notation System*, 2011, *Sphere Seven at Three Points in Its Rotation* (detail)

Drawing in Space

Stephanie Barron and Britt Salvesen

Nobel Prize–winning physicist Richard Feynman often stated, "What I cannot build, I cannot understand," and the graphic diagrams he developed in 1948 to represent particle physics are still in use today in quantum-field theory and in other fields as well. Similarly, Noa Eshkol constructed three-dimensional spherical models as aids to teaching her comprehensive and ultimately abstract movement-notation system. Sharon Lockhart, in turn, photographed these spheres, deploying one of her own preferred representational systems as a means of understanding Eshkol's. Lockhart's decision to create still photographs of the spheres—rendering them graphically, rather than dynamically—relates to her previous projects and points toward her understanding of Eshkol's practice. The meanings generated by the various representational systems used by both artists coalesce elegantly in relation to movement itself: from the spheres and the photographs, through the wall carpets and archival materials, we arrive at Eshkol's dances as seen by Lockhart.

Lockhart's photographs, collectively titled *Models of Orbits in the System of Reference, Eshkol-Wachman Movement Notation System* (2011), are in some ways the most enigmatic component of the present exhibition, yet they serve an anchoring function, both conceptually and contextually. At the end of 2009, on her second research trip to Israel in conjunction with the project, Lockhart found in the archive of Eshkol's home-studio in Holon seven spherical models, each about six to twelve inches in diameter, hidden away on shelves among hundreds of textiles, notebooks, and other artifacts. Designed by Eshkol and architect Avraham Wachman and built to their specifications under the supervision of Amos Hetz, who later became a professor of movement notation at the Jerusalem Academy of Music and Dance and Seminar HaKibbutzim College of Education in Tel Aviv, the spheres are accoutrements to an entirely original notation system devised by Eshkol and Wachman in the 1950s: Eshkol-Wachman Movement Notation (EWMN).

Using combinations of numbers and geometrical symbols on a ruled spreadsheet, EWMN is based on the understanding that every limb has a fixed range of motion from the axis of the body. The spheres render the different types of movement—rotary, plane, and conical—in the simplest terms. Seen out of context, these objects might strike the art historian as readymades, holding their own alongside the Constructivist sculpture of Aleksandr Rodchenko, Antoine Pevsner, Naum Gabo, and Barbara Hepworth. As articulated by Gabo and Pevsner in their "Realist Manifesto" (1920), these artists asserted that their work included the fourth dimension of time, through transparent constructions that unfold in space.[1] In addition to the morphological similarity between some of these sculptures and Eshkol's spheres, connections may be found in the utopian aspirations implied by their

1. Gabo also explored actual kinetic sculpture. See Martin Hammer and Christina Lodder, *Constructing Modernity: The Art and Career of Naum Gabo* (New Haven: Yale University Press, 2000); and Teresa Newman, *Naum Gabo: The Constructive Process* (London: Tate Gallery, 1976).
2. In other words, verbal language (which has to be learned) is transcended by spatial calligraphy (which can be perceived by all). The ideal of a universal visual language must have exerted a particular appeal in an era of emigration. Gabo and Pevsner emigrated from Russia to England; Wachman, from Poland to what would become the state of Israel.

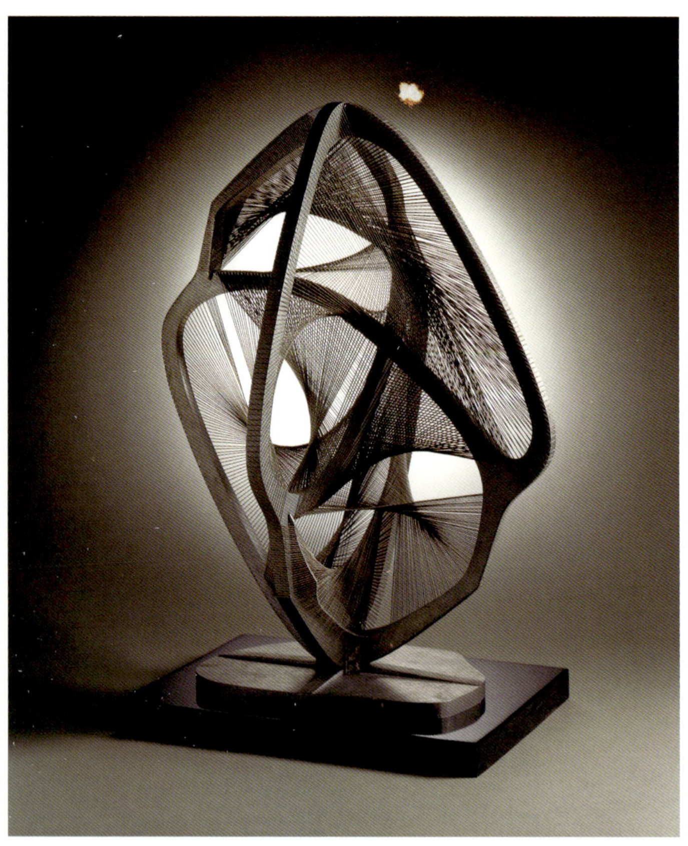

Fig. 1. Naum Gabo, *Linear Construction in Space, No. 4*, 1959, steel, 19 x 13 x 3 inches (48.3 x 33.0 x 7.6 cm), Los Angeles County Museum of Art, Gift of Anna Bing Arnold, M.79.14

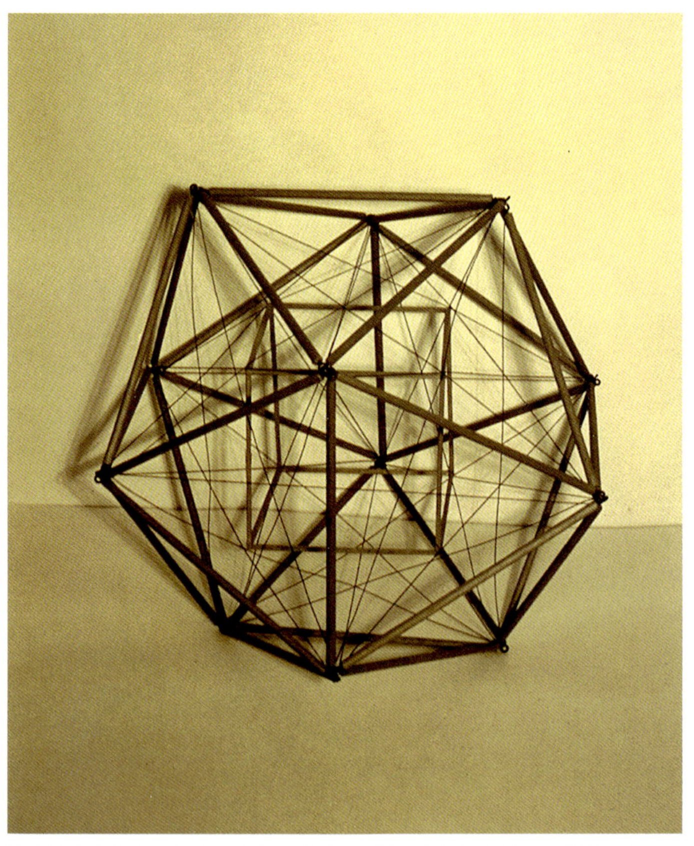

Fig. 2. *Cube in the Icosahedron*, photograph of a model made by Rudolf Laban, 1940s, reference L/F/7/4, from the Rudolf Laban Archive held at the National Resource Centre for Dance, University of Surrey©

universal legibility.[2] Gabo's work *Linear Construction in Space, No. 4* (1959, fig. 1), moreover, exemplifies his practice of producing multiple versions on a sculptural theme, another means of extending the work sequentially.

Suggestive though they may be as objects, for Eshkol and Wachman the spheres were purely functional, tied to pedagogical precedents in their respective disciplines of dance and architecture. Wachman, for his part, would have understood the role of three-dimensional models in design programs such as the Bauhaus as a means to develop the students' spatial imagination.[3] Eshkol went to England after World War II to learn the Labanotation system devised in 1928 by Rudolf Laban, the Hungarian-born dancer who initially trained as a sculptor and later incorporated spherical and geometric structures into his teaching to indicate the analogy he perceived between movement and crystallization (fig. 2).[4] While Labanotation views the body as a set of joints connected by limbs, EWMN views it as a set of limbs connected at joints. In EWMN each limb is associated with a particular longitudinal axis. EWMN is more corporeally precise than Labanotation: the intersection of axes used to orient each longitudinal axis is uniquely fixed at that end of the axis that is closer to the center of the body.[5] Hence the utility of the three-dimensional spheres, which represent the paths traced by moving limbs as membranes.[6] Both dance composer and architect wished to eliminate the expressive flourishes and potential ambiguities found in traditional hand-drawn notation methods, and the abstract rationality of the spheres supported this endeavor.[7]

When Lockhart discovered the seven spheres in Eshkol's archive, they had been unused for decades. She cleaned away the dust and rust and took them to a studio, where

3. See Oskar Schlemmer, *The Theatre of the Bauhaus* (Middletown, Conn.: Wesleyan University Press, 1961); Claire Rousier, *Oskar Schlemmer: L'homme et la figure d'art* (Pantin, France: Centre national de la danse, 2001); and Melissa Trimingham, *The Theatre of the Bauhaus: The Modern and the Postmodern Stage of Oskar Schlemmer* (New York: Routledge, 2011).

4. Christine Macel, "Rudolf von Laban," in *Danser sa vie: Art et danse de 1900 à nos jours* (Paris: Centre Pompidou, 2011), 148. Examples of Laban's cubes, dodecahedrons, etc., can be viewed on the Digital Dance Archives website, http://www.dance-archives.ac.uk/collection (search "Rudolf Laban").

5. Norman I. Badler and Stephen W. Smoliar, "Digital Representations of Human Movement," *Computing Surveys* 11, no. 1 (March 1979): 19–38. Another unique aspect of EWMN is that it can be used to compose as well as record dance.

6. See Michal Shoshani, "Foundations and Unique Aspects of Eshkol-Wachman Movement Notation," in this book.

7. According to John Harries, who worked with Eshkol to illustrate many texts on EWMN, the system "does not rely on arbitrary aesthetic assumptions." He hoped to take a similar approach to the description of visual art objects; see Harries, "A Proposed Notation for Visual Fine Art," *Leonardo* 8, no. 4 (Autumn 1975): 296.

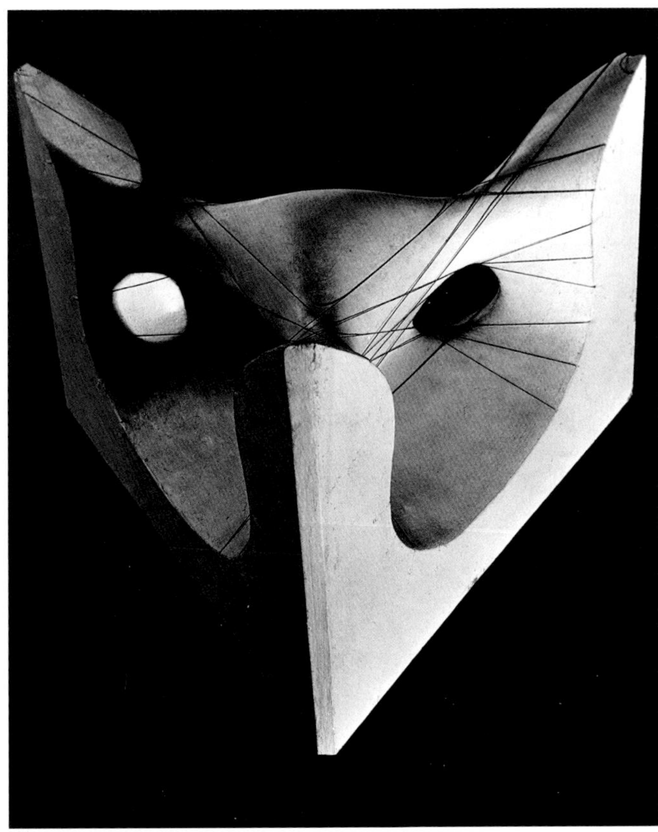

Fig. 3. Man Ray, *Mathematical Object: Ruled Surface*, 1934, gelatin-silver print

she suspended them from the ceiling with monofilament before a neutral gray backdrop, allowing them to rotate naturally in order to observe the progression of changing planes and lines. Having determined the different perspectives, she halted the rotation at each of these salient points and, using strobe illumination, made exposures with a 4x5-inch camera. Precedents for Lockhart's photographic isolation of the models exist, including Man Ray's *Mathematical Objects* series of the mid-1930s, depictions of algebraic models he found in the Institut Henri Poincaré, Paris (fig. 3).[8] Where Man Ray courted enigma by transforming object into fetish, however, Lockhart seeks clarity by connecting object to practice. Her counterintuitive, strategic decision to make still photographs of objects designed to move must be seen in the context of her previous work and in relation to the other components of the Eshkol project.

The logic emerges in Lockhart's presentation of the photographs in groups of two, three, four, and five to recapitulate the progression of movements illustrated by each sphere. Seemingly quite similar, the photographs must be studied intensely to discern the differences among them, even before beginning to ponder what the objects might be or mean. This kind of attentiveness is crucial throughout Lockhart's body of work, much of which records movement—particularly repetitions and the resulting entropic changes—over time and space. Examples include the rhythmic practice drills performed by a girls' basketball team in the film *Goshogaoka* (1997) or the more naturalistic bending and reach of the clam digger in the more recent film *Double Tide* (2009). These films trigger a contemplative process in which the viewer attempts to hold a moment in mind while anticipating and absorbing its successor.

8. A more recent entry into the genre has been made by Hiroshi Sugimoto, with his *Conceptual Forms* of 2004. These photographs portray similar mathematical models, imported from the West to Japan during the late nineteenth century. The cross-cultural and cross-temporal parallels are interesting.

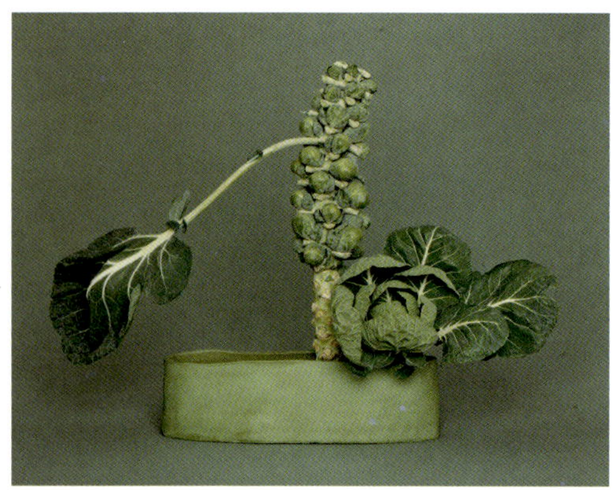
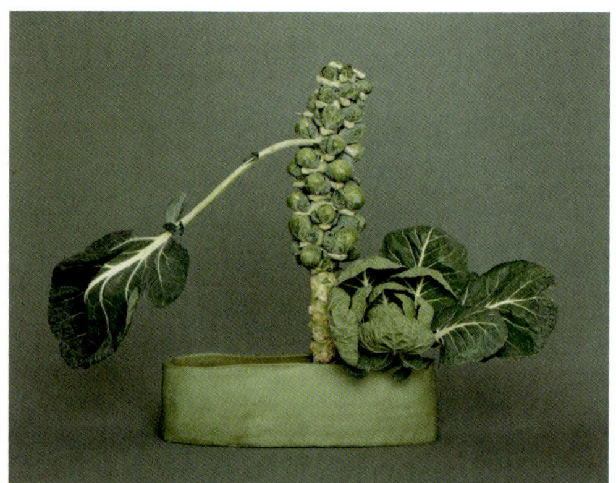
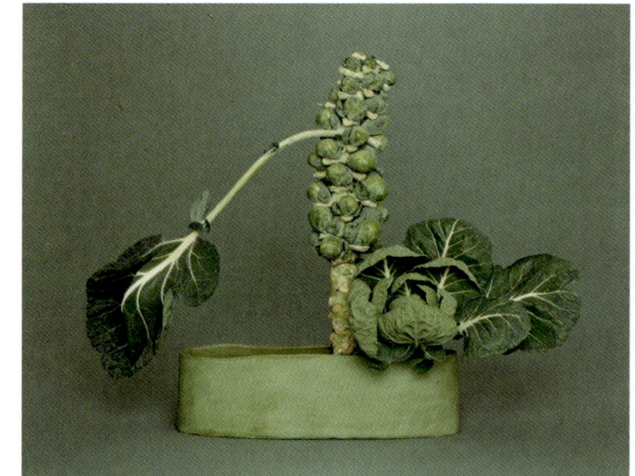

Fig. 4. Sharon Lockhart, *NŌ-no Ikebana, arranged by Haruko Takeichi, December 1, 2002 (December 2–3)*, 2003, three chromogenic prints, 22½ x 28 inches (57.2 x 71.1 cm) each

With even greater deliberation, Lockhart layered photographic and filmic time in the series of still images, *NŌ-no Ikebana* (2003), which depicts the gradual changes effected by time on an arrangement of Brussels sprouts. Lockhart's collaborator in this instance was Haruko Takeichi, a practitioner of a particular avant-garde form of ikebana that employs agricultural products rather than more traditional flowers and branches. "In a way," Lockhart remarks of Takeichi's process, "her breaking one plant into pieces mirrors the breaking up and rearrangement of time I do with the photographs."[9] Responding to the organic nature of her subject, Lockhart allowed these photographs to register subtle changes in the plants' color and morphology over the course of a month, ultimately dividing nineteen photographs into four groupings of between three and seven prints (fig. 4). These configurations presage the *Models of Orbits* groupings, in which the rotation of the spheres implies change over time, now in a controlled manner reflective of Eshkol's practice.[10]

Lockhart's work can be thought of as still and moving at the same time. Or, to put it another way, when she deploys both photography and film in large-scale projects, her ability to find dynamism in still imagery and stasis in moving imagery comes to the fore. This is not merely a matter of style or staging, although her work does have a recognizable visual signature. Instead, the calibration of photographs with films is based on the project's overall content. For *Lunch Break* (2008), for example, she made eighteen still photographs of the lunch boxes carried by employees of Bath Iron Works, the Maine shipyard where she developed the project, establishing a range of standardized compositions and then presenting the prints singly, in diptychs, or in triptychs. Seen in connection with two film installations (one eighty minutes long, the other forty-one) and two additional photographic series, the photographs of lunch boxes, which she conceived both as still lifes and as portraits, represent what Lockhart terms the "rituals, personal choices, skills, and interests" of the workers in their own idiom, free of cliché.[11] The coolness of the photographs contrasts with the warm connection between artist and workers.

In the present project, the affinity between photography and film, and between Lockhart and Eshkol, lies in the aesthetic realm, with personalities and social settings basically removed. The minimalism of Eshkol's practice—bare stage, highly structured movements, and metronome "score"—feels particularly at home with Lockhart's precise, often austere approach. *Models of Orbits* may be considered in light of Lockhart's association with structuralist filmmaking and Eshkol's affiliation with modernist dance. In structuralism, systems establish a work's shape, and this shape in turn gives rise to

9. This quotation is from a manuscript version of an interview between Lockhart and Scott MacDonald. The interview was published in Scott MacDonald, *A Critical Cinema 5: Interviews with Independent Filmmakers* (Berkeley: University of California Press, 2006), 311–32, but the passage from which the quotation was taken was ultimately not included. In this interview and elsewhere, Lockhart also discusses the related film, *NŌ*.
10. Reflecting on *NŌ-no Ikebana* now, Lockhart recognizes a parallel between the radicality of Toshie Yokoi (who pioneered *NŌ-no ikebana*) and of Noa Eshkol (who similarly stripped away idealized notions of beauty from her dances). Sharon Lockhart to the authors, email, January 24, 2012. Breaking with how ikebana was traditionally taught, Yokoi brought her innovations to rural communities, with the result that today some three hundred female agricultural workers practice the art.
11. Sharon Lockhart, in "James Benning Interviews Sharon Lockhart," in *Sharon Lockhart, Lunch Break* (St. Louis: Mildred Lane Kemper Art Museum, Washington University in St. Louis, 2010), 107.

content; in modernism, the ideal work of art is whole unto itself, independent of narrative and context. As Eshkol wrote, "In order to reach the mature stature of an art such as music, the composition of dance will have to enter a phase in which the material itself is explored. The focus of this exploration should be upon the search for structures rather than the 'expression of the emotion' so often demanded of and claimed for artistic composition."[12]

Not only has Lockhart depicted the spheres in a highly systematic manner, they are themselves already structuralist in their formalization of gestural content. Even viewers not versed in EWMN can identify these objects as symbolic signs in a semiotic system; by analogy with more familiar pictorial and alphanumeric lexicons, we infer that these apparently abstract signifiers point to things (in this case, movements) in the physical world. But instead of establishing a congruent relationship between signifier and signified, Lockhart examines the space between them. In this way she acknowledges the allure of two aesthetic doctrines—canonical modernism and structuralism—while also signaling the void that can remain when the work of art claims autonomy. The space between the spheres, a potent part of the composition, may gain its place in the composition from Lockhart's sensitivity to the Japanese concept of *ma*, the sense of space between forms—and, significantly, of intervals between instants. The space is not so much articulated, but rather felt by the viewer experientially.

Lockhart has steadily augmented these formalist legacies to evolve a practice with profound humanist implications. No matter how refined the installations and their components, she finds her subject matter within communities, and each element in a realized project must represent an aspect of the collective as distilled through the artist's sensibility. The spheres, like the lunch boxes, are objects just as much as they are symbols: handcrafted and designed to serve a utilitarian purpose. Lockhart, with her long immersion in contexts of labor, instantly recognized them as tools. Today such a device would be digitally produced and deployed, but the virtual object could never retain the marks of use the way these material artifacts do. When Eshkol brought the spheres into the classroom and, later, included them in displays accompanying the Chamber Dance Group's performances in Israel and abroad, she and her colleagues would posit the congruence between the ribs and planes of the spheres and the limbs of the body. Being three-dimensional and mobile, the spheres could indicate the body itself moving in and through space. At one level, therefore, the spheres gave the dancer a way of picturing, or conjuring mental images of, every possible movement he or she could perform.

As Lockhart learned through her research, EWMN has been used not only in dance instruction but also to record and analyze many kinds of movement (for example, sign language, athletic activity, and patterns indicative of autism). While the dancer may be able to imagine potential movements in discrete units, the observer witnesses actual movements in a flowing sequence. Lockhart suggests both perceptual processes with her photographs of the spheres. She isolates the instant in two-dimensional, sharply focused prints, and then reintroduces time and space by creating groupings of three, four, and five views of each sphere. She is not illustrating the notation system: these groupings do not correlate to Eshkol's dances, nor to any performed movement sequence. Rather, she is pointing out that while the spheres can precede or record movement, they do not suffice to replace it. Bodies themselves, as seen in the film in Lockhart's film installation *Five Dances and Nine Wall Carpets by Noa Eshkol* (2011), are required for full realization. The spheres, therefore, are a fulcrum or pivot point in the dynamic flow of thought and action: necessary symbolic abstractions that facilitate the channeling of intuition, the choreography of gesture, and the experience of community across time and space.

12. Noa Eshkol, cited in the introduction to *Theme & Variations: Dance Suite, Book 1* (Holon, Israel: Movement Notation Society for the Noa Eshkol Foundation for Movement Notation, 2010), 6.

Sharon Lockhart, *Models of Orbits in the System of Reference, Eshkol-Wachman Movement Notation System*, 2011
Sphere One at Two Points in Its Rotation

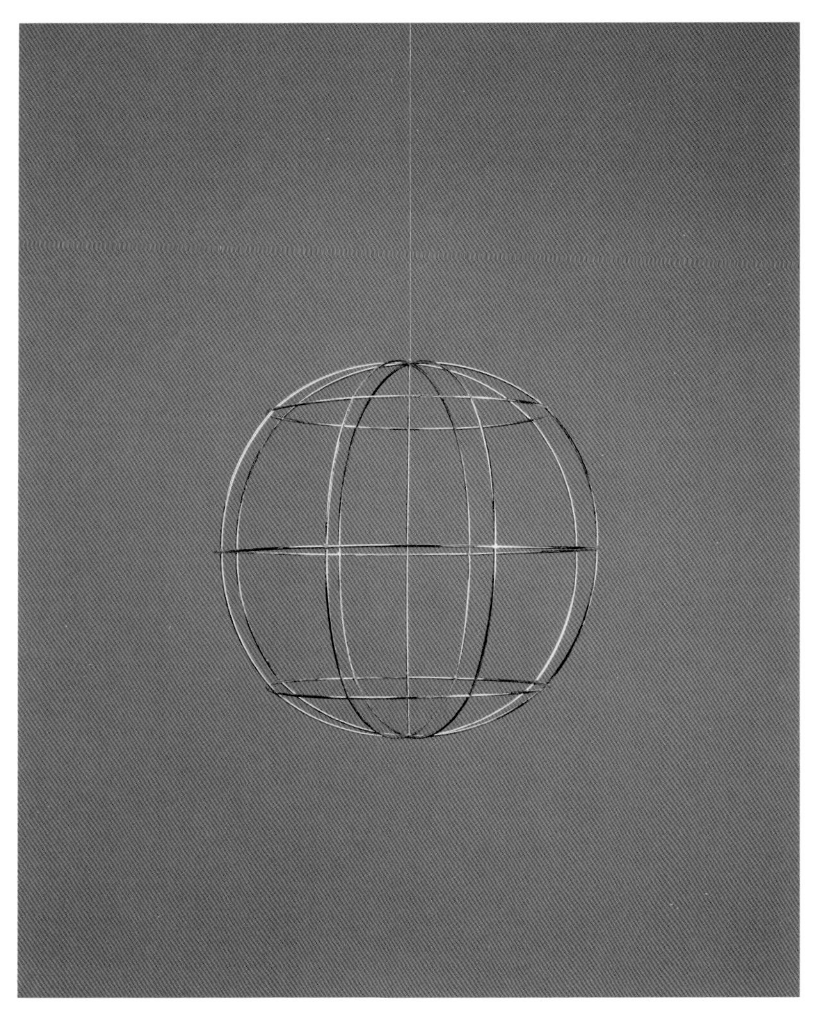

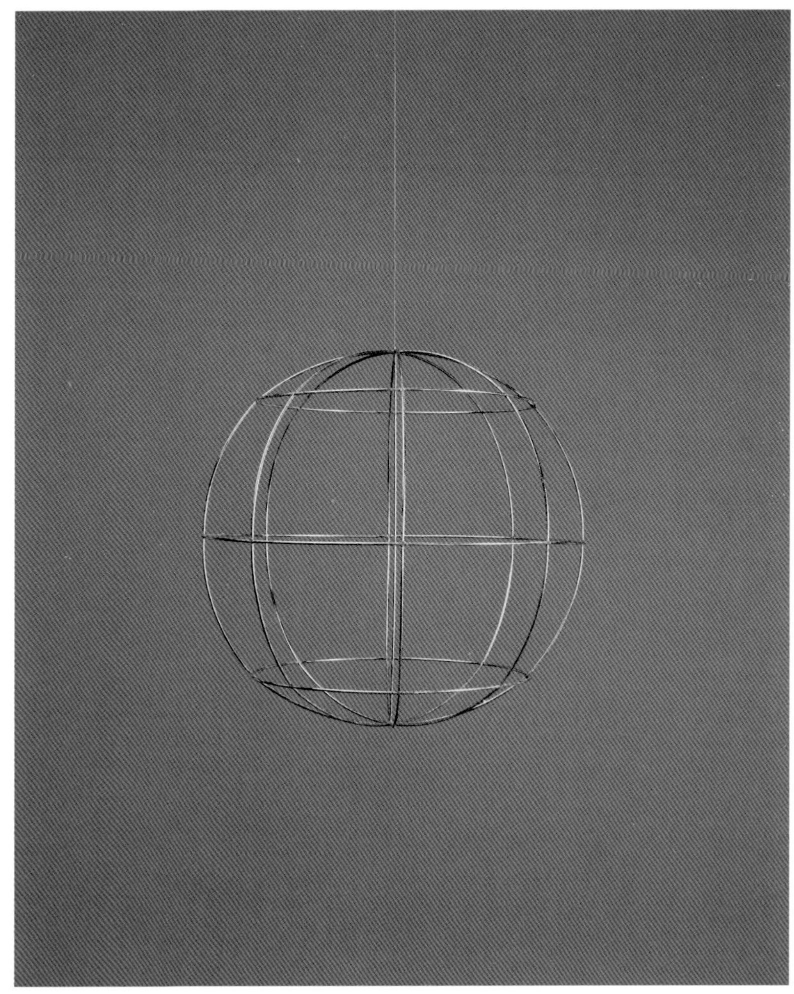

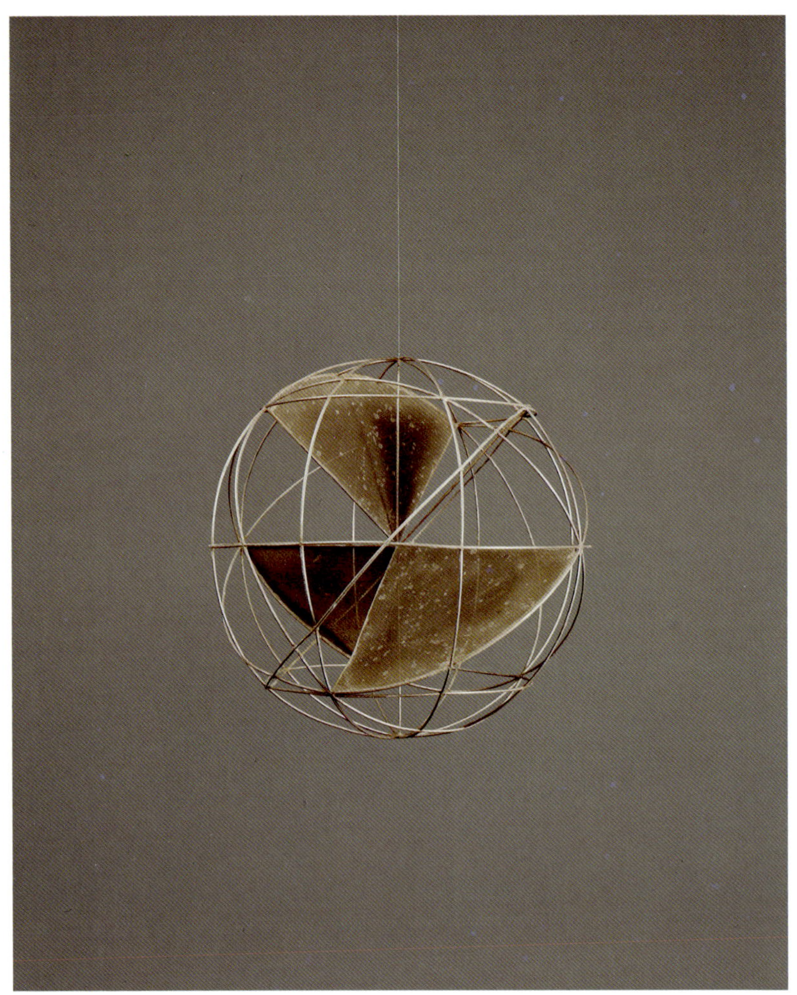

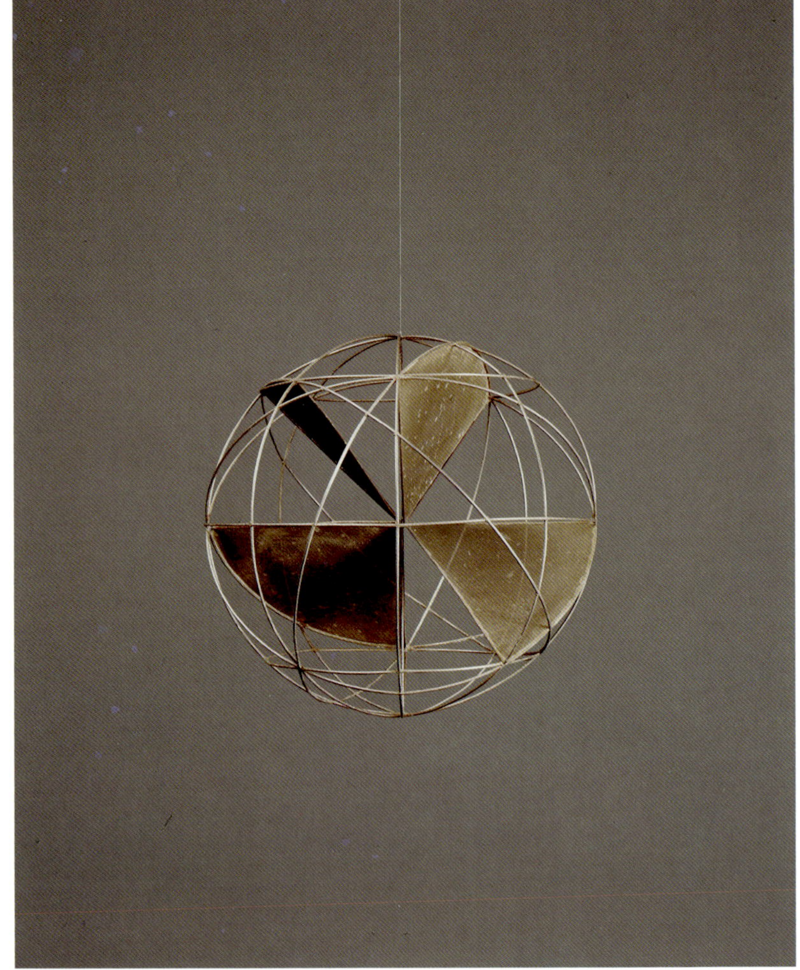

Sphere Two at Four Points in Its Rotation

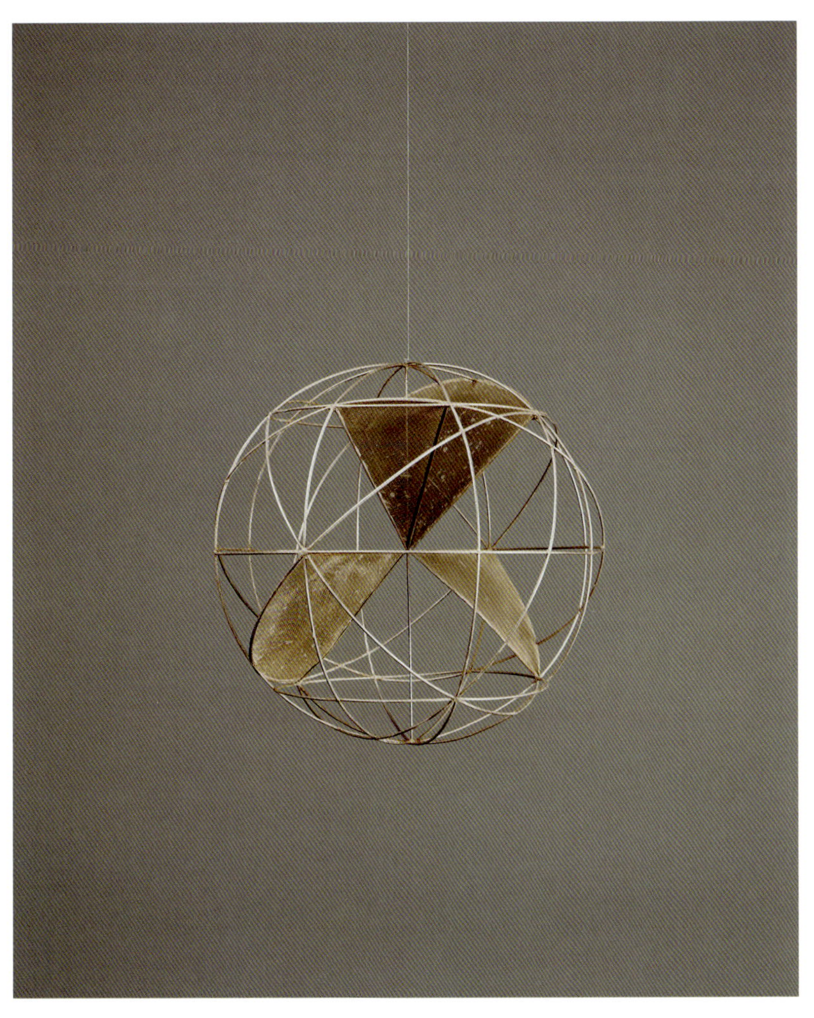

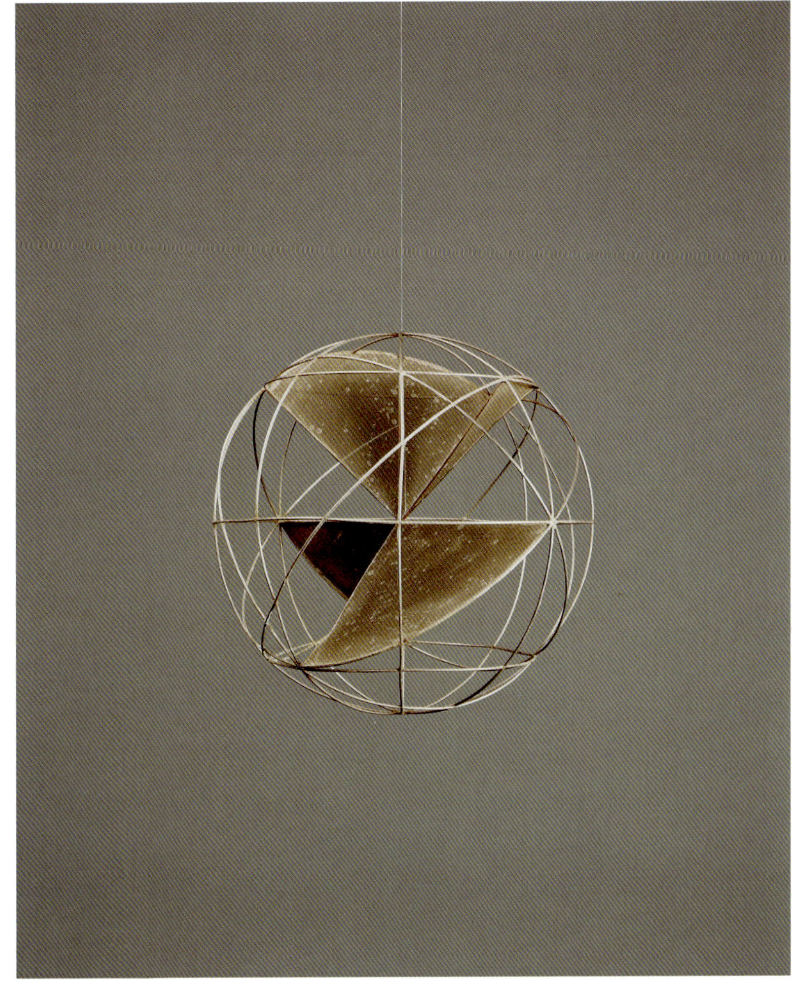

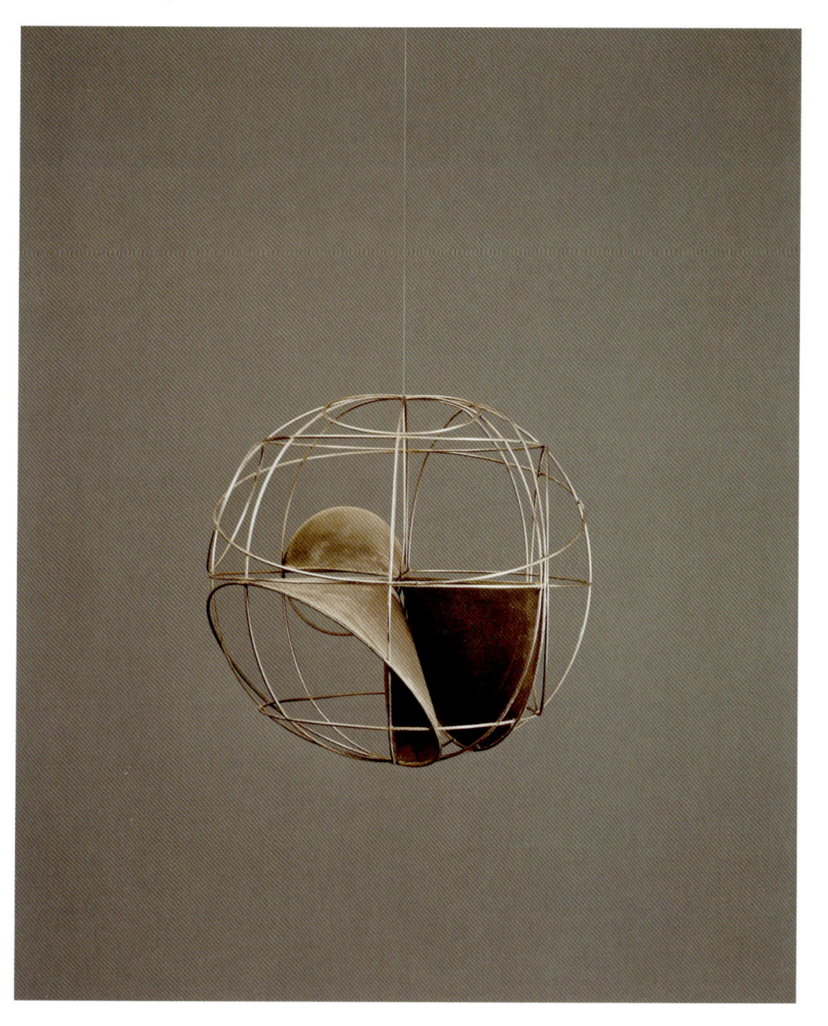

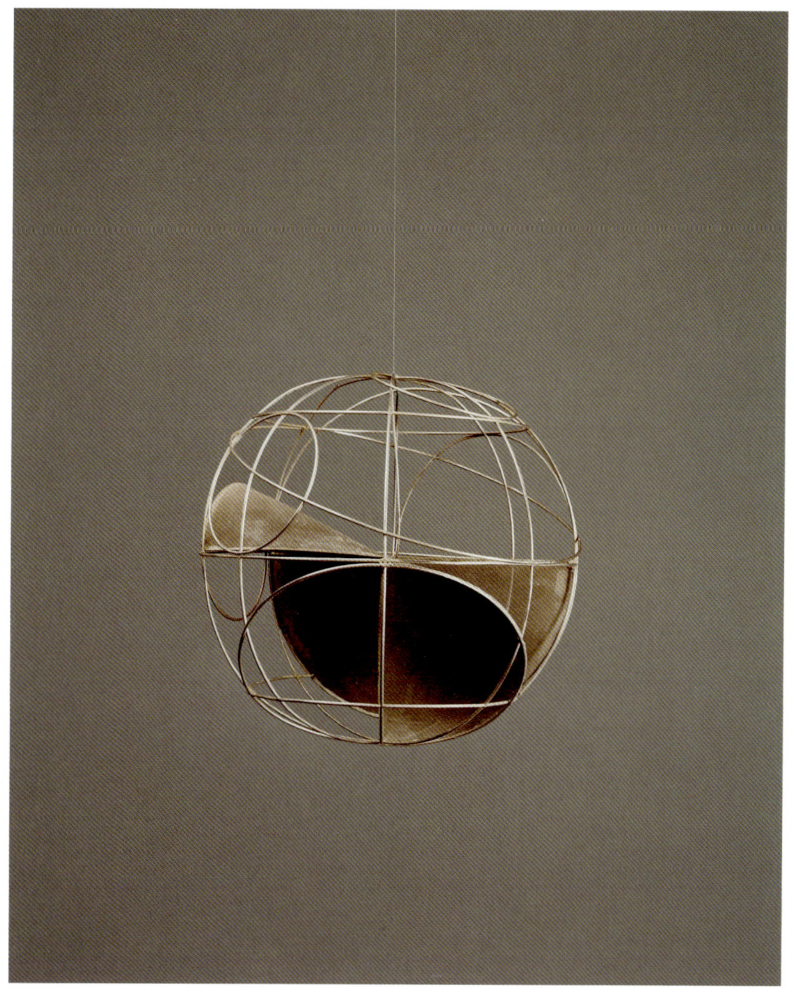

Sphere Four at Two Points in Its Rotation

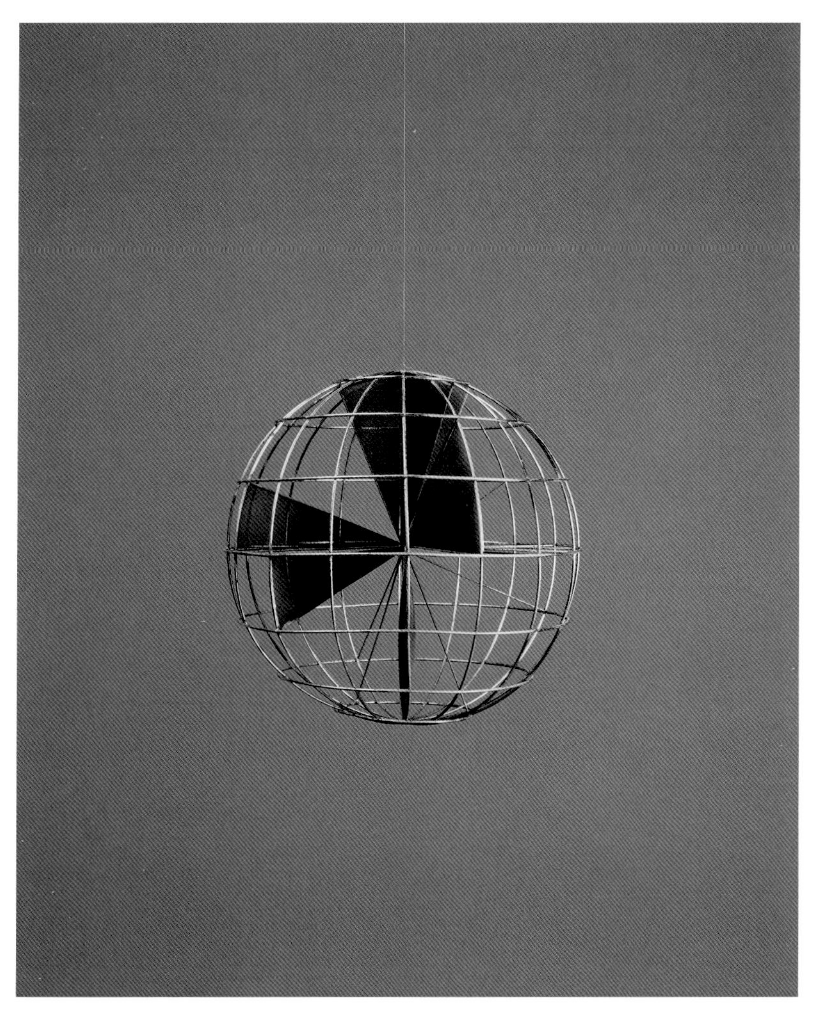

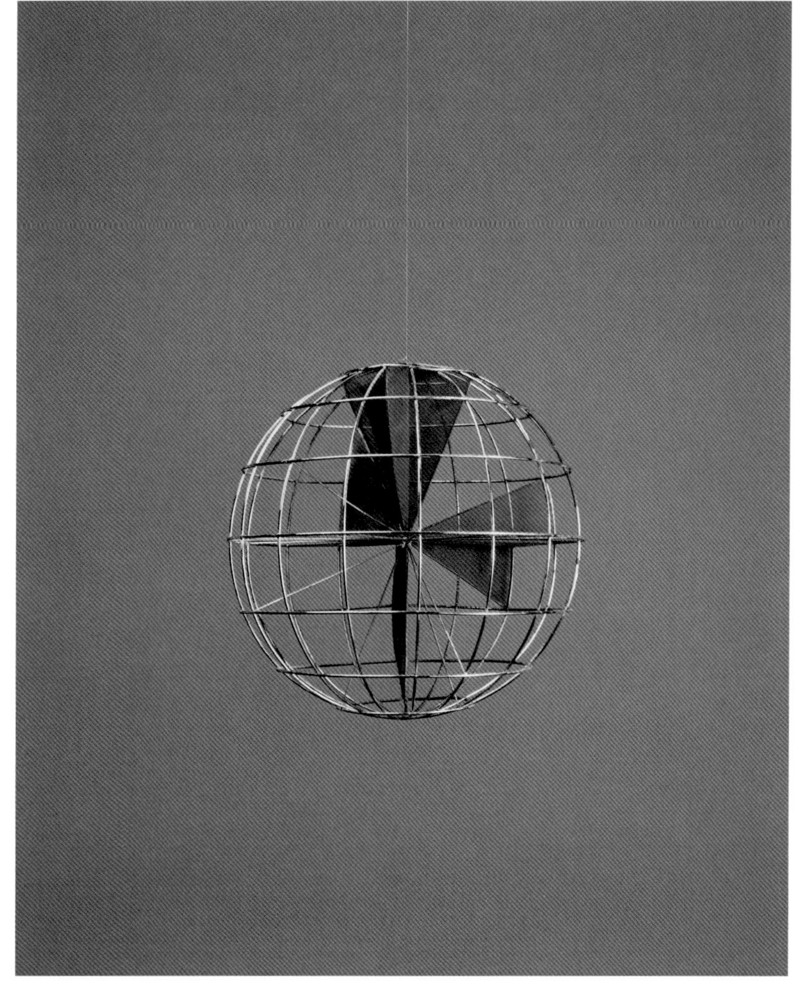

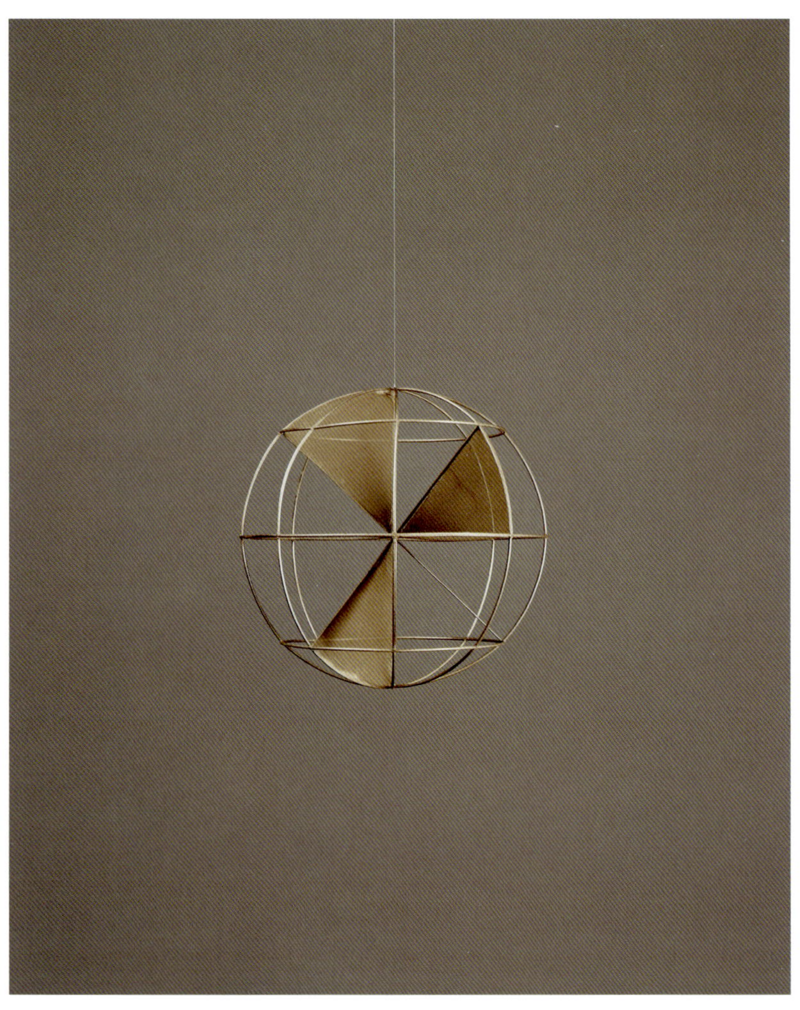

Sphere Five at Three Points in Its Rotation

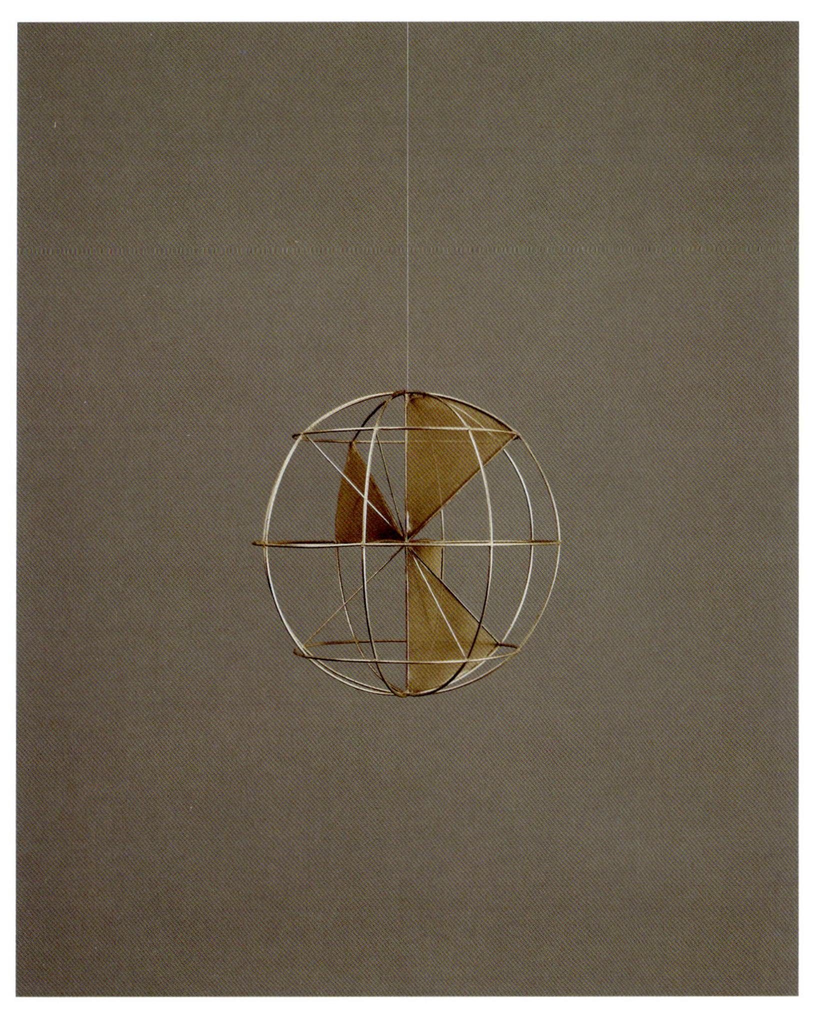

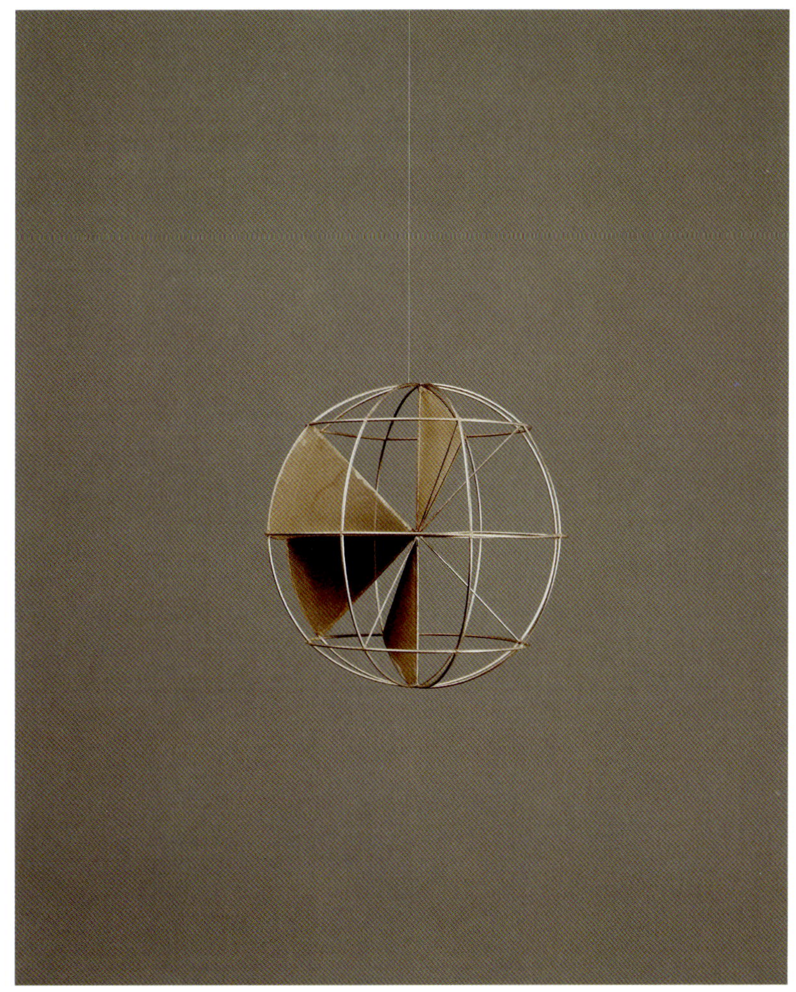

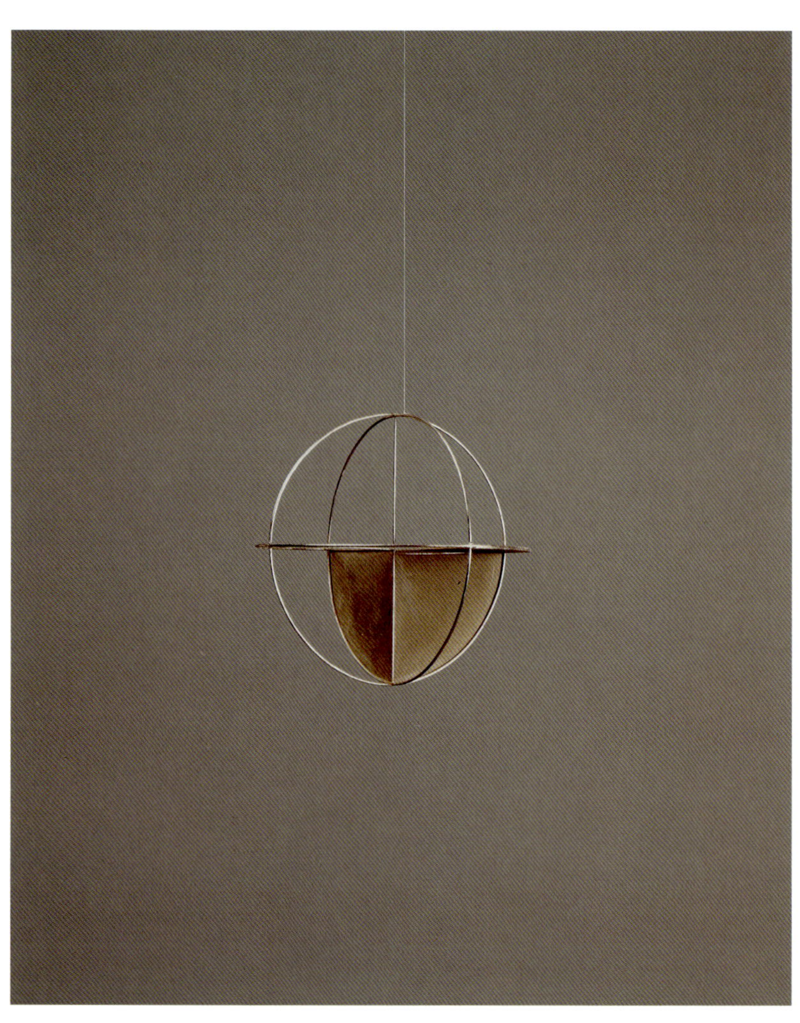

Sphere Six at Three Points in Its Rotation

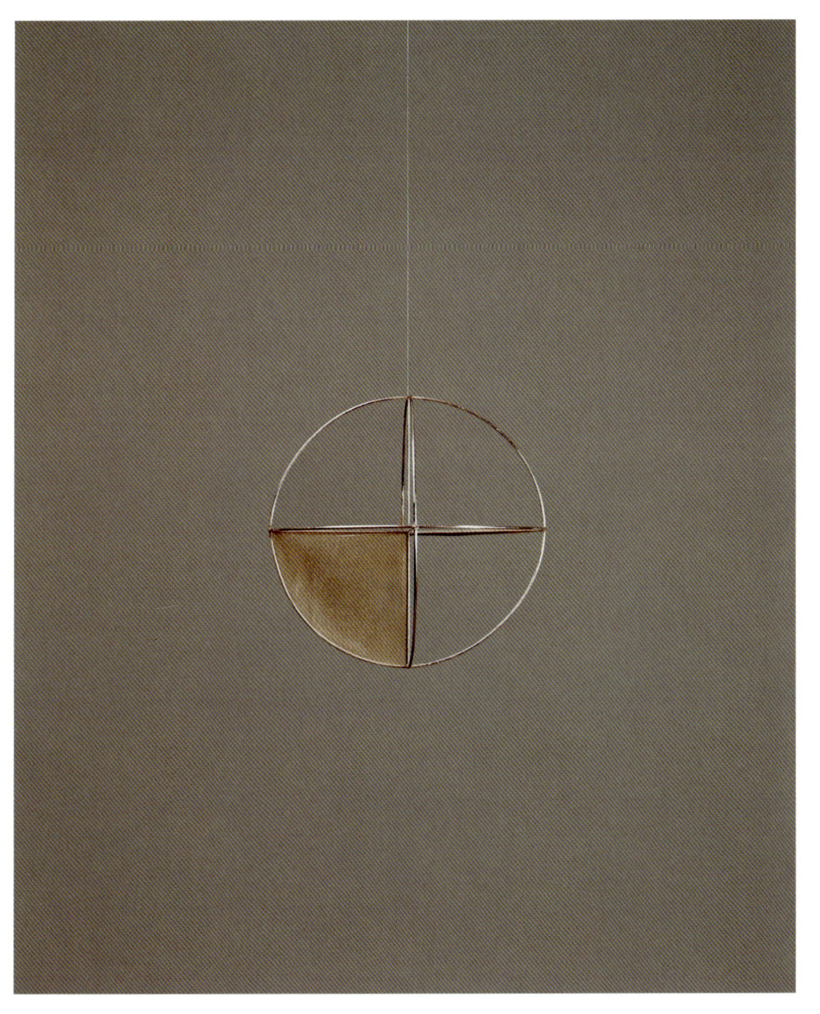

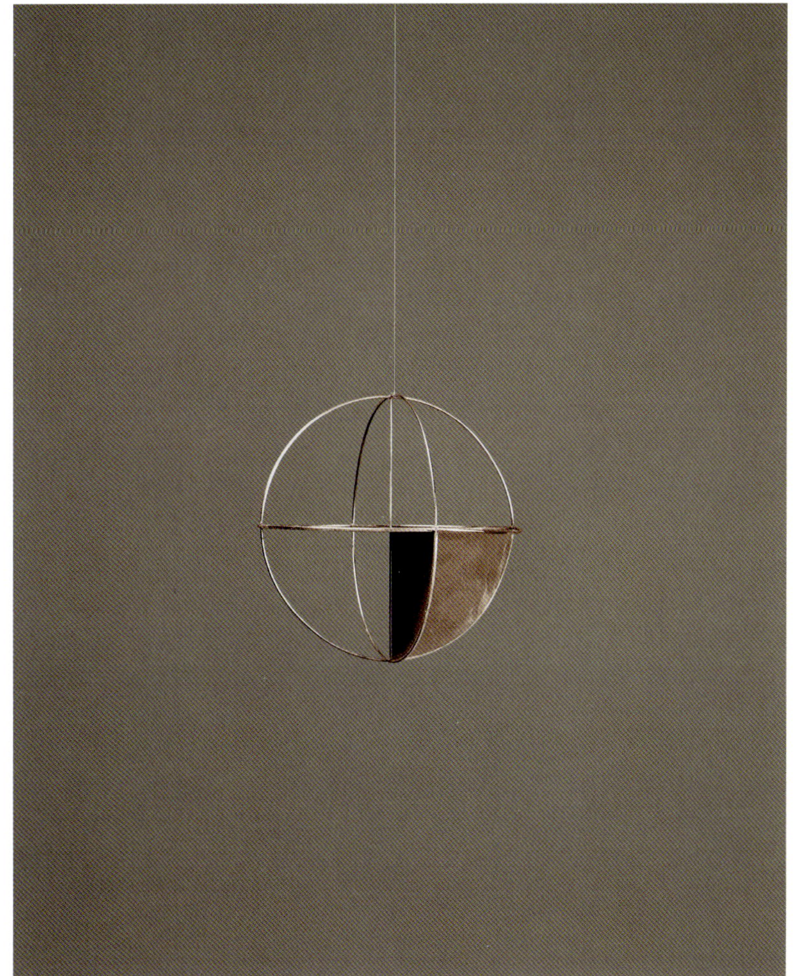

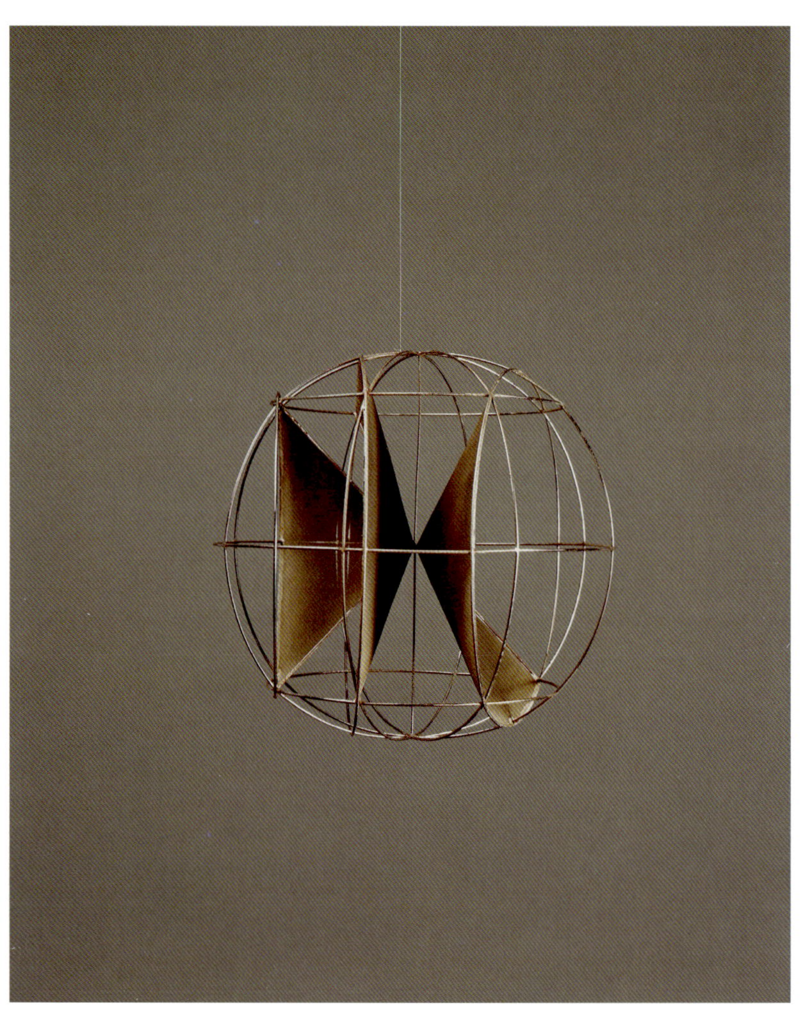

Sphere Seven at Three Points in Its Rotation

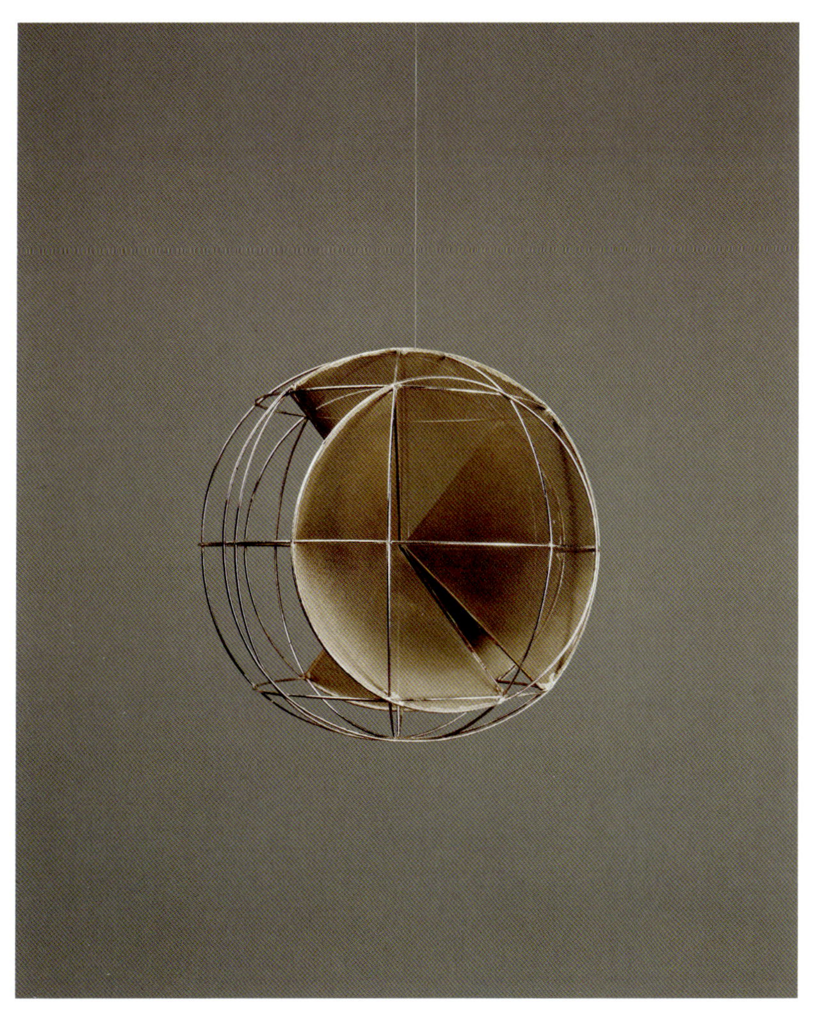

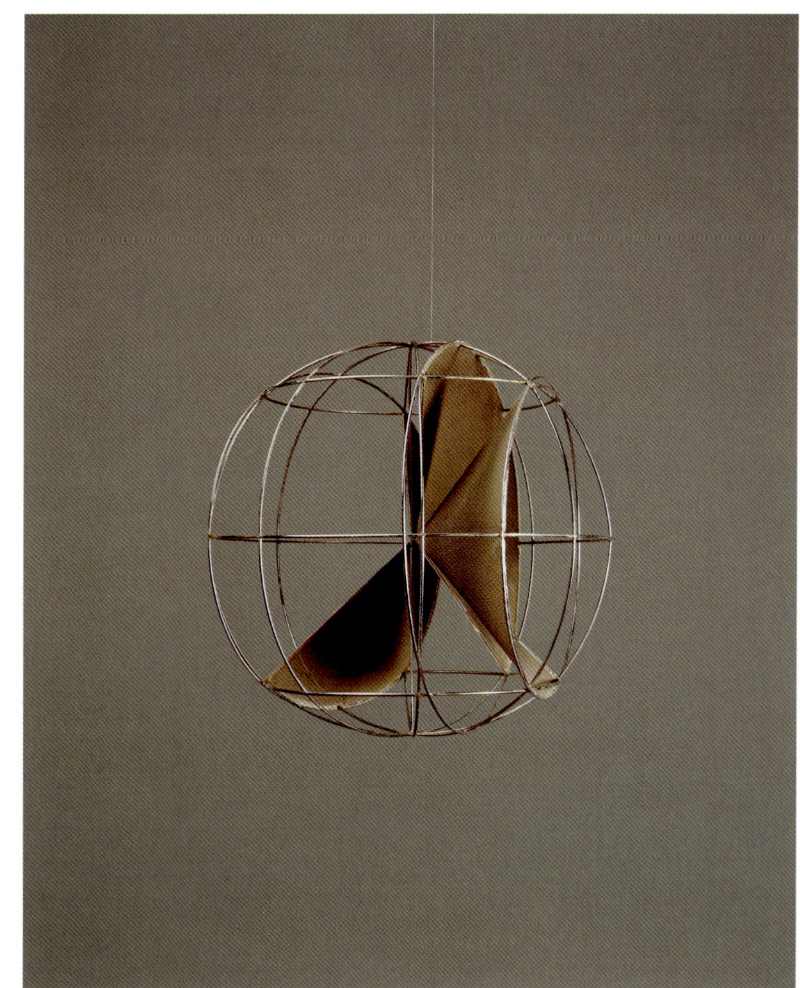

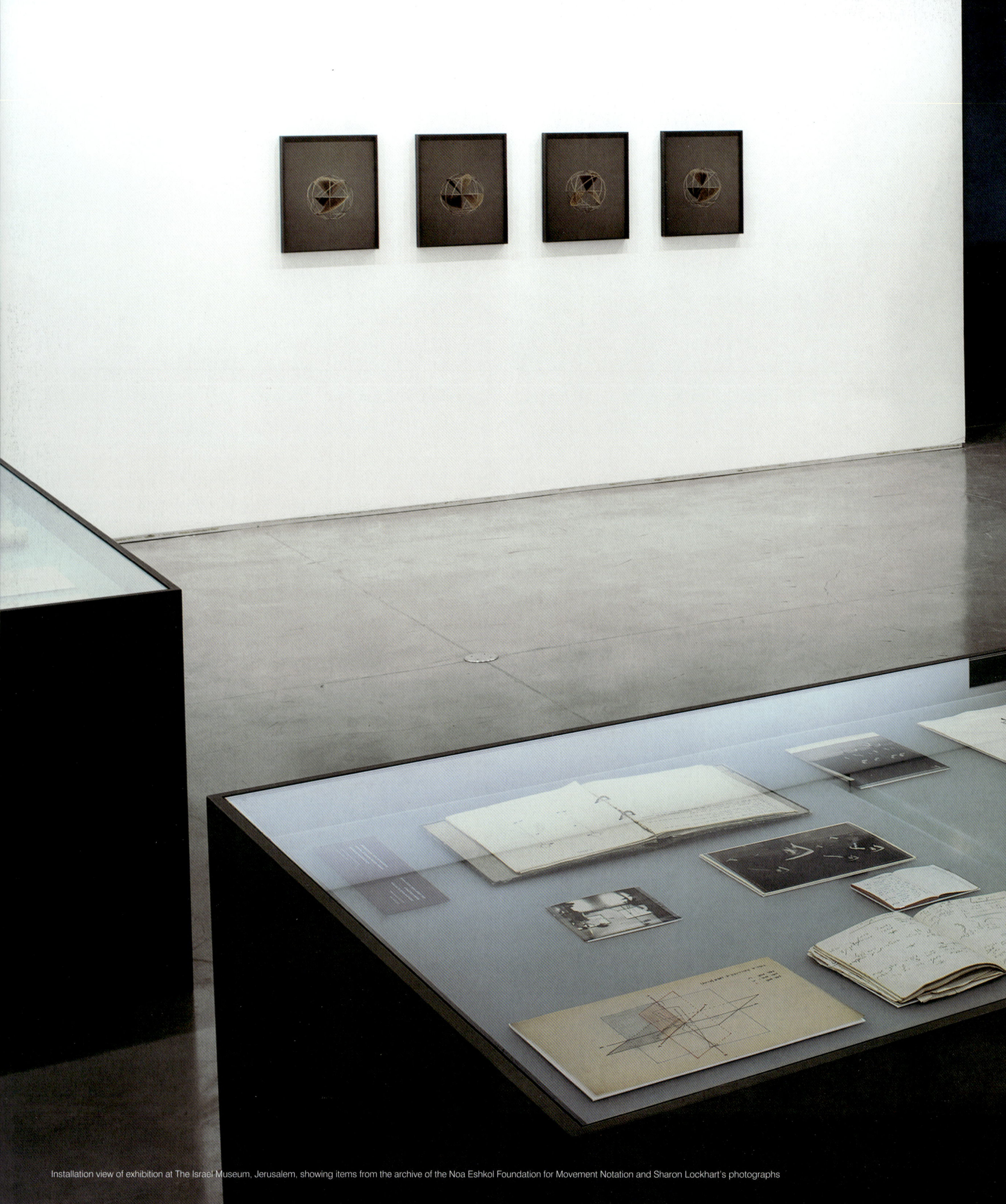

Installation view of exhibition at The Israel Museum, Jerusalem, showing items from the archive of the Noa Eshkol Foundation for Movement Notation and Sharon Lockhart's photographs

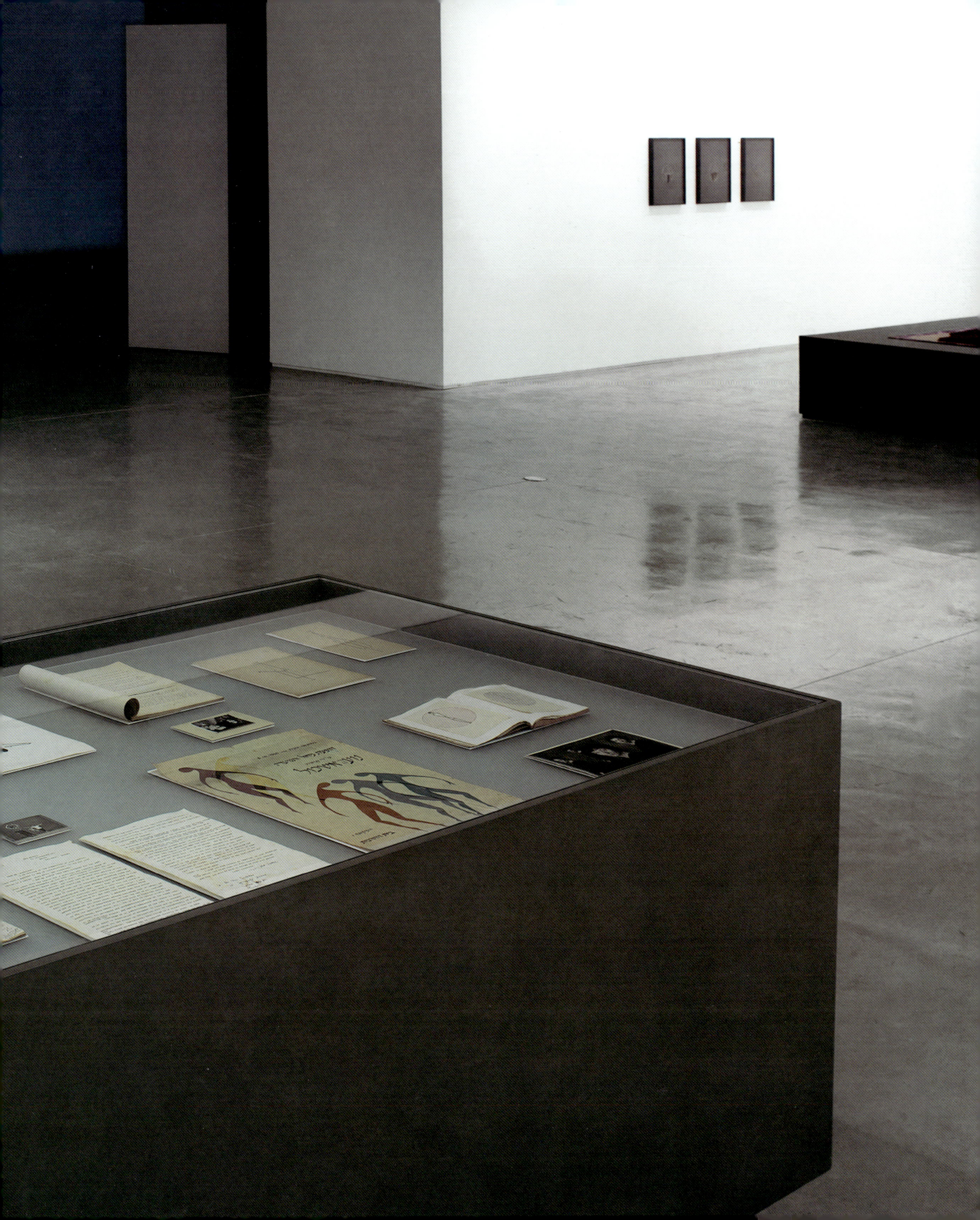

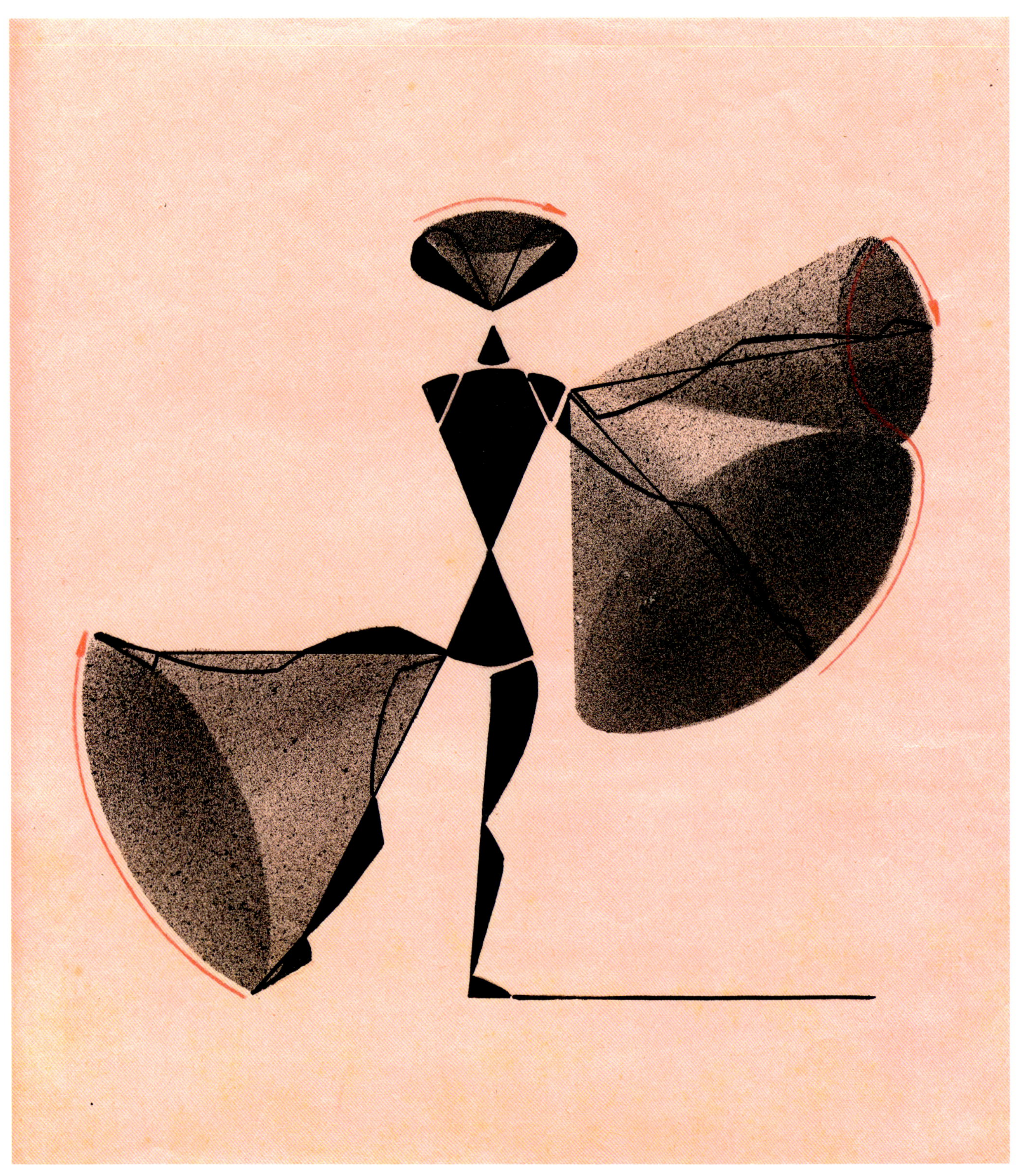

John Harries, *Conical Movement*, 1956–57; this drawing was adapted as an illustration for Noa Eshkol and Abraham [Avraham] Wachman, *Movement Notation* (London: Weidenfeld and Nicholson, 1958), fig. 8 ("Curved Movement")

Foundations and Unique Aspects of Eshkol-Wachman Movement Notation

Michal Shoshani

When a certain event raises our interest to the point where it becomes desirable to remember it, describe it, and above all to think and calculate or to compose within it . . . then a fitting substitute is required for the actual event: this substitute is a symbol. —Noa Eshkol[1]

Eshkol-Wachman Movement Notation (EWMN) is an objective method for analyzing human movement and representing it by means of symbols. This method was designed by Noa Eshkol and Avraham Wachman, the latter serving as Dean of the Faculty of Architecture at the Technion—Israel Institute of Technology. EWMN was first presented in Eshkol and Wachman's 1958 book *Movement Notation*, which was published in London. Over time, it was developed and honed by Eshkol as a tool for analysis and research and for dance composition.

This method is based on an analytic process that disassembles movement into its basic elements—body, space, and time. These elements are represented by means of a small selection of graphic signs and numerals. Different combinations of these symbols allow for the description of every perceptible body movement, while creating a shared language that may be used in a range of fields concerned with the study and performance of different types of movement. Like other forms of nonverbal notation, such as musical or mathematical notation, movement notation offers a means of both exploring and recording potential movement combinations that have yet to be used by creators, movement teachers, and researchers.

Mapping the Space of Movement

Movement notation is designed to describe the spatial relations between the parts of the human body, and the changes they undergo in time. The parts of the skeleton each have a constant length, and are connected to one another by means of joints. Owing to these structural qualities, the free extremity of any single moving limb will always delineate a curved orbit—a circle or part of a circle—on the surface of an imaginary sphere.

In order to define the spatial location of such an orbit, this imaginary sphere is mapped using a system of vertical and horizontal coordinates, much like those used on a globe. The horizontal plane that bisects the sphere parallel to the ground is divided into equal sections by the lines radiating outward from its center in different directions. One of the lines on this horizontal plane is selected as the starting point

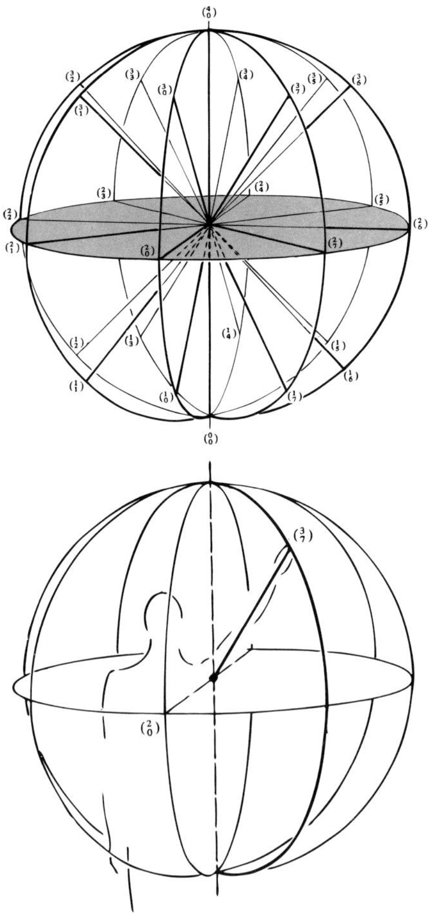

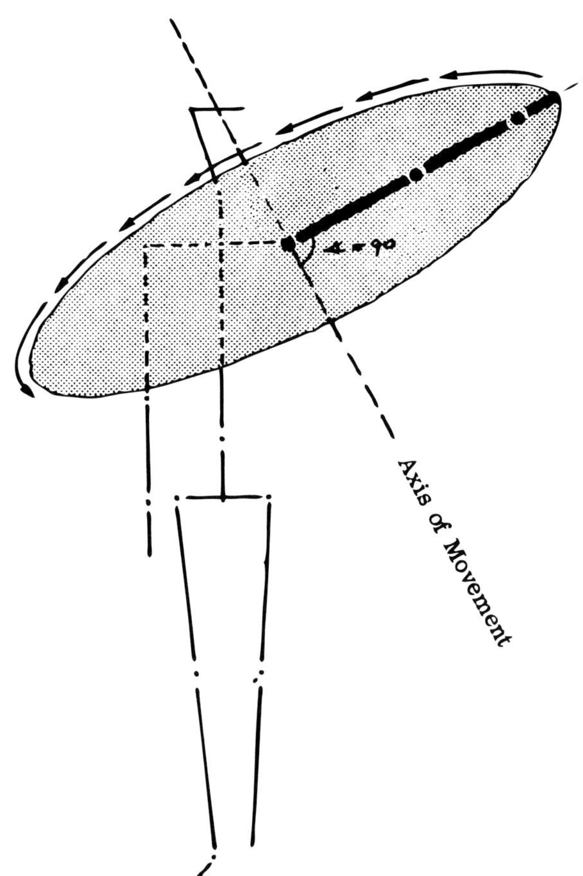

Fig. 1. Top: Illustration by John Harries, adapted from Noa Eshkol, *Right Angled Curves: Dance Suite, Eshkol-Wachman Movement Notation* (Holon: Movement Notation Society, 1975), p. 10; bottom: p. 12

Fig. 2a. Illustration by John Harries, adapted from Noa Eshkol, *Moving, Writing, Reading* (Holon: Movement Notation Society, 1973), p. 24

for all measurements. This direction is labeled (0). Additional lines are marked, clockwise, by the consecutive numbers (1), (2), and so forth (in a positive sense of movement).

Perpendicular to these horizontal radii are the vertical planes. The numerical name of each vertical plane is derived from that of the horizontal line to which it corresponds: plane (0), plane (3), and so forth. Every vertical plane is divided into the same intervals that divide the horizontal plane. The lines that divide it are similarly marked by consecutive numbers, beginning with the lowest line, which is numbered (0). The combination of the number marking the name of the plane and the number above it, which marks its distance from the lowest line (0), defines its location on the sphere of movement and is enclosed in parentheses to indicate a "position." Mapped in this manner, the sphere of movement forms a system of reference. The movements of the different limbs, as well as their static positions, are defined in relation to this system.

The spheres are most commonly divided by intervals of 45°—the most natural angle for human perception. Fig. 1 describes the standard system of reference, on a scale of 1=45°. This system includes 26 defined positions. It also contains a secondary net of coordinates, which divides the intervals into a half, a third, and two-thirds by means of three simple signs. These signs are affixed to the numbers defining a given position, much like "flat" and "sharp" in music. Together, these signs allow for the notation of 482 positions. It is possible to choose a different unit of division, in accordance with the type of movement being described: 1=30°, 1=15°, and so forth. The human eye has difficulty discerning units that are smaller than 10°, yet such units may be recorded by means of precise instruments and computers.

The Movement of a Single Limb

The transition from one position to another is a movement, and every movement may seemingly be described by a sequence of positions. Yet movement from one position to another may take place along one of several orbits. In order to address this possibility, which was ignored or remained unidentified in other notation methods, Eshkol and Wachman define two axes necessary for the analysis of every movement:

1. "The axis of the limb," a longitudinal axis that runs between two joints, or between a joint and the free extremity of the moving limb.
2. "The axis of movement," an imaginary axis that radiates outward from the joint of the same moving limb.

The spatial location of the axis of the limb and the axis of movement is defined by means of positions on the system of reference. By

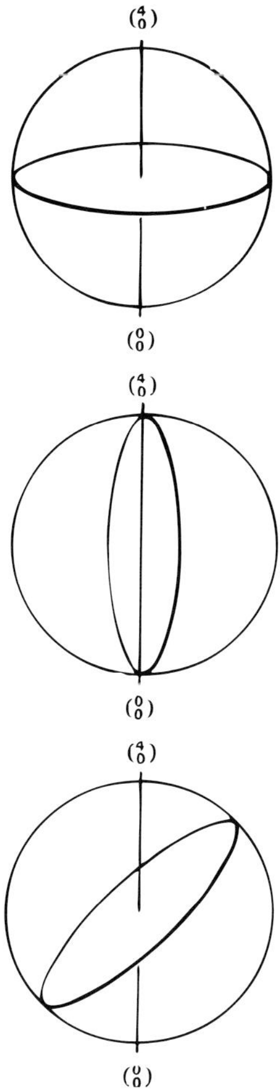

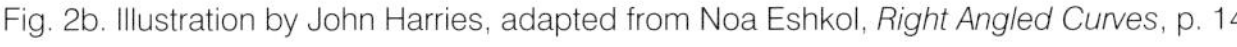

Fig. 2b. Illustration by John Harries, adapted from Noa Eshkol, *Right Angled Curves*, p. 14

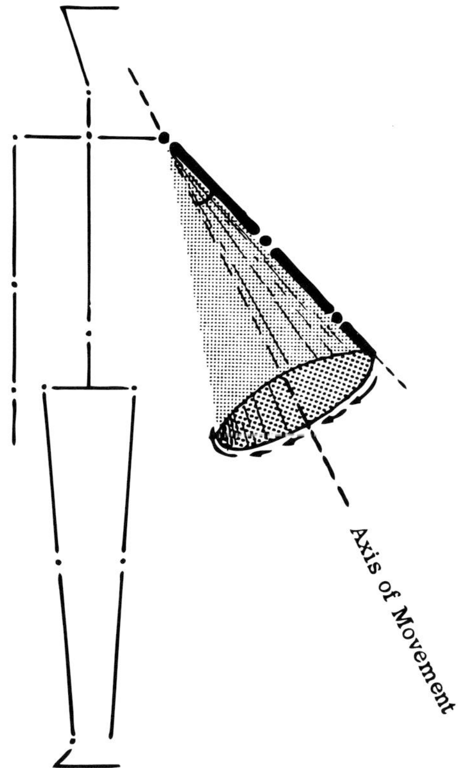

Fig. 3. Illustration by John Harries, adapted from Noa Eshkol, *Moving, Writing, Reading*, p. 23

defining the angular relation between these two axes, Eshkol and Wachman were able to reduce the number of all possible movements performed by a single limb to only three types:

1. "Plane movement" (figs. 2a and 2b): in this type of movement, the relation between the axis of the moving limb and the fixed axis of movement is 90°. It includes the horizontal plane, the vertical planes, and the diagonal circles positioned at different inclinations, which are called "intermediate planes." These are the largest possible circles delineated by a single limb. In the course of the movement, every point along the moving limb delineates an imaginary circle parallel to the circle delineated by its extremity; when they fuse, they form a sort of flat, planar membrane, which gives this type of movement its name.
2. "Rotatory movement": in this type of movement, the angular relation between the axis of the limb and the axis of movement is 0°, and the two axes become one. The limb does not change its location in space, but rather rotates around its own longitudinal axis.
3. "Conical movement" (fig. 3): in all other circles of movement, the angular relation between the axis of the limb and the axis of movement changes, yet it is always larger than 0° and smaller than 90°. The membrane-like surface created in the course of such movements is shaped like a cone, whose vertex is the joint of the moving limb; the base of this cone is a circle, whose diameter is defined by two positions on the sphere of movement.

The possibility of noting conical movements and reading them in a simple and precise manner is unique to EWMN. The inventors of other notation methods, such as Vladimir Stepanov and Pierre Conté, noticed the existence of such movements, yet were unable to find the tools to define and notate them, and thus did not use them as materials for dance compositions.[2] Indeed, with the exception of a few familiar movements, conical movements only appear in dance repertoires by chance. In Eshkol's dances, these movements enlarge the reservoir of movements and enhance the texture of the dance composition. The EWMN method makes them available to other dance creators.

In order to illustrate the imaginary membrane-like surfaces created by the planar movements and cones, Eshkol and Wachman created a series of models that each demonstrate a range of possible movement orbits, as they may appear within the system of reference concerning a single limb. These models appear in Sharon Lockhart's photographs as "models of possible movement orbits within the system of reference."

Winter

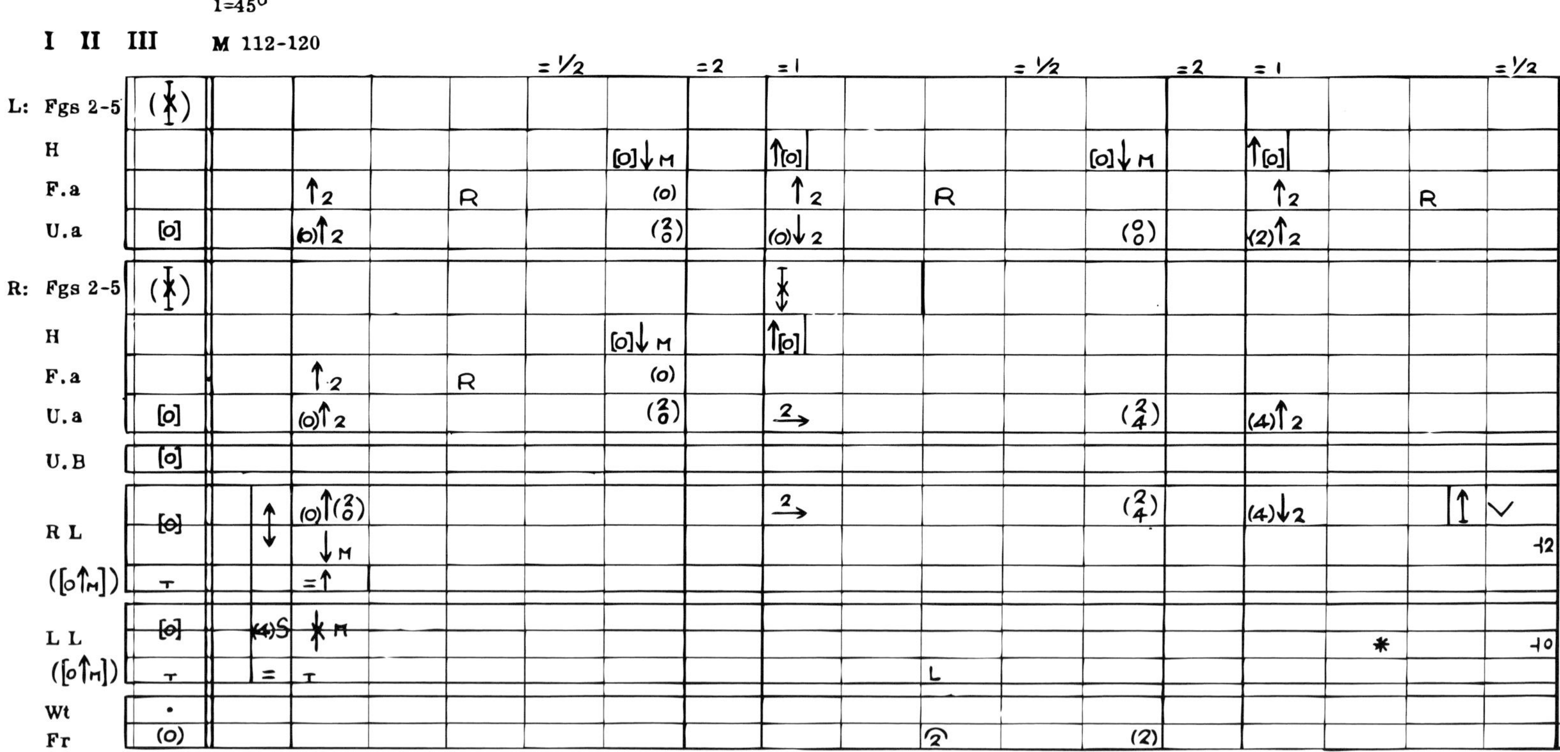

Fig. 4. Score from the dance suite *Right Angled Curves*, notated by Noa Eshkol

The Organization of Relations between Moving Limbs

The instructions concerning all the movements of a single limb—the type of movement, the sense of movement, the amount of movement (the number of intervals), and the duration of movement—are noted as combinations of signs on a special manuscript page, in a row bearing the name of the limb (fig. 4). The vertical lines on this page divide the temporal continuum into predefined units (beats). The movement of the entire body is equal to the ensemble of all movements performed in time by the individual limbs, and to their interweaving relations.

Eshkol and Wachman distinguish between limbs with a free extremity whose movement is independent and limbs that are interconnected at the joint, so that the movement of one limb influences the spatial location of the other limb and its orbit of movement. This latter type of movement is called "simultaneous movement."

In order to analyze simultaneous movement, the influential limb is referred to metaphorically as the "heavy limb," and the one impacted by its movement is called the "light limb." When the light limb remains motionless, it is carried along by the movement of the heavier limb, and its location in relation to the system of reference, as well as the orbit delineated by its free extremity, changes passively. When several adjacent limbs move simultaneously, the movement of each limb delineates part of a circle, while the orbit created by their simultaneous movement might be very complex (fig. 5).

Eshkol was fascinated by these orbits and found them highly interesting both in their own right, as trajectories concealed within the three-dimensional space of movement and because of their contribution to her dance compositions. She sought to detect some sort of logic or order that would enable these movements to be studied, categorized, and perhaps even given expression by means of another notation method. In 1968–69, she conducted a systematic study of simultaneous movements at the University of Illinois at Urbana-Champaign. The results of this study were partial, yet it produced a beautiful and impressive collection of computer simulations that reveal the existence of a remarkably rich and complex world of forms. These movements play an important role in Eshkol's dance compositions, endowing them with their original formal character and complexity. Although they cannot be envisioned in advance, they can be expressed through a description of the individual movements of which they are composed, thus calling the viewer's attention to their existence, and further enriching his or her experience.

Translated from the Hebrew by Talya Halkin

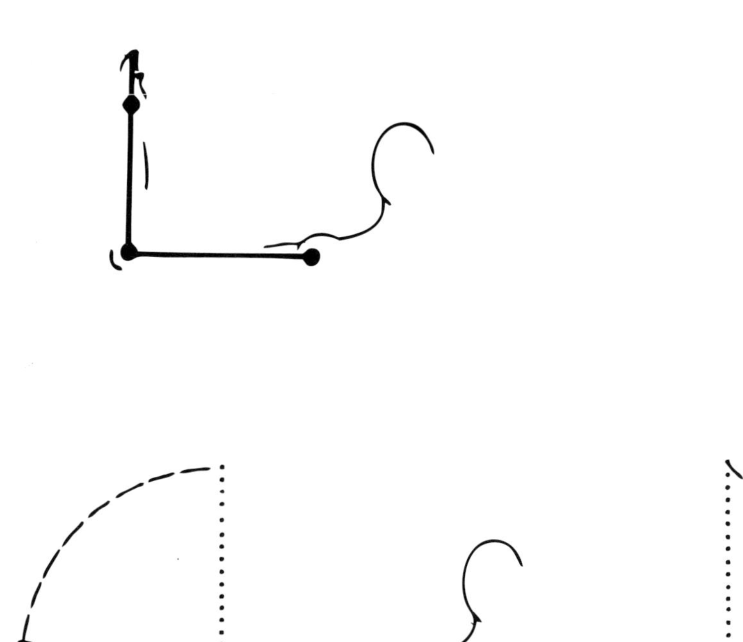

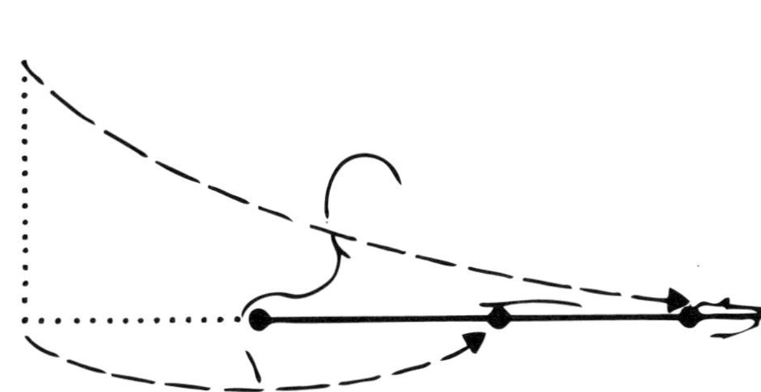

Fig. 5. Illustration by John Harries, adapted from Noa Eshkol, *Right Angled Curves*, p. 20

1. Noa Eshkol and Abraham [Avraham] Wachman, *Movement Notation* (London: Weidenfeld and Nicolson, 1958), viii.
2. See V. I. Stepanov, *L'alphabet des mouvements du corps humain* (Paris: M. Zouckerman, Paris, 1892) and Pierre Conté, *Écriture* (Paris, 1931).

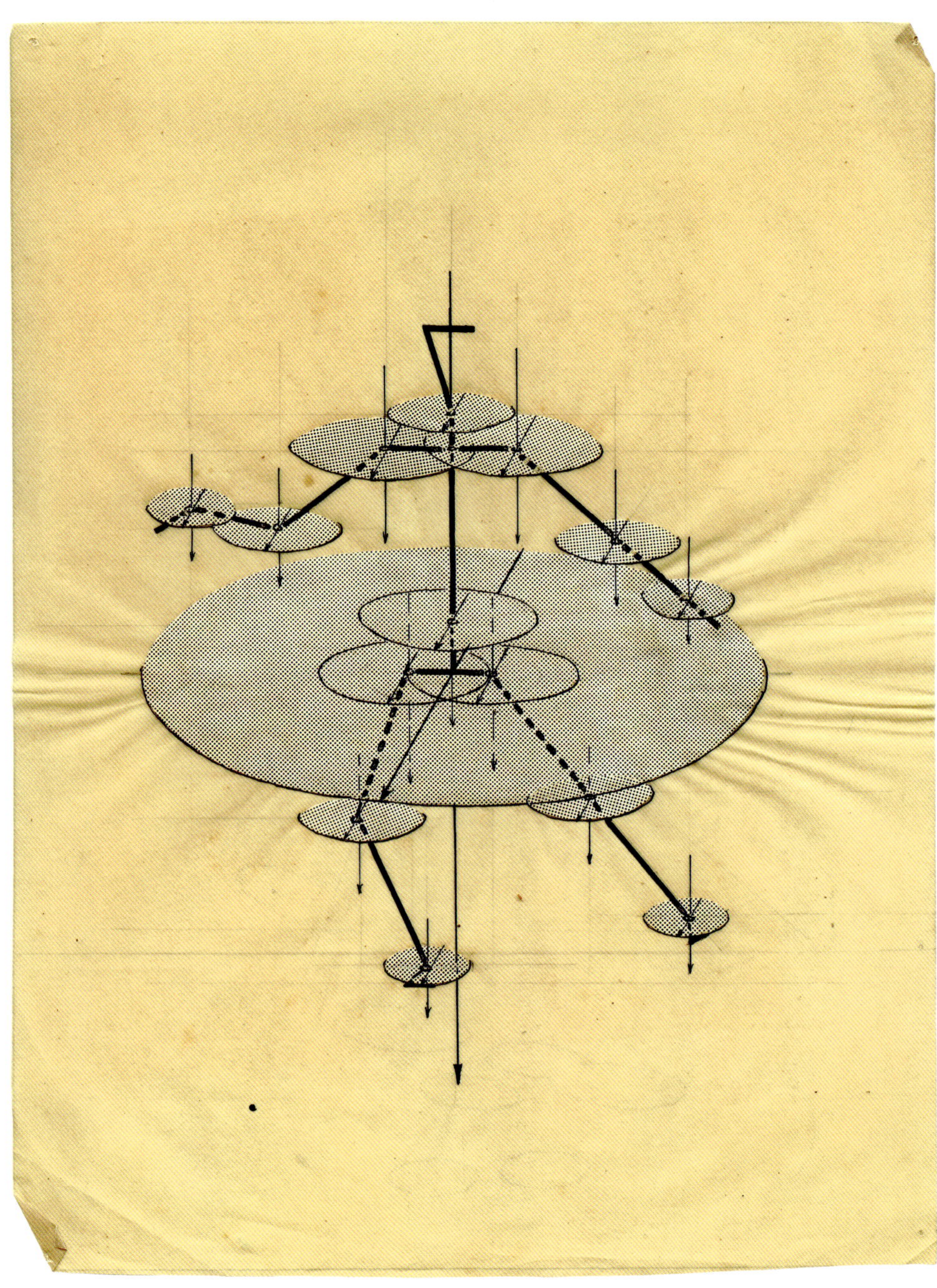

John Harries, *The individual systems of reference of the body limbs are parallel to each other and to the overall reference system*, 1956–57; this drawing was adapted as an illustration for Noa Eshkol and Abraham [Avraham] Wachman, *Movement Notation* (London: Weidenfeld and Nicholson, 1958), fig. 14 ("The Main and Private Systems of Reference")

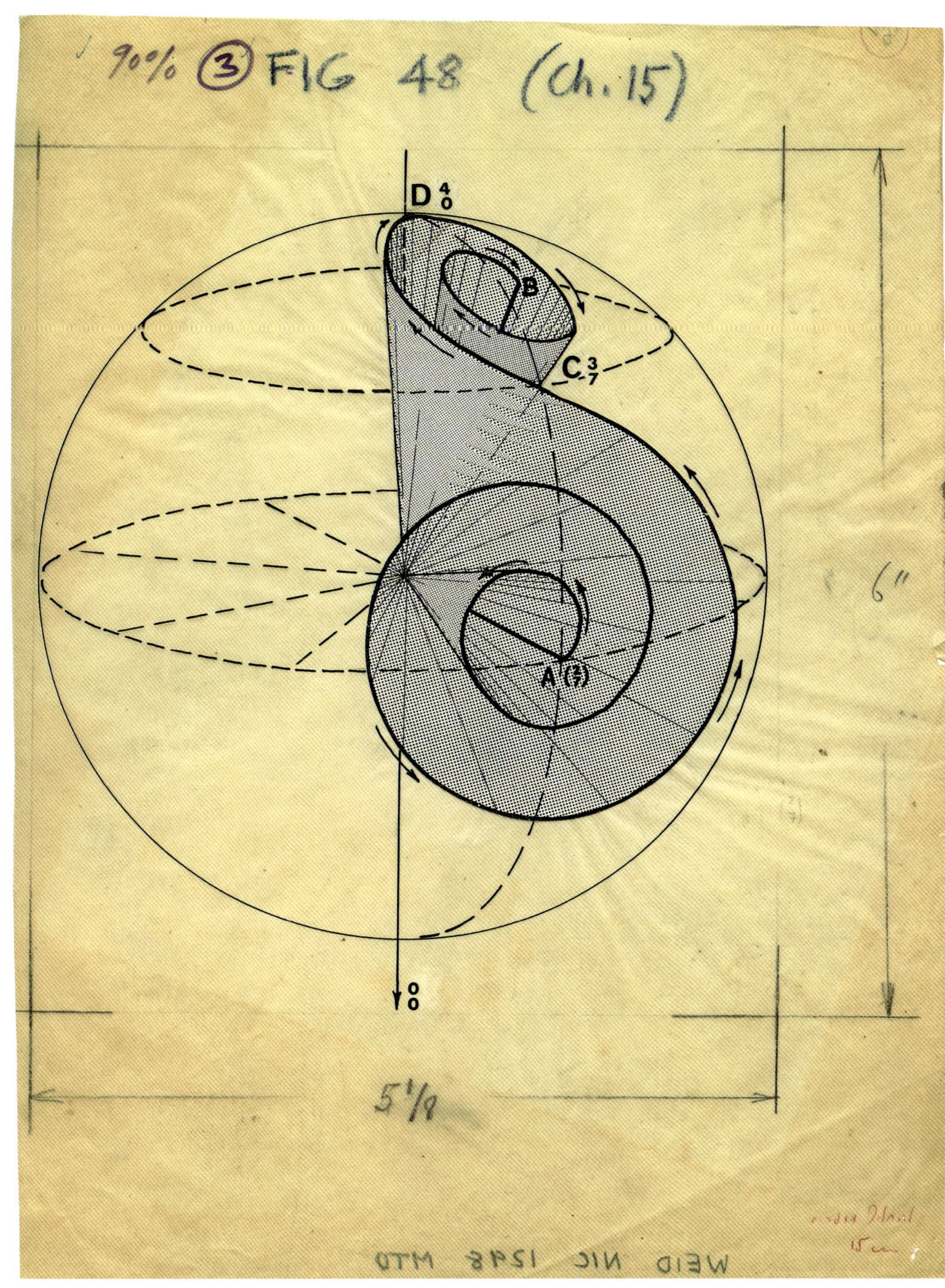

John Harries, *The limb begins to move from A, through points C and D and ends at B. From A to C the limb produces an augmenting spiral; from C to B a diminishing spiral*, 1956–57; this drawing was adapted as an illustration for Noa Eshkol and Abraham [Avraham] Wachman, *Movement Notation* (London: Weidenfeld and Nicholson, 1958), fig. 48 ("Spiral Movement")

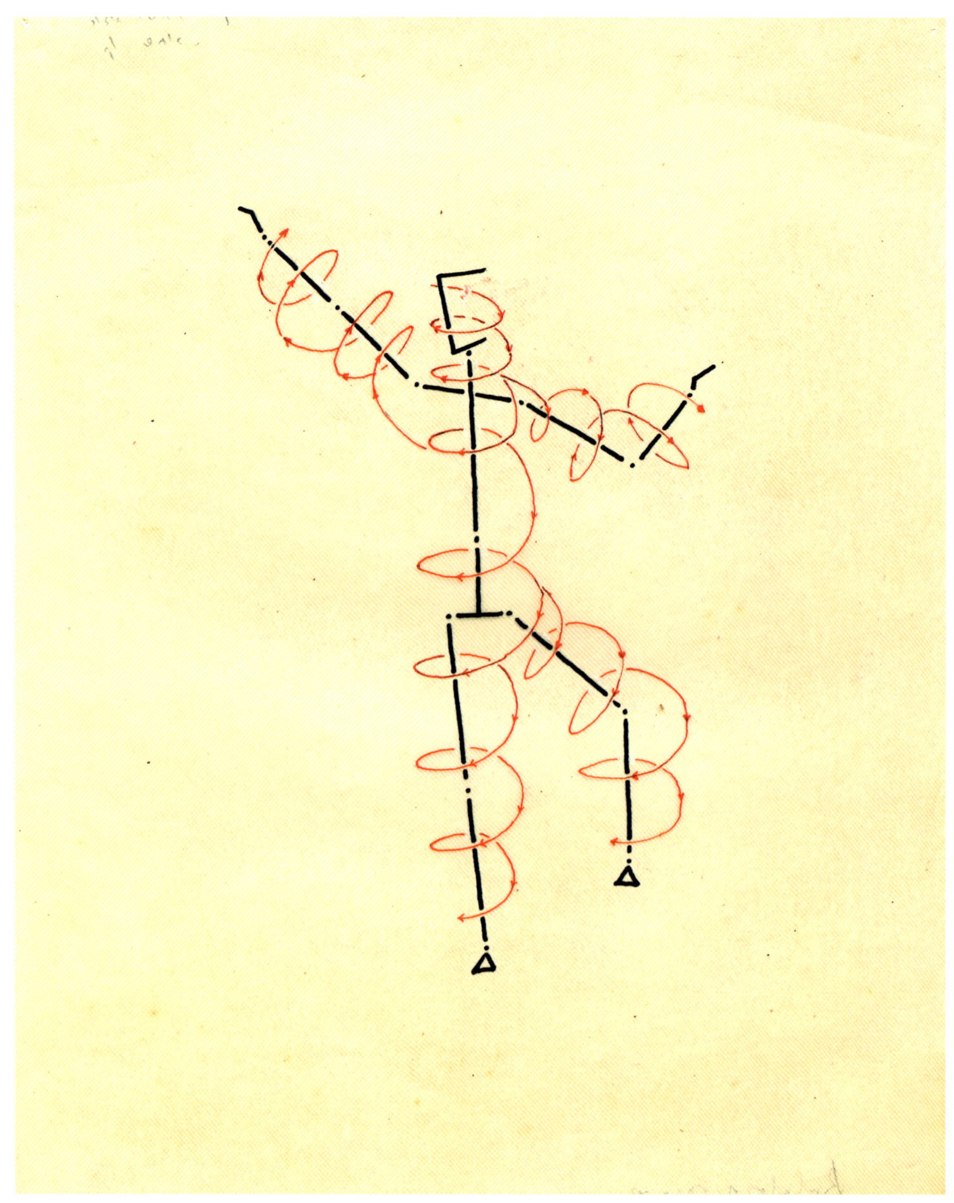

John Harries, *Sense of the Rotary Movement*, 1956–57

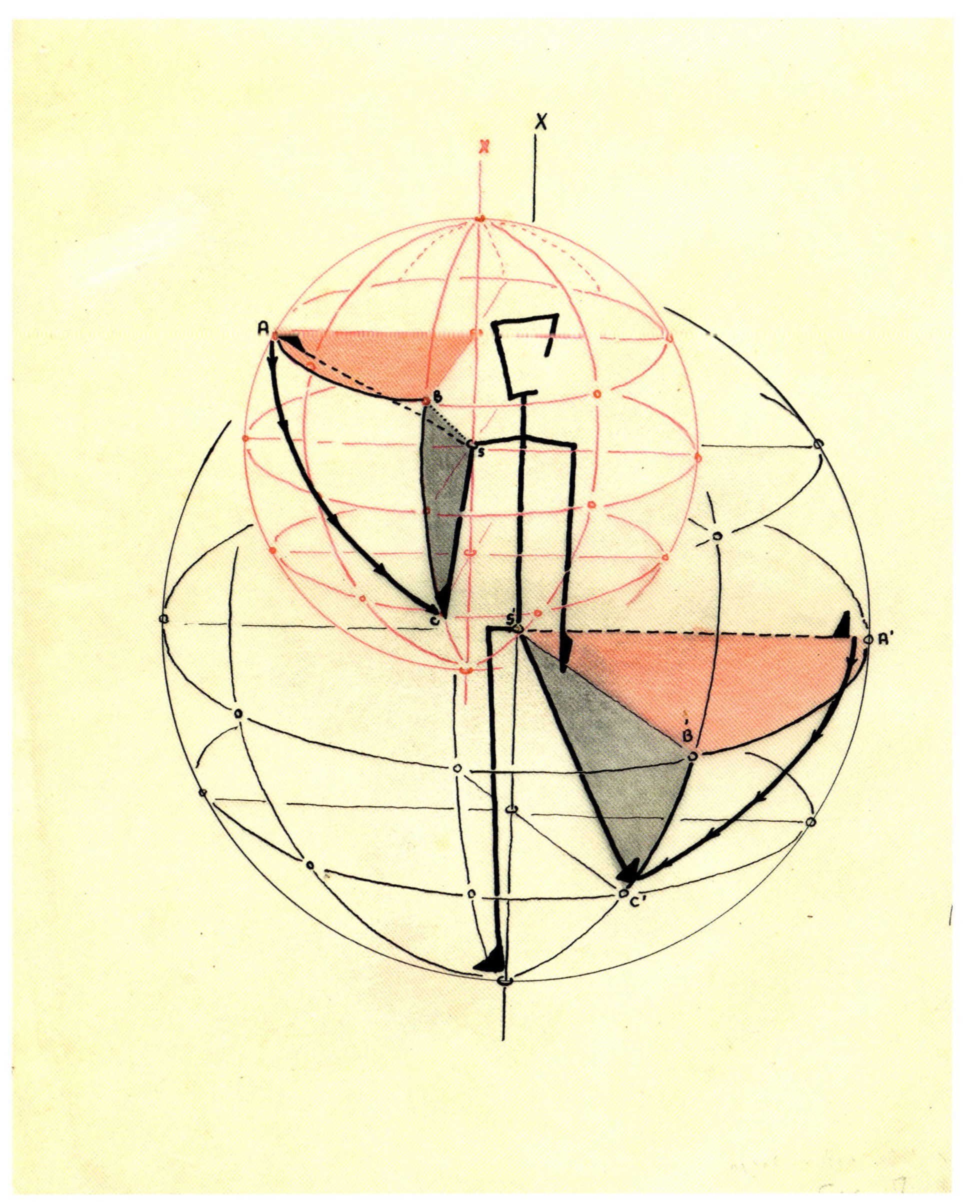

John Harries, *Intermediate Plane Movement*, 1956–57

On Collaboration: A Conversation with Sharon Lockhart

Sabine Eckmann

SABINE ECKMANN: I'd like to start by talking about the ways in which you have collaborated in the past with communities and people usually unassociated with the art world, but who have importantly become the subjects of your works. Your film and photography projects, which are always shown in museum and gallery spaces in the form of strictly designed installations, such as *Pine Flat* (2005) and *Lunch Break* (2008), illuminate to some degree how you work with your chosen community. It's striking how the people you engage with, framed by an often-static camera, emerge as themselves. In this sense much of your work is quite contrary to how we usually conceptualize staged photographs and films. Your approach could almost be understood as the very deconstruction of this convention, insofar as the strength of your work lies in the fact that your subjects seem unaware of the artistic and technological apparatus that captures them. In the context of your collaborations it appears critical that you give the people you work with their own space to be who they are, and in turn they let you be who you are and do what you need to do as an artist. Much of the actual collaboration then happens beyond or behind the camera. The resulting works ambiguously both reveal and conceal this collaboration at the same time. When conceiving these projects, how does this tension between real-life collaboration and artistic translation influence the creation of the works themselves?

SHARON LOCKHART: Tension is definitely something I work hard to create, but I think it's also sometimes merely a side effect of the process I go through. As you say, there's something distinct about my intervention as an artist. My work is not "reality": it's somehow formalized, or a translation of real life. In the past I've spoken a lot about how I choreograph movements or work with movement advisers and about how what looks like something spontaneous is actually highly orchestrated. I have a sense, however, that you're getting at something else. I think it's also obvious from the work that blatant fictionalizing is not something that interests me. I want viewers to know that there's a conversation between the subjects of the films or photographs and me, the artist—but not in an overt, over-the-top, heavy kind of way. It's important to me that the translation is seamless, but at the same time present. Equally, the part of the process in which I work with a community, a person, or a group of people is very enjoyable for me as an artist; it's the part that really produces the work. More and more, I see the work as the interaction. The final form it takes is a link to the process.

ECKMANN: When I recall *Lunch Break*, I think of an artistic meditation about time off from the daily routine of regulated labor at the beginning of the twenty-first century.[1] I also think about how experimental film and photography intersect and inform each other. The workers themselves—their lives and personalities—don't come to mind immediately. What seems aesthetically significant is that the main film has characteristics of static photographs and that the photographs, through serial variations, recall films. At first these artistic approaches appear unrelated to your actual collaboration with the workers, but I'm wondering if there isn't a connection. That would also hold true for *Pine Flat*, for example. We can understand your collaboration with the workers as a situation that focuses on belonging to a special social group and as one that is about experiencing something new: namely, the process of engaging with an artist and becoming part of an artwork. The actual artworks also concentrate on this tension, in that the photographs and films are very much about themselves, but also about the interpenetration of each other. This is, of course, my view—the view of a critic, curator, and art historian. I would be curious to know how you see your aesthetic collaboration with the people who become the subjects of your films and photographs and who surface in your final installations.

LOCKHART: That's an interesting insight. I've never thought about how the relationship between the mediums of film and photography might be reflected in the collaborative process between my subjects and myself. But yes, there's definitely an interpenetration between the cohesiveness of the group and its externalization for an outside audience. The initial

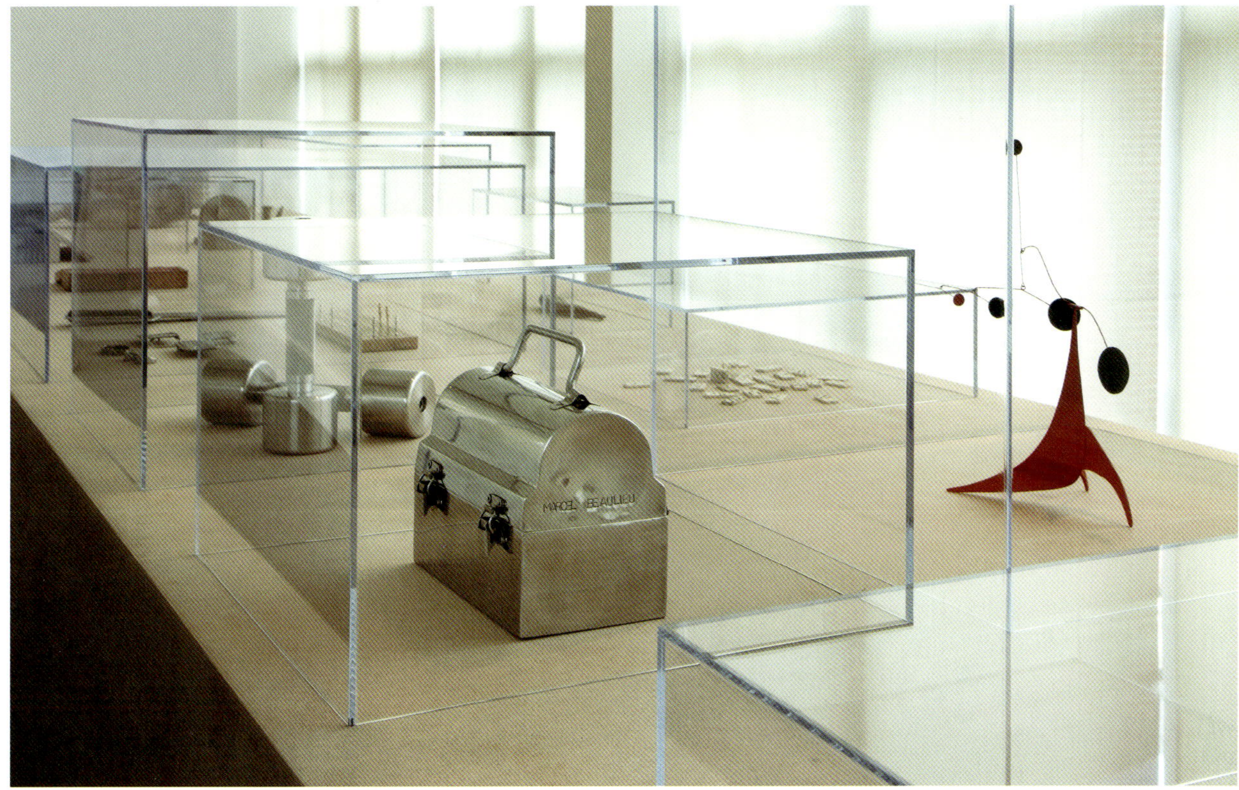

Fig. 1. Installation view of *Sharon Lockhart: Lunch Break*, Colby College Museum of Art, Waterville, Maine, 2010

stage of my process is to develop a group dynamic—for me to become part of the group. In doing that, both the group and I are changed. I'm educating them about my goals and methods, and they're educating me in the same way. Together we're creating a solidarity that can then be externalized in the films and photographs. When I think back to the projects and images I've discarded over the years, I realize it was almost always because I felt that I had not established that intermediary group. The resulting images were all flawed in one of two ways: either I had failed to create that solidarity, or I had not communicated the aesthetic side of the equation successfully enough for it to find its form in the final work. With most of the projects I've taken part in, I would say the subjects fully understood the problematics at play. They understood that there was something at stake in how things looked, but also in how the work might be approached by a viewer.

ECKMANN: I like your notion of solidarity. Not only do your works convey a heightened sense of humanity, but they also instill the idea that in the realm of art, one can create better, and more humane, worlds, despite the coexistence of certain social and political realities, which are invoked as well. Yet recently your collaborations have taken a fairly different turn. At the installation of *Lunch Break* at the Colby College Museum of Art in Maine, you included objects that some of the workers who participated in the project had created, such as lunch baskets and tools.[2] These objects entered into a dialogue with Colby's collection by assuming their own place within the exhibition, and in so doing extended your project. Was there a decisive moment that triggered or encouraged you to turn to the workers as artists by engaging them on your, rather than their own, terms? Was this a turning point in your work: did it transform the nature of how you collaborate with communities?

LOCKHART: I didn't see the inclusion of the workers' objects in the Colby exhibition as being on my terms; it seemed to me part of the collaboration. Just as with the films and photographs, I'm always setting the terms of the collaboration, but I'm also trying to open up a space my collaborators can feel comfortable entering. As I got to know the workers, I found that many of them were artists of some sort. Perhaps it was self-selection—the ones who gravitated toward me might have been artistically inclined. Colby had asked me to curate a room in the exhibition using their collection, and when I started researching the objects they had, I saw connections with objects the workers had made. For instance, I ended up including from the museum's collection a small sculpture by Alexander Calder made with World War II–scrap metal, displayed next to a 1980 stainless-steel lunch box by Marcel Beaulieu, one of the workers (fig. 1). I think the interaction started earlier, however, when I was creating the series of photographs of the workers' lunch boxes, which were so personal and creative. Their owners really understood what I was after and that I saw them as artworks—that I saw the ritual of lunch in an artistic way. It wasn't much of a leap from there to include the workers' crafts and artworks in the exhibition.

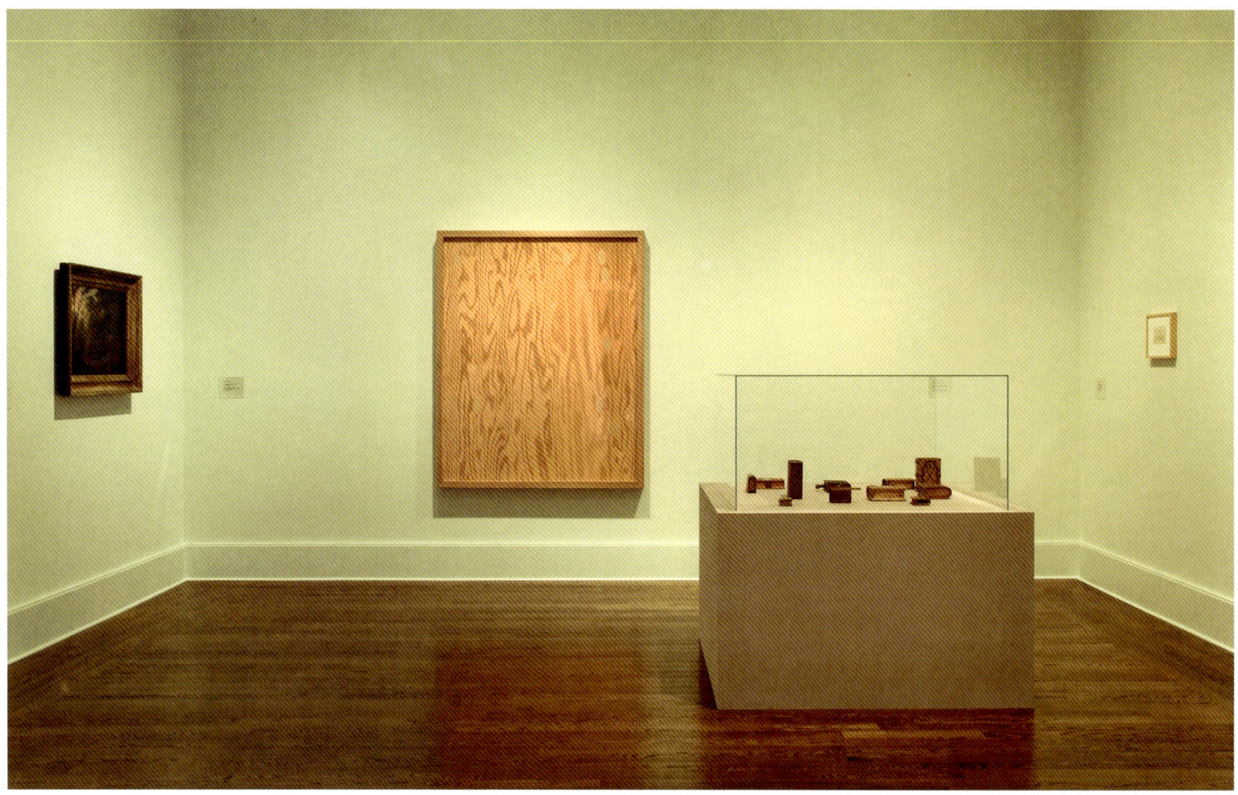

Fig. 2. Installation view of *Sharon Lockhart: Lunch Break*, Colby College Museum of Art, Waterville, Maine, 2010

In retrospect, yes, this might have been a turning point in my practice. It's hard to say when it's your own work. It definitely opened up a new way of seeing the collaboration, by showing that the experience we call art can be found in all kinds of places. The Colby show became a conversation with the community, but also a conversation between different kinds of artworks—historical objects like carved spruce-gum boxes and Sherrie Levine's knot paintings, for example (fig. 2). This shift also grew out of the newspaper you and I did together, the *Lunch Break Times*, free copies of which were distributed to the public. For a year I collected articles from people who had worked on the project—artists, art historians, and workers from all over Maine—both to give a voice to the participants and to create an object that could reenter the working world outside the museum. The inclusion of the audience's voice in the museum, through their objects and their articles in the paper, created a dynamic for the exhibition different from what I'm used to. People were coming to see what they did as much as they were coming to see what I did. I found the experience exhilarating.

ECKMANN: This is the right context to think more about what the inclusion of objects made by your collaborators means in relation to your installations and their presentation within a museum context. These interventions differ from project to project. As part of the *Lunch Break* exhibition at the Secession in Vienna, for example, you showed James Benning's baseball-card collection together with your photographs of his beer-bottle collection. This provided a connection to the context of American working-class culture that defines *Lunch Break*. It also resonated with the knickknacks and personal items that the workers had assembled in the independent businesses they operated in the shipyard, and with the stickers they attached to their actual lunch boxes. With both the workers' objects seen in the *Lunch Break* films and photographs and Benning's collections represented in the Secession installation, the collected items form a kind of portrait of the owner. In the context of the museum, they also invited consideration about collecting and who collects what, in part owing to the different mediums through which they are displayed: on the one hand as a particular hybrid between installation art and exhibition design, and on the other hand through photography, all the while establishing a dialogue between both.

At Colby, as you just described it, you expanded on that approach, intermingling objects from the collection with objects the workers had created based on a curatorial process that looked for similar aesthetic sensibilities (fig. 3). Through this equal footing you mobilized, but also did away with, the history of institutional critique. Perhaps more in line with the Benning project, you also displayed an actual lunch box together with your photographs of the lunch boxes. (By the way, it's striking how your photographs, as formally strict as they are, appear more personal than the actual lunch box itself.) But I want to turn to the role of the specially designed vitrines, in which the workers' objects and selections from the collection were displayed. They seem to embrace a multiplicity of connotations as they relate to and are part of

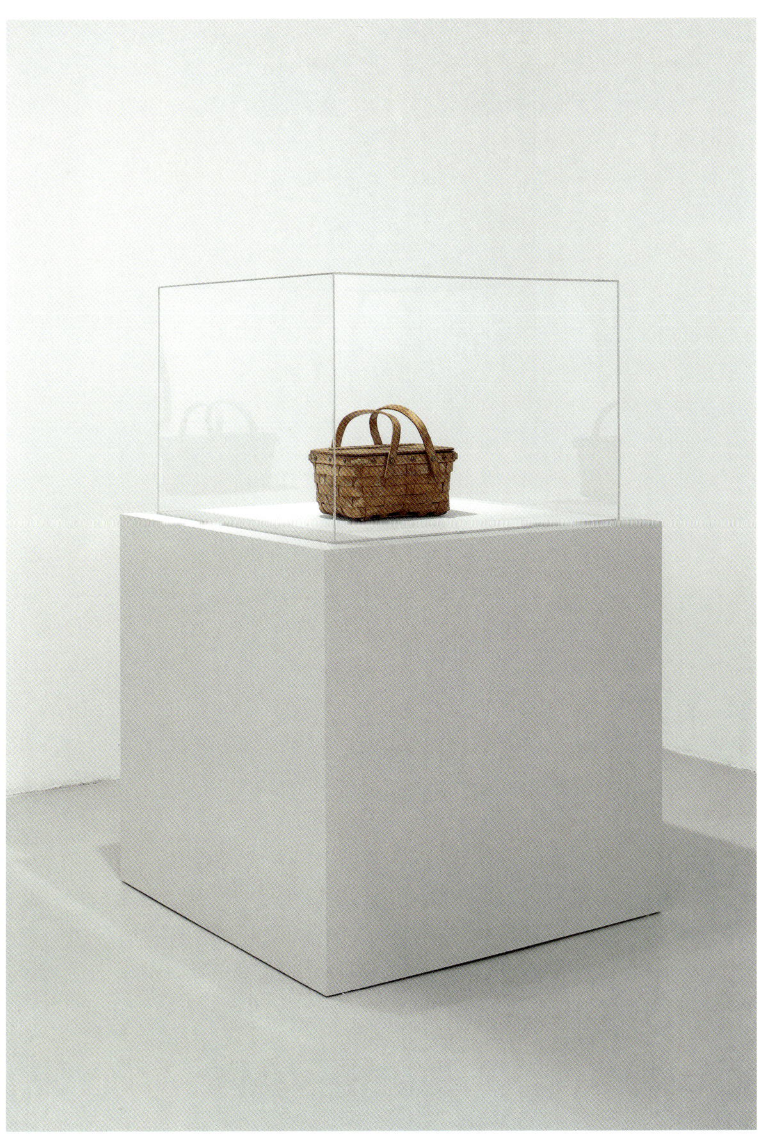

Fig. 3. Installation view of *Sharon Lockhart: Lunch Break*, Gió Marconi, Milan, 2011, showing lunch box made by Bath Iron Works machinist Butch Greenleaf

the curatorial process, yet they also evoke the displayed objects themselves. Aren't they containers and abstract sculptures at the same time, in this sense twisting not only the history of institutional critique but also the way the viewer experiences the objects created by the workers?

LOCKHART: I think it's easy for some to look past the way in which the vitrines, and also the enclosed architectural structures on which the films are projected, are sculptural in some sense, so I'm glad you pointed that out. I do think of them as containers and abstract sculptures at the same time. They may be seen as framing devices for the work included in them, but they have a relationship to both the architecture and the institution that frames them, and I'd like viewers to think about those relationships. On the other hand, I'm not interested in pointing out how the museum is a privileged place or reaffirming the hierarchies it creates through some kind of negation.

With the Benning room in the Secession it was easier to see that I wasn't referring to such hierarchies because he and I are on an equal footing as artists, and the nod to both of our activities of collecting (through photography, film, or the standard accumulation of objects) was a way of establishing a methodology for viewing a very similar engagement with the shipyard workers. Collections are both an aesthetic undertaking and a conversion of the objects collected into a text. Perhaps that's why the photographs seem more personal than the actual objects: because we're so used to converting a photograph into a text about the person or object it represents, and the objects themselves are more likely to be read as "just objects." If one can appreciate this and not separate the objects from the overall project as addenda, then I think the vitrines and the objects inside them actually reframe the photographs themselves as personal, as a collection, and as a text. In fact, they seem to be more of a text about the person than the objects themselves. This is part of what I was trying to do with the Eshkol installation. It might be easy to miss the way I was engaging with her as a person and an artist, and with her collaborators, through just the films and photographs. But by including the archival material and carpets, I felt that I was shifting the viewer's attention away from what I was doing aesthetically in the works that I created toward what I was doing conceptually, which was creating a space for a cultural/social interaction with Eshkol and her dancers. That my authorship disappeared, in a way, would strengthen the viewer's perception of my actual project and the complex relationships of authoring and interdependencies it implied.

ECKMANN: Many of your projects prior to this one engaged with a contemporary community on the verge of disappearance, such as the blue-collar working class at the beginning of the twenty-first century or adolescents on the cusp of adulthood. Many were also driven by a particular ethnographic interest, as in *Goshogaoka* (1997) and *Teatro Amazonas* (1999). Eshkol, however, is an artist from the past. One way you collaborate with her is through her own close collaborators, the dancers. Yet you also engage with her through her artworks (the

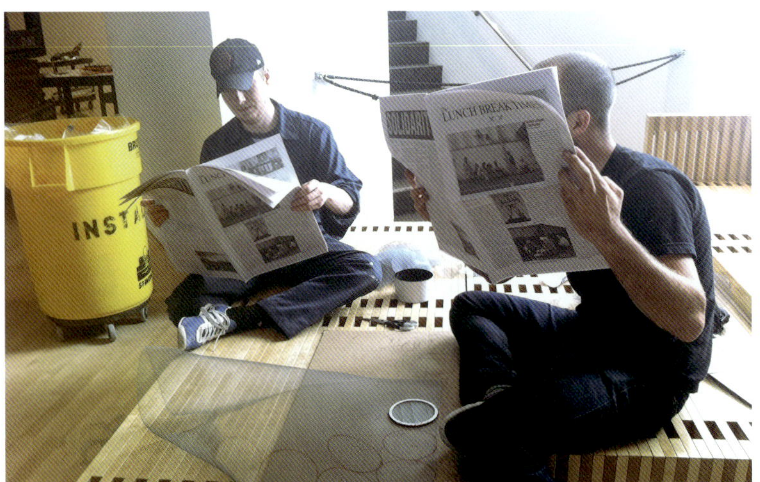

Fig. 4. Members of the crew reading the *Lunch Break Times* during installation of *Sharon Lockhart: Lunch Break*, San Francisco Museum of Modern Art, 2011 (left: Travis Kerkela; right: Dave Vetrano)

dance compositions and the wall carpets), pedagogical devices such as the notation system and the wire-and-mesh spheres (small mobiles that visualize abstract movement), as well as her personal archive, which includes her sketches and notes in relation to notation system and personal items such as photographs and her diaries. How does this process of collaborating with someone you never met impact the work? In your mind, is it shaped by the structures and methods of memory and the imagination? What role do the living dancers play in your conversation with Eshkol and the creation of the work?

LOCKHART: This project is perhaps different in that there are two points of collaboration: Eshkol and her dancers. It may seem odd, but I hadn't actually separated the two in my mind. My association with Eshkol seemed so natural and personal when I was introduced to her production. I immediately felt a connection, and it was only later that I came to know the distinction between her creations and those of her collaborators. Bringing up the question of memory and the imagination seems appropriate, because in truth that's the only way I will ever know her. The projects I've done with the work of Morris Louis, Duane Hanson, and On Kawara are similar, in that I saw something I connected with and tried to pull that out and make it visible. Eshkol was different because I had the voices of the dancers to bring her to life for me. The dancers are central to my conversation with Eshkol. They knew her; it's through their memory of her in part that I know her, too. And it was their commitment to Eshkol's vision that drew me to her as much as Eshkol's own work. They were lifelong collaborators with her (some for forty years), performing her dances and sewing her wall carpets. That she established a collaborative relationship with them seemed to be an important connection to my own interests. They've created a wonderful practice in her absence, keeping her house as a workplace and managing it together. They are like a collective with a shared responsibility for her legacy, which was deeply inspiring to be a part of. This was the place where the real-life collaboration we were speaking of earlier could happen. In the end it was our bond that informed the project as much as my bond with Eshkol's work.

ECKMANN: In *Sharon Lockhart | Noa Eshkol* the artwork itself is the collaboration, as indicated in the title that gives authorship to both Eshkol and yourself, an imaginative dialogue with Eshkol and her lifelong passion for minimalist body movement. This theme is realized through your focus on the meaning and structure of movement, yet also through the inclusion of other creative aspects of Eshkol's life, like the carpets, into your multichannel installation work. Do you see this as a continuation of what you began by including the workers' objects in the Colby installation, or are the two projects entirely different from each other?

LOCKHART: There's definitely a connection. Incorporating Benning in the Secession installation of *Lunch Break* was the beginning, but it was more of an aside. Then developing the Colby show and the *Lunch Break Times*, including the second edition for the San Francisco Museum of Modern Art (fig. 4), allowed me to see the possibilities for incorporating voices that had an equal footing to mine as part of the work. The Eshkol project expands that idea. I tried to emphasize that by the title of the exhibition, which gives us equal authorship. I really see it as a two-person exhibition, although I created the frame for both of us. Perhaps this goes back to your earlier comment that I was creating a space for the workers on my own terms. Everyone told me that this collaboration could never have taken place if Eshkol were alive. Aside from the fact that she was incredibly uncompromising, she may not have understood my reframing of her work.

ECKMANN: The re-creations of Eshkol's dances, which have rarely been performed publicly, are now captured on film, where they achieve permanence, in contrast to the ephemeral quality of an actual dance performance. It seems to me that in the actual installation, in which the films are projected onto large-scale volumes that architecturally shape the space, you have transformed these performances (fig. 5). Together with the plinths in the installation, which are used to display the carpets but also serve as stage-design elements for the performance of the dances, your collaboration with Eshkol also materializes through a reconfiguration of space. You connect the carpets as sculptures with the compositions of the dances and the bodies of the dancers, something Eshkol didn't do, and with time: the past is the basis for a new present. I think this is very important because it distinguishes *Sharon Lockhart |*

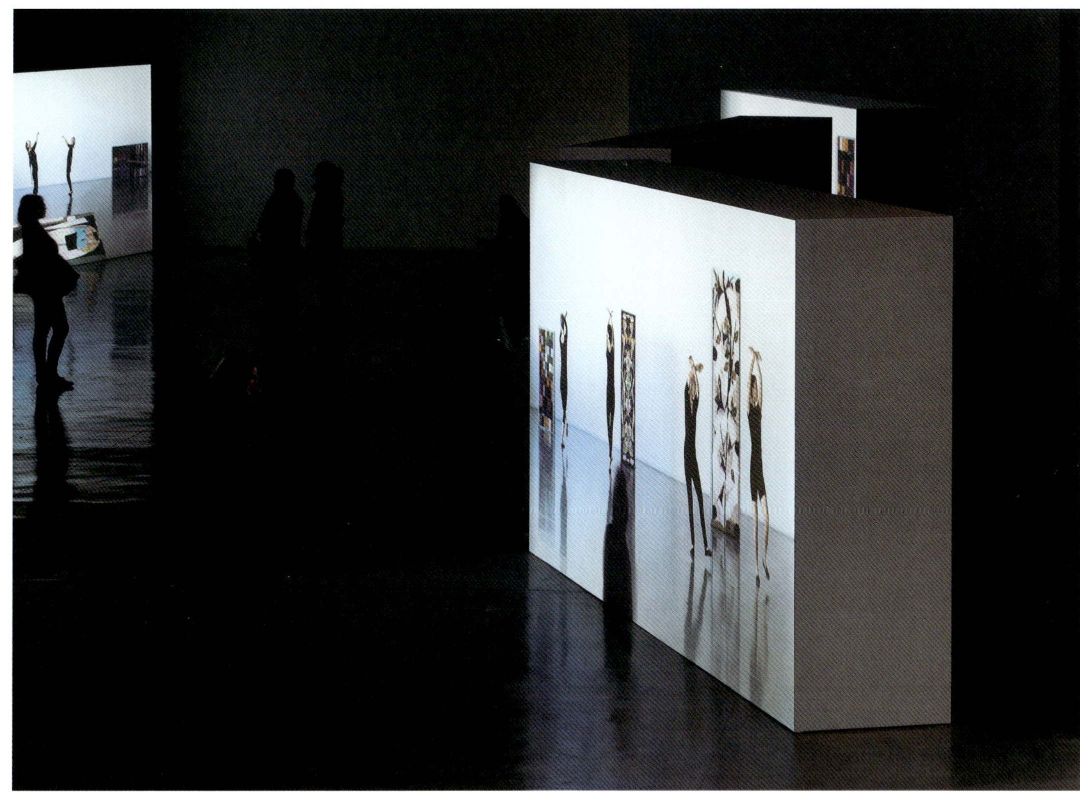

Fig. 5. Installation view of exhibition at The Israel Museum, Jerusalem, showing Sharon Lockhart's *Five Dances and Nine Wall Carpets by Noa Eshkol*, 2011

Noa Eshkol as a collaboration, an exchange and dialogue between two artists, rather than a re-creation of Eshkol's work and life. What's interesting is that you were able to assert a relation between the fleetingness of memory and the precarious nature of the imagination and the rigid, highly structured, and three-dimensional composition of both the individual films and the installation itself. This work with memory and imagination perpetually penetrates our spatial environment, the here and now in which we live. This causes me to ask if we could also understand this project in terms of deferred action (in German, we say *Nachträglichkeit*), in the sense that through the means of memory, the past materializes in the present as different, yet still joined to its origin.

LOCKHART: The reframing I was just speaking of alters Eshkol's original production in a way that is appreciably different from what her place in the course of history would've allowed her to see. At the same time I was trying to be as true to her process as I could. I recognize that I was drawn to her by historical precedents with which I identified, including many ideas and forms that I was familiar with from my study of mid-twentieth-century art, but that the work would function only if I could surpass that history and create something really new. In this sense, I relate to what you refer to as *Nachträglichkeit*, which I read as a past that somehow haunts the present. All of the components I contributed to the exhibition—the projections, the architectural elements, the photographs, the archive—were just framing devices for what I saw as my own historical precedents.

ECKMANN: Could you explain the role of the historical precedent a little more? In many of your works you engage with a present-day community that often escapes our attention and knowledge. To a certain extent this is also true for Eshkol, as the dancers continue her legacy, which is relatively unknown. But then there is also this aspect that engages in a creative exploration of Eshkol's dance compositions and art, and the way you give her coauthorship over the project. How does this relate to the importance of historical precedents for you?

LOCKHART: I spend a lot of time looking at work that precedes my own. For example, I spent a lot of time looking at postmodern dance and Jean Rouch's work when I made *Goshogaoka* (1997). Yet, the work I make is very much a reworking of the research material. The connection to the past, as you say, creates something uncanny about the repetition. It is familiar but different. In the case of Eshkol, I identified with her approach to dance and also to textiles. She liked to have a structure and then work from there: the textiles were all made from scraps or deconstructed found textiles. She never cut fabric. In the dances, she broke the body down into essential elements that were then recombined in a very mechanical way. In both cases, there are connections to practices that have influenced my own work: Minimalism, postmodern dance, and structuralist film. However, she never fit properly into those movements. Maybe this is what made the material so fertile for me. More than any other project, it allowed me to foreground my process.

ECKMANN: In your work sculptural elements become part of a multidisciplinary endeavor, as you emphasize yourself. For the films, as well as for the installation itself, it's striking how the large-scale volumes turn your films, Eshkol's carpets, and even her personal archive into experiential components. In that sense, I think that they're more than framing devices. I believe that they heighten Eshkol's presence throughout the space. In short, they seem to make the coauthorship possible. Let me give you an example of what I mean. In *Four Exercises in Eshkol-Wachman Movement Notation* (2011), we see the dancer "interacting" with four large-scale architectural elements that reference the dancer's body as much as they, in an abstract manner, embody Eshkol's approach to movement. Not that different is the way in which the dancers engage with the architectural elements to which the carpets are attached in the film *Five Dances and Nine Wall Carpets by Noa Eshkol* (2011). In both cases, you give Eshkol a presence not only through her dances and her carpets but also through these sculptures, as they underscore a Minimalist, yet embodied, experience of movement. I wonder if one could call this a creative, or maybe imaginary, reconstruction?

LOCKHART: It's hard for me to answer that question. As I've said, my comprehension of what Eshkol was doing cannot be exactly what she herself thought of it. Since the experiential elements of the installation are what I most think of as my own, I mistrust them the most in relation to who Eshkol was and what she intended in her work. I tried very hard to be true to my idea of her, and it certainly was my understanding that this Minimalist approach was a central concern and that she wanted viewers always to remain conscious of their relationship to the performer.

ECKMANN: Along those lines, I'm wondering how the viewer finds herself in the role of collaborator. Only by moving through time (through the films and the motions of the dancers) and space (through the display of the films and carpets as three-dimensional elements) is the viewer able conceptually and physically to experience your collaboration with Eshkol.

LOCKHART: I would hope so. I wanted everything to have a very specific relation to the body. This was something with which Eshkol was so completely in tune. She conceived of the dances as "chamber dances," in that they were supposed to take place in a room with a small audience so that the relationship of bodies (viewers and dancers) would be contained and reflexively apparent. This was the organizing principle for the Center for Contemporary Art exhibition in Tel Aviv.[3] The exhibition occupied two spaces. On the second floor of the exhibition space, we installed the film *Four Exercises in Eshkol-Wachman Movement Notation*. The architectural elements for this installation consisted of a volume for the projection, a volume for the projector, and a bench (just beyond the projector volume was a vitrine displaying a selection of the daily diaries that Eshkol and the dancers maintained). These elements related to the gray volumes that viewers could see in the film, which were sized to the height and armspan of the film's only performer, the dancer Ruti Sela, and were presented in arrangements within the frame that highlighted the physical path each dance exercise occupied in space. For example, all three architectural elements were painted gray, and the projector volume and the bench had the same footprint as the volumes in the film. Thus, the three elements physically extrapolated the experience of the film into the installation.

From the open balcony on the second floor, viewers could look down into a gallery that we transformed into a performance space (figs. 6–7), where a series of performances, workshops, and lectures, as well as the dancers' own practices, took place. We designed bleachers for the audience at one end of the gallery, leaving a space roughly the same size as the studio where the dancers practice and bringing their daily routine in Holon to the public. Viewers could experience a real relationship to bodies performing, both when the space was occupied by the dancers and when it was empty, to be filled with bodies like their own. The dances themselves are meant to make you aware of how your body moves.

All of the architectural interventions, which I designed with the architectural firm EscherGuneWardena Architecture, were meant to create a very specific movement through space. At the Israel Museum, one entered the exhibition through the volumes in which the films are projected, which are arranged in a processional way, and, once one moves into the archive room, the plinths with the carpets and the vitrines with the archival materials are arranged so as to create an awareness of their place in the wider architecture. I would hope that the architectural interventions in both spaces operate with the conceptual goals of the works to create a space for viewers to consider themselves within a community and a history. Eshkol's work sparked for me an understanding of how she was able to create a practice that was collaborative with her partners, attentive to the world around her and its history, and yet completely uncompromised in its relation to institutions. I wanted to honor that commitment while opening up the work to a public that was held at arm's length.

1. *Lunch Break* consists of two film installations and three distinct series of photographs that explore the social life of workers during times of retreat from production. The first film, *Lunch Break* (2008), is eighty minutes long, during which the camera travels in extreme slow motion through a seemingly endless corridor, encountering workers and their environment during their lunch break. The second film, *EXIT* (2008), employs, by contrast, a static camera, and is divided into five discrete sections, each of which, over the duration of forty-one minutes, shows workers exiting the factory during the five workdays of the week. The first series of photographs consists of diptychs, triptychs, and single images that portray workers' lunch boxes. A second series of photographs is devoted to the independent businesses run by the workers encountered in the longer film. And the third series comprises deliberately composed group portraits of workers. In the United States the exhibition *Sharon Lockhart: Lunch Break* originated at the Mildred Lane Kemper Art Museum in 2009, and was organized by Sabine Eckmann. It then traveled to the Colby College Museum of Art in Maine (2010) and the San Francisco Museum of Modern Art (2011). In Europe the Vienna Secession showed *Lunch Break* in 2008.

2. In addition to a selection of the films and photographs from *Lunch Break*, the Colby exhibition incorporated works by Maine artists and artisans drawn from its own collection, other Maine museums, and private lenders. These works included paintings, sculptures, drawings, prints, and folk art depicting the Maine landscape, the factory town, maritime themes, and people at work and at leisure. They also included historical objects by Maine artisans, such as spruce-gum boxes and earthenware, as well as objects made by some of the workers involved in the production of *Lunch Break*.

3. In Israel, *Sharon Lockhart | Noa Eshkol* was presented at The Israel Museum, Jerusalem, from December 13, 2011 to April 14, 2012; concurrently, an extension of the project occurred at the Center for Contemporary Art, Tel Aviv, from December 15, 2011 to February 23, 2012.

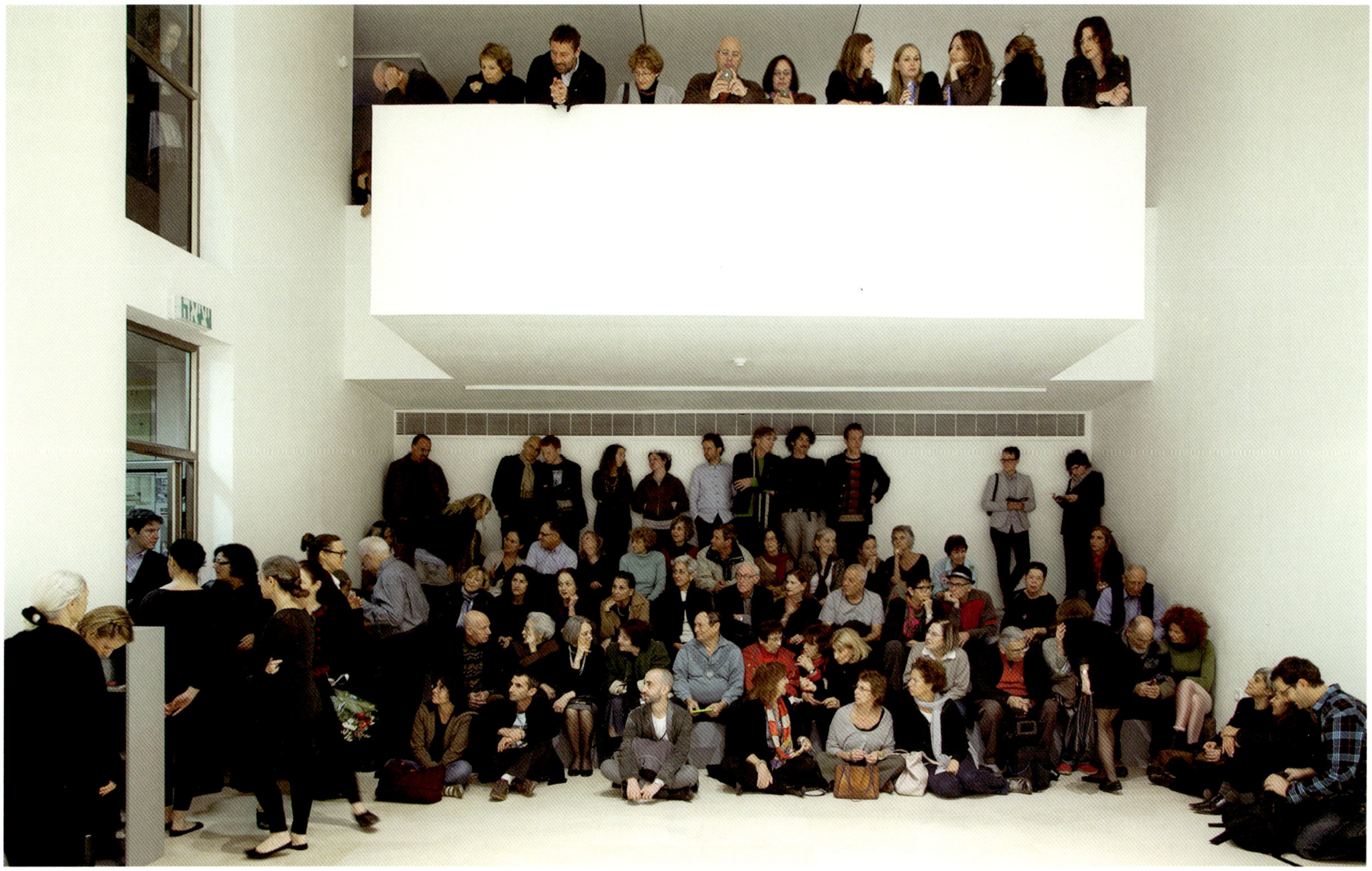

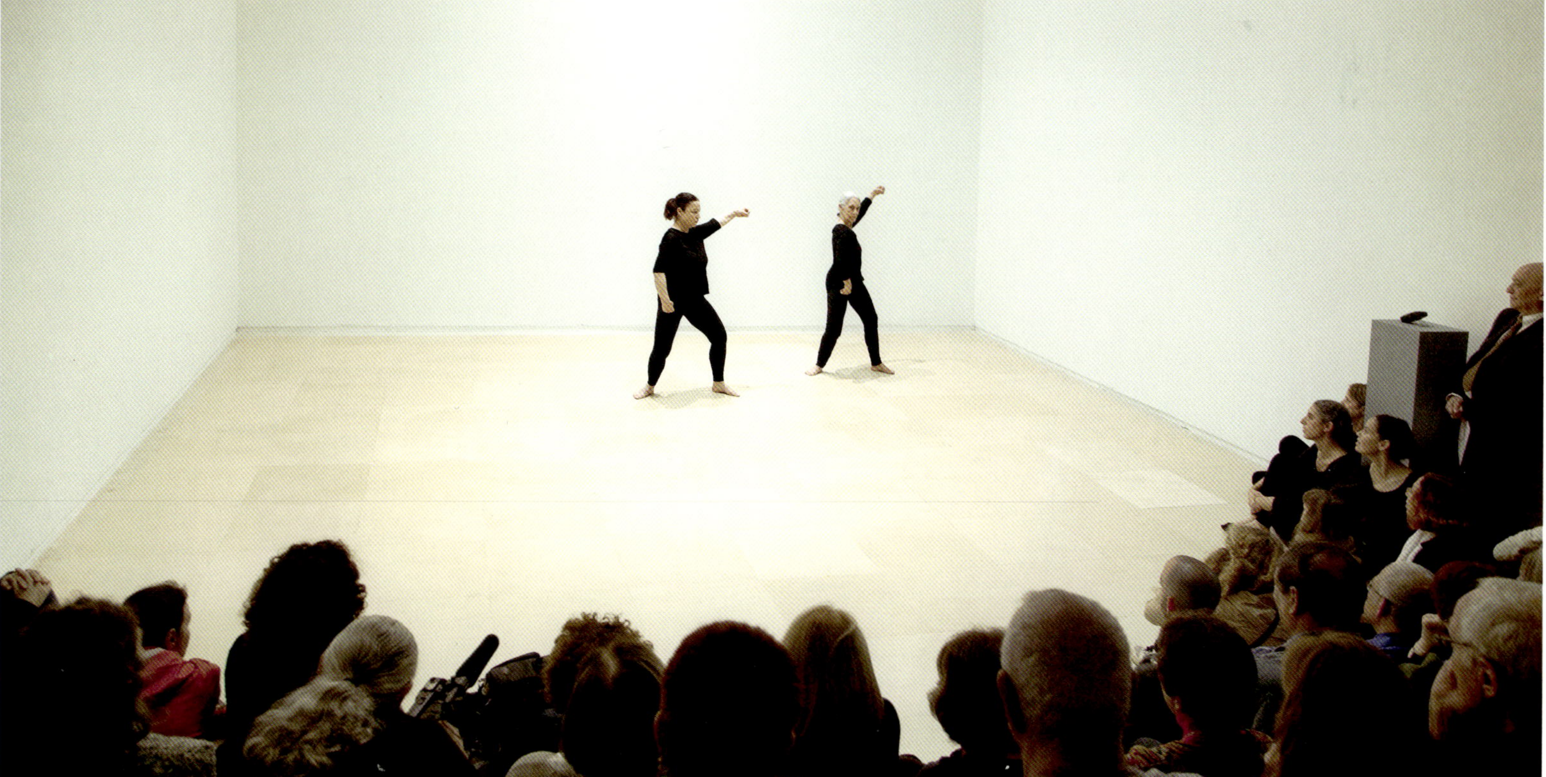

Figs. 6–7. Installation views of exhibition at Center for Contemporary Art, Tel Aviv, showing performances in the exhibition space

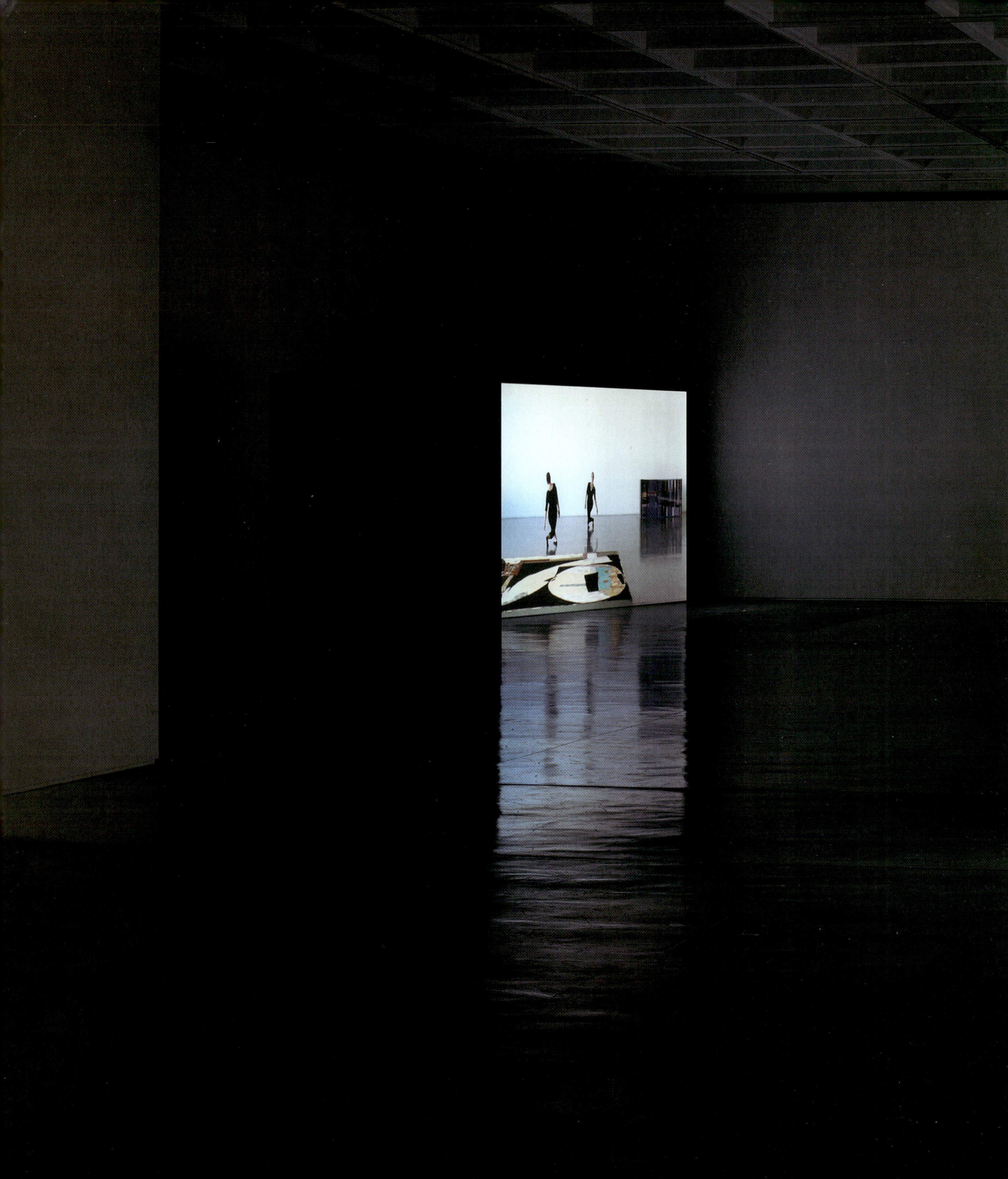

Installation view of exhibition at The Israel Museum, Jerusalem, showing Sharon Lockhart's *Five Dances and Nine Wall Carpets by Noa Eshkol*, 2011

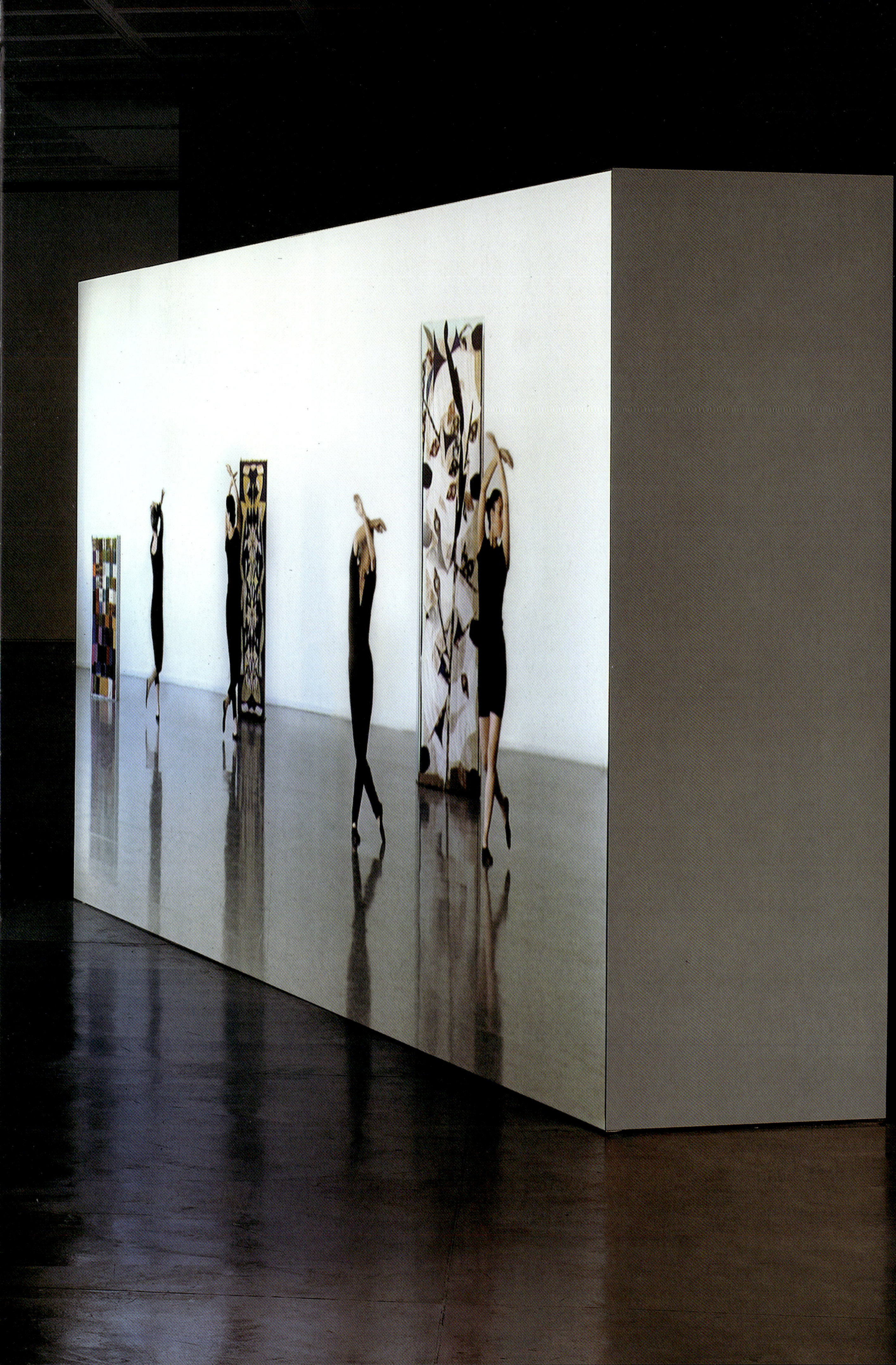

Noa Eshkol

Noa Eshkol was born in 1924 in Kvutzat Degania Bet in what is now Israel. Her father was Levi Eshkol (1895–1969), who was born in Russia and moved to Palestine in 1914 as part of the Second Aliyah (1904–14). He served as Israel's prime minister from 1963 until his death in 1969. Her mother was Rivka Marshak (1895–1951), also born in Russia. After her parents divorced in 1927, Eshkol was raised by her mother. When Eshkol was four, she and her mother moved to New York, where the latter taught Hebrew; they returned home three years later. In the early 1940s, the two moved to a small house in Holon, where Eshkol lived for the rest of her life.

Eshkol was a highly cultured woman who read widely in many fields. As a youth, she studied piano with Frank Peleg, who taught her the role of notation in music. From 1943 to 1945 she attended the Tille Rössler School in Tel Aviv. About this time she began to believe that for dance to attain the seriousness of music, a system of notation analogous to music notation was essential. Rössler introduced her to the work of Rudolf Laban, inventor of a system of dance notation known as Labanotation. In 1946 Eshkol moved to England to study Labanotion. She attended the Art of Movement Studio, founded by Rudolf Laban, in Manchester and then the Sigurd Leeder School of Modern Dance, established by Laban's student, the German dancer, choreographer, and teacher Sigurd Leeder, in London. In England she also met Moshe Feldenkrais, the inventor of the Feldenkrais Method, a system for improving movement through the cultivation of self-awareness.

In 1951 Eshkol returned to Holon. From 1951 to 1953 she taught at the Drama School of the Cameri Theatre, Tel Aviv, known for its experimentalism. Later she taught movement and movement notation at other institutions in Israel, including Beit Zvi Drama School, Tel Aviv (1960–61; 1963), Jerusalem Academy of Music and Dance (1960–61; 1964–65), and Seminar HaKibbutzim College of Education, Tel Aviv (1965–75), which became her educational home.

In the 1950s Eshkol developed the Eshkol-Wachman Movement Notation (EWMN) system with Avraham Wachman (1931–2010). They documented its fundamentals in *Movement Notation* (London: Weidenfeld and Nicolson, 1958), and Eshkol continued refining the method for the rest of her life. In 1954 she established the Chamber Dance Group, for which she composed dances using EWMN. She was one of the original dancers but stopped dancing in the late 1950s to focus on teaching and composition. The group's changing membership included Ilana Banai, John Harries, Amos Hetz, Racheli Nul-Kahana, Naomi Polani, Ruti Sela, Ilana Shaked, Mirale Sharon, and Shmulik Zaidel, among others. In 1965 the group premiered Eshkol's first dance suite composed using EWMN, *Theme and Variations* (originally known as *Preludes and Fugues*), the subject of the book *Theme & Variations: Dance Suite, Book 1* (Holon, Israel: Movement Notation Society for the Noa Eshkol Foundation for Movement Notation, 2010). The group performed throughout Israel and less frequently abroad, including at the Place in London in November 1969 and the Festival dei Due Mondi (Festival of the Two Worlds) in Spoleto, Italy, in summer 1972. It became inactive in 2000, after Nul-Kahana's departure left Sela as the sole dancer, but resumed activity in 2007.

In 1968 Eshkol founded the Movement Notation Society, which has published numerous books by her and her colleagues, including *The Hand Book: The Detailed Notation of Hand and Finger Movements and Forms* (1971), *Right Angled Curves: Dance Suite, Eshkol-Wachman Movement Notation* (1975), *Rubáiyát: Dance Suite* (1979), and *Movement Notations: A Comparative Study of Labanotation (Kinetography Laban) and Eshkol-Wachman Movement Notation* (1979).

In 1968–69 Eshkol was awarded a Fulbright fellowship and served as visiting professor in the physical education and electrical engineering departments at the University of Illinois, Urbana-Champaign, where she investigated simultaneous movement using computer technology. In 1969 the Chamber Dance Group toured colleges and universities in the Midwest. In 1972 Eshkol was appointed professor in the Faculty of Visual and Performing Arts at Tel Aviv University, where she established a movement-notation research center that operated out of her home.

In 1973, at the beginning of the Yom Kippur War, Eshkol created her first "wall carpets," which reflect her broad knowledge of the history of art, among other fields; she titled some of them in homage to artists. Exhibitions include *Noa Eshkol: Wall Carpets* (Danish Museum of Decorative Arts (now Designmuseum), Copenhagen, 1980); *Wall Carpets from Fabrics* (Museum of Art Ein Harod, Israel, 1996); *Fabrics on Fabrics* (Hamumche Gallery, Tel Aviv, 1998); and *Textile Tales* (The Open Museums, Tefen Industrial Park, Israel, 2010, cat.).

In August 1984 the first International Congress for Movement Notation brought over two hundred theorists and practitioners of Labanation, Benesh Notation, and EWMN to Tel Aviv University to examine the state of the field. The congress was initiated, organized, and hosted by Eshkol, with the cooperation of The Dance Notation Bureau, London, headed by Muriel Topaz, and the Benesh Institute, London, headed by Monica Parker.

On October 14, 2007, Eshkol died of complications from lung cancer. In her will, she provided for the establishment of the Noa Eshkol Foundation for Movement Notation, which preserves her legacy.

Sharon Lockhart

Sharon Lockhart was born in Norwood, Massachusetts, in 1964; grew up in Massachusetts and Maine; and has lived in Los Angeles since 1991. From 1984 to 1986 she attended the New England School of Photography (NESOP) in Boston, where she was introduced to the work of artists such as Cindy Sherman and Sherrie Levine, which piqued her interest in how contemporary artists use the medium of photography. In 1986, on an extended world trip, she first visited Israel, where she worked on a *moshav* (a cooperative settlement of small individually owned farms). In 1987 she enrolled at the San Francisco Art Institute, from which she received her BFA in 1991. Having previously studied photography at NESOP, she focused her studies on video, performance, art history, and critical theory, including feminism, which has continued to influence her practice. She then moved to Los Angeles to attend Art Center College of Design in Pasadena, receiving her MFA in 1993. Her most influential teachers were Mike Kelley, Timothy Martin, and Stephen Prina, as well as critic Diedrich Diederichsen. From Kelley she learned how to develop projects through intensive research; Martin advanced her awareness of theory and became a mentor who has advised her on the theoretical foundations of all of her major projects; and Prina introduced her to structuralist film, including the films of Hollis Frampton. For her graduate thesis on the history of medical photography and its relation to horror film, she studied documentary and ethnographic film. This research led her to the work of filmmaker Jean Rouch—one of the founders of cinema vérité, ethnofiction, and visual anthropology—and to a broader interest in ethnography, which has informed many of her projects.

Lockhart's extensive body of work includes projects that involve years of in-depth research and collaboration with communities and that result in the creation of both photographic series and films. These works are conceptually rigorous, formally precise, and socially and historically grounded, often dealing with the subject of labor. She frequently produces different versions of her films for screenings in cinemas and for exhibition in museums and galleries. The films for exhibitions are typically presented in installations designed in response to the architecture of the site.

Lockhart's first long-term photography and film project was *Goshogaoka* (1997). For this project she collaborated with a girls' basketball team from a high school in a Tokyo suburb and the choreographer Stephen Galloway, who choreographed basketball routines for the team that evoke the movements of postmodern dancers such as Yvonne Rainer and other dancers associated with Judson Dance Theater, in whom Lockhart has long been interested. Similarly, for the film *NŌ* (2003), also shot in Japan, she worked with a movement coordinator, who helped her analyze the movements of two farmers as they cover a field with a coat of hay by working their way forward in lines across the field, creating piles that compensate for the perspectival foreshortening of the camera's optics. The result is a choreographed version of their daily work and a visual interaction with the landscape.

Other projects include *Teatro Amazonas* (2000), for which Lockhart and two anthropologists interviewed over six hundred individuals in Amazonas, Brazil; *Pine Flat* (2006), which focuses on a group of children in a rural community in the Sierra Nevada of California over the span of four years; and *Lunch Break* (2008), a collaboration with the workers of Bath Iron Works, the largest shipyard in the state of Maine. With *Lunch Break* she began to take a greater interest in the curatorial dimension of her projects—an interest manifested by her selection of objects by other artists and artisans for display alongside her own works in the *Lunch Break* exhibition at the Colby College Museum of Art in Maine in 2010, and in the present exhibition.

Lockhart's work has been the subject of numerous one-person exhibitions, including *Teatro Amazonas* (Museum Boijmans Van Beuningen, Rotterdam, 2000, cat.), *Sharon Lockhart* (Museum of Contemporary Art, Chicago, 2001, cat.); *Pine Flat* (Walker Art Center, Minneapolis, 2006, cat.); and *Lunch Break* (Secession, Vienna, 2008; Mildred Lane Kemper Art Museum, St. Louis, 2010, cat.). Her films have been screened in film festivals around the world, including the Museum of Modern Art's New Directors/New Films series, Sundance Film Festival, and Internationale Filmfestspiele in Berlin, among many others. In addition, Lockhart has been a committed teacher from the beginning of her career. Her first teaching position was at the Merz Akademie in Stuttgart in 1996; for the past several years she has served as associate professor in the University of Southern California's Roski School of Fine Arts.

Compiled by John Alan Farmer

Works Exhibited

Sharon Lockhart

Five Dances and Nine Wall Carpets by Noa Eshkol, 2011
5-channel film installation (35mm film transferred to HD, sound), continuous loop, edition of six and two artist's proofs
(IMJ and LACMA only)

Models of Orbits in the System of Reference, Eshkol-Wachman Movement Notation System, 2011
Chromogenic prints, edition of six and two artist's proofs
20 ½ x 16 ½ inches (52.1 x 41.9 cm) each

- *Sphere One at Two Points in Its Rotation* (two prints)
- *Sphere Two at Four Points in Its Rotation* (four prints)
- *Sphere Three at Five Points in Its Rotation* (five prints)
- *Sphere Four at Two Points in Its Rotation* (two prints)
- *Sphere Five at Three Points in Its Rotation* (three prints)
- *Sphere Six at Three Points in Its Rotation* (three prints)
- *Sphere Seven at Three Points in Its Rotation* (three prints)

(IMJ and LACMA only)

Four Exercises in Eshkol-Wachman Movement Notation, 2011
Single-channel film installation (HD video, silent), continuous loop, edition of six and two artist's proofs
(CCA only)

All works by Sharon Lockhart courtesy of Blum & Poe, Los Angeles, Gladstone Gallery, New York and Brussels, and neugerriemschneider, Berlin

Noa Eshkol

The Four Seasons, 1970s
Cotton, corduroy, wool, and synthetic fibers
61 ¾ x 122 inches (157 x 310 cm)
(IMJ only)

Umbrella Flower, 1970s
Wool, cotton, corduroy, and nylon
81 ⅞ x 63 inches (208 x 160 cm)
(LACMA only)

Celebrating Circle (Wedding), 1980s
Cotton, cotton velvet, devoré velvet, polyester
100 ⅜ x 152 ⅝ inches (255 x 387.5 cm)
(LACMA only)

King Mooky I, 1980s
Cotton, corduroy, wool, and synthetic fibers
68 ⅞ x 59 ⅝ inches (175 x 151.5 cm)
(IMJ only)

Chinese Circus, 1990s
Cotton, corduroy, wool, and synthetic fibers
156 ¼ x 108 ⅝ inches (397 x 276 cm)
(IMJ only)

Plane Tree, 2000
Cotton
118 ⅛ x 58 ⅞ inches (300 x 149.5 cm)
(LACMA only)

All wall carpets by Noa Eshkol courtesy of the Noa Eshkol Foundation for Movement Notation, Holon, Israel, and neugerriemschneider, Berlin

Archival materials

Drawings

All drawings are by John Harries and are India ink on paper unless otherwise indicated

Avraham Wachman
Building a Spatial System of Reference, 1950s
The horizontal and vertical planes are divided into 90° (left) and 45° (right)
India ink and colored pencils on paper

The Stick Figure, 1950s
Longitudinal axis of the limbs—zero position

The Stick Figure, 1950s
The right arm has moved from zero position to position (2.2); the left leg has moved from zero position to position (0.2)

Intermediate Plane Movement, 1956–57
Vertical and planar deviation of the arm and the leg within their own individual systems of reference
India ink and colored pencils on paper

Movement in the Vertical Plane (Plane 0), 1956–57
Collage and India ink on paper

Plane Movement, 1956–57
Movement of one limb "drawing" a circle in space
Collage and India ink on paper

Conical Movement, 1956–57
Conical membranes, produced by the movement of the arm and of the leg

Sense of the Rotary Movement, 1956–57

Carrying, 1956–57
The back, the heavy moving limb, changes its relation to the "stationary" pelvis, carrying along the arms and the head, which do not change their interrelationship

Score for *Peacock 2*, one of the *Peacock* dances performed by Chamber Dance Group 1 (Movement Quartet), 1954–55
Notated by Noa Eshkol and John Harries

Score for *Bird*, two-part illustration for Noa Eshkol and Abraham [Avraham] Wachman, *Movement Notation* (London: Weidenfeld and Nicolson, 1958), 1956–58
Notated by Noa Eshkol and John Harries

Layout of classical ballet scores, 1968
India ink and Sellotape on paper
Notated by Noa Eshkol and Racheli Nul

Notation Symbols, 1992
32 notation symbols whose combinations enable the notation of every movement

Other Materials

Notebook by Noa Eshkol, 1949–50
Includes unrealized teaching program and description of the movement possibilities of each and every part of the body with reference to human anatomy

Program from the first performances of Chamber Dance Group 1 (Movement Quartet), 1954–56
Director: Noa Eshkol; performers: Noa Eshkol, Naomi Polani, Mirale Sharon, and John Harries

First Hebrew draft of *Movement Notation* by Noa Eshkol and Avraham Wachman, 1955
Submitted as a proposal for publication to the Weizmann Institute of Science

Eshkol-Wachman Movement Notation System, demonstrated by the Chamber Dance Group
Poster designed by Amos Hetz for performance of Noa Eshkol's Chamber Dance Group at Ohel Theater, Tel Aviv, 1956
Lithograph

Poster for performance of Noa Eshkol's Chamber Dance Group at Ohel Theater, Tel Aviv, 1956
Lithograph

Noa Eshkol and Abraham [Avraham] Wachman, *Movement Notation*, 1957
Comparative study of Labanotation and Eshkol-Wachman Movement Notation, supplement no. 1
Booklet exhibited at the Royal Festival Hall, London, in exhibition on dance notation

Noa Eshkol and Abraham [Avraham] Wachman, *Movement Notation* (London: Weidenfeld and Nicolson, 1958)
First edition of first book on Eshkol-Wachman Movement Notation

Movement Orbits, 1969
Computer printouts showing the spatial tracks created by simultaneous movement, produced while Noa Eshkol served as visiting professor at the University of Illinois, Urbana-Champaign

Additional archival materials were exhibited at The Israel Museum, Jerusalem and the Los Angeles County Museum of Art

All archival materials courtesy of the Noa Eshkol Foundation for Movement Notation, Holon, Israel

Notes on Contributors

Talia Amar is associate curator of contemporary art at The Israel Museum, Jerusalem. Her exhibitions include *Out of the Labyrinth* (2000); *Rising Sun, Melting Moon: Contemporary Art in Japan* (2005–6); *Yinka Shonibare MBA: Earth, Wind, Fire, and Water* (2010–11); and collection exhibitions.

Stephanie Barron is senior curator of modern art at the Los Angeles County Museum of Art, where she has organized more than fifty exhibitions, including *David Hockney: A Retrospective* (1988); *"Degenerate Art": The Fate of the Avant-Garde in Nazi Germany* (1991); *Exiles + Emigrés: The Flight of European Artists from Hitler* (1997); *Made in California: Art, Image, and Identity 1900–2000* (2000); *Magritte and Contemporary Art: The Treachery of Images* (2007); and *Art of Two Germanys/Cold War Cultures* (2009).

Eva Díaz is assistant professor of contemporary art at Pratt Institute in New York. Her forthcoming book, *The Experimenters*, examines how the interdisciplinary group of artists at Black Mountain College proposed new models of art practice around the concept of experimentation. Her writing has appeared in the *Art Bulletin*, *Art Journal*, *Art in America*, *Cabinet*, *Frieze*, and *Grey Room*, and she is a regular contributor to *Artforum*.

Sabine Eckmann is director and chief curator at the Mildred Lane Kemper Art Museum at Washington University in St. Louis, where she also teaches in the Department of Art History and Archaeology. Among her many exhibitions and publications are *Exiles + Emigrés: The Flight of European Artists from Hitler* (1997); *Caught by Politics: Hitler Exiles and American Visual Culture* (2007); *Reality Bites: Making Avant-garde Art in Post-Wall Germany* (2007); *Art of Two Germanys/Cold War Cultures* (2009); and *Sharon Lockhart: Lunch Break* (2010).

Britt Salvesen is curator of photography and prints and drawings at the Los Angeles County Museum of Art. Her LACMA exhibitions include *New Topographics: Photographs of a Man-Altered Landscape* (2009); *Outside the Box: Edition Jacob Samuel* (with the Hammer Museum; 2010); and *Catherine Opie: Figure and Landscape* (2010).

Michal Shoshani graduated from the Rubin Academy of Music and Dance, now the Jerusalem Academy of Music and Dance (JAMD), in 1966 and received an MA in dance research from the University of Surrey in 1995. She has conducted extensive research on movement notations and taught movement and movement notations at JAMD and Seminar HaKibbutzim College of Education in Tel Aviv, among other institutions. She worked with Noa Eshkol from 1967 to 2007, has authored and co-authored several books for the Movement Notation Society, and now heads the Noa Eshkol Foundation for Movement Notation's archive.

Photography Credits

All works by Sharon Lockhart courtesy the artist and Blum & Poe, Los Angeles, Gladstone Gallery, New York and Brussels, and neugerriemschneider, Berlin.

Additional photography credits: photo © Center for Contemporary Art, Tel Aviv, by Youval Hai: front cover; photo © The Israel Museum, Jerusalem, by Oded Löbl: pp. 8–9, 18–19, 30–31, 42–43, 70–71, 94–95, 111, 114–15; photo © Estate of Robert Rauschenberg/Licensed by VAGA, New York, NY, photo by Herb Migdoll, Cunningham Dance Foundation: fig. 3, p. 15; photo © The Israel Museum, Jerusalem, by Elie Posner: fig. 4, p. 16; fig. 5, p. 41; pp. 45, 46–47, 48; Photo: Jacob (Jack) Rosner © The Israel Museum, Jerusalem, fig. 2, p. 35; Photo: Yaacov Ben-Dov © The Israel Museum, Jerusalem, fig. 3, p. 36; photo © Los Angeles County Museum of Art, by Sam Kahn: pp. 49, 51, 52–53; photo © The Noa Eshkol Foundation for Movement Notation, Holon, Israel: fig. 1, p. 33; fig. 4, p. 38, photo by T. Brauner; pp. 54, 56, photo by Derry Moore; p. 58, photo by Geula Dagan; p. 60, photo by Derry Moore; p. 62, photo by John Harries; p. 96; figs. 1 and 2a, p. 98; figs. 2b and 3, p. 99; fig. 4, p. 100; fig. 5, p. 101; pp. 102–05; photo © Tate, London 2012; The Work of Naum Gabo © Nina & Graham Williams: fig. 1, p. 74; photo © Man Ray Trust / Artists Rights Society (ARS), New York / ADAGP, Paris / Telimage – 2012: fig. 3, p. 75; photo Alex Slade: pp. 107, 108, 113; photo Filippo Armellin: p. 109

Curators' Acknowledgments

Our first thanks are to Sharon Lockhart for creating the remarkable body of work inspired by her encounter with the practice of Noa Eshkol. She has brought her customary focus, precision, and sensibility to all facets of the exhibition and the publication, and it has been a pleasure to work with her. The project would not have happened without the efforts of studio assistant Meredith Bayse, who has been unfailingly helpful, ever-enthusiastic, and supremely well organized, juggling demands from colleagues on two continents with great aplomb. At The Israel Museum, Jerusalem, we thank James Snyder and Suzanne Landau for their support; Paulina Galper, Shirly Yahalomi, and Amit Bauml for their central role in realizing the exhibition; and Tami Michaeli for her wise editing. At LACMA, we thank Michael Govan for his deep commitment to the project; Lauren Bergman and Ryan Linkof, who helped us with myriad details for the publication; and Eddy Vajarakitipongse and Peter Kirby for their technical assistance. We are delighted that following the presentation in Los Angeles the exhibition will travel to The Jewish Museum in New York. Architects Frank Escher and Ravi GuneWardena of EscherGuneWardena Architecture, who have long collaborated with Sharon, again brought their particular sensitivity to the exhibition design.

Preparing this publication under extremely tight deadlines, and managing texts in two languages, has only happened through the tremendous work of editor John Alan Farmer and designer Conny Purtill. Mary DelMonico of DelMonico Books•Prestel took a personal interest in seeing this book to fruition, for which we are deeply grateful. Authors Eva Díaz, Sabine Eckmann, and Michal Shoshani graciously accepted our invitation to write; they, too, deserve sincere thanks. The conversations Sharon and Meredith conducted with the dancers over the course of several visits to Israel provide an informative window into the nature of Eshkol's practice. We are extremely grateful to the project's supporters, who responded with enthusiasm to funding requests; they are included in the directors' foreword. This exhibition and catalogue allow a wider audience to experience the special quality that Noa Eshkol and her dancers embodied through the lens of Sharon Lockhart.

Stephanie Barron
Senior Curator of Modern Art, LACMA

Britt Salvesen
Curator of Photography, LACMA

Talia Amar
Associate Curator of Contemporary Art, The Israel Museum, Jerusalem

Artist's Acknowledgments

I first thank Diana Shoef of the Center for Contemporary Art, Tel Aviv, who introduced me to the work of Noa Eshkol. She insightfully knew that this work would resonate with me on many levels, and she and her colleagues provided invaluable assistance as I began to develop the project. My deepest appreciation goes to the members of the Noa Eshkol Foundation for Movement Notation, who welcomed me into their extraordinary world. I am exceptionally grateful to the foundation's chairman, Mooky Dagan, who generously shared his extensive knowledge of Eshkol with me, and to Racheli Nul-Kahana, Ruti Sela, Shmulik Zaidel, Michal Shoshani, Mor Bashan, Noga Goral, Or Gal-Or, Hamutal Peled, and Sara Sheffi for their close collaboration, tireless effort, and enduring support. Racheli Nul-Kahana deserves special thanks for her exceptional work conserving the dances and training the dancers. My sincere gratitude go to Clay Lerner, my assistant at the start of this project, as well as to my wonderful crew in Israel, including Tully Chen and Itai Neeman; thanks also to Ohad Naharin, artistic director of Batsheva Dance Company, for his support. In addition, I thank my postproduction team in Los Angeles: Dane Davis, Aaron Morgan, Tom Ozanich, Walt Rose, and Fil Ruting. An Advancing Scholarship in the Humanities and Social Sciences grant from the University of Southern California provided crucial support for the realization of the work, for which I am very grateful. The attention to detail of the outstanding staff of The Israel Museum, Jerusalem and the Center for Contemporary Art resulted in perfect installations. At The Israel Museum, Jerusalem, I thank Talia Amar, Amit Bauml, Tania Coen-Uzzielli, Suzanne Landau, James Snyder, and Shirly Yahalomi; at the Center for Contemporary Art, Sergio Edelsztein. At LACMA the exceptional commitment, intellectual brilliance, and fierce support of Stephanie Barron and Britt Salvesen made possible both the presentation of the work in Los Angeles and the publication of this catalogue. My deep gratitude goes to authors Eva Díaz, Sabine Eckmann, and Michal Shoshani for their outstanding contributions to this publication.

The vision, inspiration, and friendship of Becky Allen, Frank Escher, John Alan Farmer, Ravi GuneWardena, and Conny Purtill were invaluable. Also integral was the support of my galleries, especially Rosalie Benitez, Tim Blum, Maia Gianakos, Barbara Gladstone, Augusta Joyce, Sam Kahn, Tim Neuger, Jeff Poe, and Burkhard Riemschneider. In addition, I am indebted to the following individuals for their generous assistance on many levels: Adam Berg, James Benning, Ido Biran, Tyler Coburn, Michelle Crisosto, Kathy Halbreich, Karen Higa, Sylvia Liska, Jean Lockhart, Tony Manzella, Timothy Martin, Sue Medlicott, Edna Moshenson, Hector Murillo, Jane Neidhardt, Jenelle Porter, Joachim Reck, Yael Saharof, Rusty Sena, Katy Siegel, Nerissa Dominguez Vales, and Flora Wiegmann. Finally, special thanks go to my phenomenal assistant Meredith Bayse, whose intelligence, dedication, and boundless energy contributed immeasurably to the realization of every phase of this complex project; to Nancy Berman and Alan Bloch for their warmth, enthusiasm, and commitment; and to Alex Slade for his love and support. I could not have done this project without them.

Sharon Lockhart

This publication accompanies the exhibition *Sharon Lockhart | Noa Eshkol* organized by Talia Amar for The Israel Museum, Jerusalem, and Stephanie Barron and Britt Salvesen for the Los Angeles County Museum of Art. It also accompanies the companion exhibition of the same title organized by Sergio Edelsztein for the Center for Contemporary Art, Tel Aviv.

Initial support for the project was provided by The Jewish Federation of Greater Los Angeles's Tel Aviv – Los Angeles Partnership; and The Philip and Muriel Berman Foundation, Los Angeles.

The exhibition at the Israel Museum is made possible by Dorit Gary and Modi Segal, Los Angeles and Tel Aviv; Judith Yovel Recanati, Herzliya, in memory of her beloved husband Israel (Rolly) Yovel; Rivka Saker and Uzi Zucker, New York and Tel Aviv; Rachel and Moshe Yanai, Tel Aviv; anonymous donors, Caesarea and Tel Aviv; donors to The Israel Museum's 2011 Exhibition Fund: Claudia Davidoff, Cambridge, Massachusetts, in memory of Ruth and Leon Davidoff; Hanno D. Mott, New York; The Nash Family Foundation, New York.

The exhibition at the Los Angeles County Museum of Art is made possible through major gifts from Daniel Greenberg, Susan Steinhauser and The Greenberg Foundation; Audrey M. Irmas; Alice and Nahum Lainer; Drs. Rebecka and Arie Belldegrun; The Philip and Muriel Berman Foundation; and The Photographic Arts Council, LACMA. Additional support was provided by Helgard Field-Lion and Irwin Field; Laura and Jim Maslon; and the Consulate General of Israel, Los Angeles.

Sponsored by

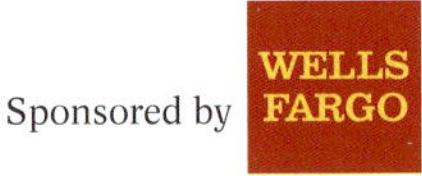

At the Center for Contemporary Art, Tel Aviv, Sharon Lockhart's film was produced with the support of Outset Contemporary Art Fund, The Philip and Muriel Berman Foundation, Ostrovsky Family Fund, and Art Partners; the programs were made possible thanks to the generosity of the Weil Family.

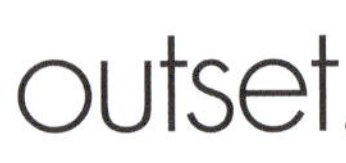

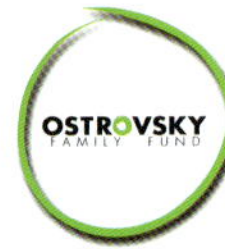

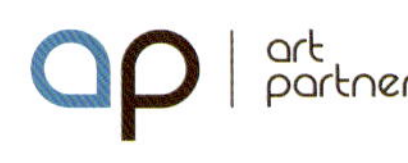

Exhibition itinerary

The Israel Museum, Jerusalem, December 13, 2011–April 14, 2012
Companion exhibition: Center for Contemporary Art, Tel Aviv, December 15, 2011–February 23, 2012
Los Angeles County Museum of Art, June 4–September 9, 2012
The Jewish Museum, New York, November 2, 2012–March 24, 2013

Copublished by

Los Angeles County Museum of Art
5905 Wilshire Boulevard
Los Angeles, CA 90036
www.lacma.org

The Israel Museum, Jerusalem
P.O.B. 71117
Jerusalem 91710 Israel
www.imjnet.org

AND

DelMonico Books•Prestel, an imprint of Prestel, a member of Verlagsgruppe Random House GmbH

Prestel Verlag
Neumarkter Strasse 28
81673 Munich
Germany
Tel 49 89 41 36 0
Fax 49 89 41 36 23 35
www.prestel.de

Prestel Publishing Ltd.
4 Bloomsbury Place
London WC1A 2QA
United Kingdom
Tel: 44 20 7323 5004
Fax: 44 20 7636 8004

Prestel Publishing
900 Broadway, Suite 603
New York, NY 10003
Tel: 212 995 2720
Fax: 212 995 2733
sales@prestel-usa.com
www.prestel.com

Library of Congress Cataloging-in-Publication Data

Sharon Lockhart | Noa Eshkol / edited by Stephanie Barron and Britt Salvesen;
with contributions by Talia Amar, Stephanie Barron and Britt Salvesen, Eva Díaz,
Sabine Eckmann and Sharon Lockhart, Michal Shoshani.
pages cm
Published on the occasion of the exhibition Sharon Lockhart | Noa Eshkol,
organized by The Israel Museum, Jerusalem and the Los Angeles County Museum of Art.
Includes bibliographical references and index.
ISBN 978-3-7913-5223-7 (hardcover : alk. paper)
1. Lockhart, Sharon, 1964---Exhibitions. 2. Eshkol, Noa--Exhibitions. 3.
Eshkol-Wachman movement notation--Exhibitions. 4. Film installations (Art)
I. Barron, Stephanie, 1950- editor of compilation. II. Salvesen, Britt,
editor of compilation. III. Lockhart, Sharon, 1964- Works. Selections. 2012.
IV. The Israel Museum, Jerusalem V. Los Angeles County Museum of Art.
N6537.L6345A4 2012
709.2'2--dc23
2012010329

ISBN 978-3-7913-5223-7

DESIGN: Purtill Family Business
EDITOR: John Alan Farmer
PRODUCTION COORDINATION: The Production Department
PRODUCTION ASSISTANT: Meredith Bayse
HEBREW EDITOR: Tami Michaeli
ENGLISH TRANSLATION: Talya Halkin and Annie Lopez
HEBREW TRANSLATION: Aya Breuer
PROOFREADER: Richard G. Gallin
COLOR SEPARATIONS: Echelon, Los Angeles

Printed in China

Front cover: Left to right: Noga Goral, Ruti Sela, and Mor Bashan performing a dance by Noa Eshkol at the opening of the exhibition *Sharon Lockhart | Noa Eshkol* at the Center for Contemporary Art, Tel Aviv, December 15, 2011.